On 'What is History?'

In this book Keith Jenkins argues that older modernist discussions about the nature of history – including those by Carr and Elton – are now partial and dated guides to contemporary debates. He advocates that they be 'replaced' by two other theorists, Richard Rorty and Hayden White.

In his introduction and first chapter, Keith Jenkins places Carr, Elton, Rorty and White within current discussions concerning the discourse of history. This 'contextualisation' is then followed by four chapters: in the first two Carr and Elton are subjected to radical critique; in the latter Jenkins introduces aspects of the works of Rorty and White, postmodern-type thinkers who in his opinion represent a possible way forward for today's historiographical concerns.

Keith Jenkins' exploration of Hayden White's work is particularly significant. For although White has long been recognised as one of the most original history theorists currently writing, his work is actually little read and little understood in many orthodox historical arenas, or by most history students. Jenkins argues that the neglect of White and the general suspicion of 'theory' among many historians are issues which need to be urgently addressed.

On 'What is History?' should enable students to gain insights into and understandings of many current debates with regard to the 'history question', insights and understandings that necessarily move us beyond those old introductory favourites, Carr and Elton, into new and vital areas of consideration.

Also available from Routledge:

Re-thinking History by Keith Jenkins
'A model of concise argument [that] poses fundamental questions concerning the nature of historiography in a post-modernist world.'
A. White, *University of East London*

'raises many interesting and important questions'
Teaching History

On 'What is History?'

From Carr and Elton to Rorty and White

Keith Jenkins

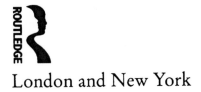

London and New York

First published 1995
by Routledge
2 Park Square, Milton Park, Abingdon, Oxon, OX14 4RN

Simultaneously published in the USA and Canada
by Routledge
270 Madison Ave, New York NY 10016
Reprinted in 1996

Transferred to Digital Printing 2006

© 1995 Keith Jenkins

Typeset in Garamond by
Ponting–Green Publishing Services, Chesham, Bucks

British Library Cataloguing in Publication Data
A catalogue record for this book is available from the
British Library

Library of Congress Cataloguing in Publication Data
A catalogue record for this book is available

ISBN 0–415–09724–X (hbk)
ISBN 0–415–09725–8 (pbk)

Contents

For Maureen, Philip and Patrick

Acknowledgements

I would like to thank Peter Brickley, Richard Brown, Andrew Foster, Keith Grieves, Guy Nelson, Richard Pulley, Geoff Seale and Alan White for their comments on the arguments I have tried to put forward in an introductory way in this book. I have attempted to take on board their critical suggestions whenever possible and those that 'have not made it' I have kept gratefully for possible future use.

The author and publishers would like to thank the following who have kindly given permission for the use of copyright material: Macmillan Press Limited, for excerpts from E. H. Carr's *What is History?*; Cambridge University Press and the Royal Historical Society for excerpts from G. R. Elton's *Return to Essentials*; Cambridge University Press and Richard Rorty for excerpts from R. Rorty's *Contingency, Irony, and Solidarity*, also *Objectivity, Relativism and Truth: Philosophical Papers Volume I*, and *Essays on Heidegger and Others: Philosophical Papers Volume II*; University of Minnesota Press for excerpts from R. Rorty's *Consequences of Pragmatism*; Johns Hopkins University Press for excerpts from Hayden White's *Metahistory, Tropics of Discourse* and *The Content of Form*. Every effort has been made to obtain permission from the publishers of G. R. Elton's *The Practice of History*. Any queries about the above should be addressed to Patrick Proctor at Routledge, London.

Keith Jenkins, 23 November 1994

Introduction: history, theory, ideology

This book has been written as something of a sequel to an earlier volume published in 1991 entitled *Re-thinking History* and, as on that previous occasion, this new work is addressed primarily (though obviously not exclusively) to advanced and undergraduate students and their teachers.[1] And I have written it because I think it is necessary to introduce such students – who may well be studying the question of the nature of history in some detail for the first time – to some of the more contentious, polemical and difficult debates which are currently in circulation, and which are arguably determining how this particular discourse is being constituted and considered today.

If, however, these comments indicate in only the very briefest of ways who I have written this book for and something of its general purpose, I do not actually want to enlarge on these intentions at this early stage. Rather what I do want to do, is to go on to explain my approach to the question of what is history, how and why I have organised it around the four people whose names appear in the book's subtitle – Edward Carr, Geoffrey Elton, Richard Rorty and Hayden White – and, more importantly perhaps, why I have put into that subtitle an element of movement, that is, *from* Carr and Elton *to* Rorty and White.

For, whilst I think that readers will find a good deal of description and exposition in this work, I shall also be running a particular argument throughout its entirety, it being within the 'movement' just mentioned that what polemical cutting edge the book has is located. For these two simple words, *from* and *to*, carry within them the weight of the thesis I shall be developing in the following pages, my position being (in brief for now) that despite the continued popularity of their texts as 'essential introductions' to the 'history question' (which is why I have thought it useful to organise this book around individual historians/theorists and not around 'schools' or 'movements' or 'concepts' or whatever)[2] I feel that Carr and Elton are no longer good enough embodiments and/or guides to the more reflexive debates on 'what is history?' currently taking place, so that they should now be effectively abandoned in favour of more relevant and generous exponents as to what is going on, exponents from whose number I have chosen to look at just two: Rorty and White.[3]

How can this 'thesis' be justified; what sort of reasons for replacing Carr and Elton can be given? Here I think that at least two types of answer, operating on two different levels, can be put. First, there is an answer that is actually a rather obvious one, but which I want to mention briefly, not only because it is apparently ignored by those still recommending Carr and Elton as 'essential reading', but also because it will allow me to 'introduce' Carr, Elton, Rorty and White. Second, there is an answer that, whilst somewhat more complicated, nevertheless takes me in the direction in which I want to go, and which I will therefore outline in more detail. For this second answer will enable me both to justify my treatment of Carr, Elton, Rorty and White with regard to the position I shall be developing, as well as letting me say something about how my argument – and thus the book which embodies it – is constructed.

I think that the level one answer as to why Carr and Elton now have to be left behind, then, is simply because the books for which they have long been best known with regard to the question of what constitutes history – Carr's *What is History?* and Elton's *The Practice of History* – are now around thirty years old and unrevised.[4] Carr's text, which first appeared in 1961, was the published version of lectures he finished drafting in 1960, and although he had written a new Preface to it by the time of his death in 1982, no changes had been made to the body of the work. Similarly, whilst Elton produced a further text in 1970 justifying the principles and practices of (his kind of) political history, and whilst he published a revisionist work *Return to Essentials* in 1991, *The Practice of History* (1967) remained effectively untouched.[5]

By virtue of the age and the unrevised character of their works, therefore, it really does not seem sensible to me that, as history teachers, we should still be suggesting to our students that their first (and sometimes their only) port of call with regard to the question of what is history should be the 'Carr–Elton debate'. Or at least it should give us pause for thought (I mean, how many other discourses introducing students to their *current* practices recommend as basic reading thirty-year-old texts?). Yet from a study of course reading lists, lecture programmes and conversations with historians, it seems that this is overwhelmingly what continues to occur. For, since their original publication dates, Carr and Elton's most famous texts have never ceased to be 'strongly recommended', have never stopped selling well, have never been unavailable and have thus never lost – certainly within the academic mainstream – their preeminent status as the works 'to raise the issues'. Consequently, it seems no exaggeration to say that Carr and Elton have long set the agenda for much if not all of the crucially important preliminary thinking about the question of what is history. And all this is well-recognised of course, as Dominick LaCapra's comments (which draw on a very different experience of introducing students to history from my own) seem to confirm:

> A standard practice in historiography seminars is to begin by assigning Elton's *The Practice of History* and Carr's *What is History?* ... as representing the alternatives in the self-understanding of the discipline. This practice is sure to generate heated debate among students, and it starts the course with a pleasant 'Steve Reeves meets Godzilla' scenario. The result is usually a more or less pragmatic and eclectic 'synthesis' of the two works that may serve as a tenuous consensus on which the seminar may proceed in its study of less 'theoretical' and 'methodological' assignments.[6]

Yet, as I say, these texts as 'representing the self-understanding of the discipline' are arguably no longer good enough today. For over the last twenty to thirty years there has developed around and about this dominant academic discourse a range of theories (hermeneutics, phenomenology, structuralism, post-structuralism, deconstructionism, new historicism, feminism and post-feminism, post-Marxism, new pragmatism, postmodernism and so on) as articulated by a range of theorists (for example, Ricouer, Foucault, Barthes, Althusser, Derrida, Greenblatt, Kristeva, Bennett, Laclau, Fish, Lyotard *et al.*) which have reached levels of reflexive sophistication and intellectual rigour with regard to the question of historical representation, which one could not even hazard a guess at from a reading of Carr and Elton's vintage texts – or from their later thoughts on the subject, come to that. From this perspective then, Carr and Elton cannot help but appear passé, all of this suggesting that we should now move on to theories and theorists of the type just mentioned – and in this particular text to Rorty and White – if we are to gain a better understanding of how the discourse of history is being currently rendered.

To those who already have some familiarity with these 'current renditions', the choice of Richard Rorty (if not Hayden White) as part of a 'Carr–Elton' replacement package may seem odd. Because, although Rorty has written extensively on the history of ideas, he is not really a historian at all but a philosopher.[7] So why in the present context choose him? Well, although one may not go all the way with Harold Bloom's view that Rorty is simply 'the most interesting philosopher in the world today', it is easy to see why Bloom should think this. For (again, over the last twenty to thirty years) the once 'analytical' Rorty has not only blended a 'personalised' Dewey-type pragmatism with readings of, say, Nietzsche and Freud, Heidegger and Wittgenstein, Foucault and Derrida, Davidson and Quine, but he has also quite deliberately absorbed and worked on aspects of semiotics, post-structuralism, deconstructionism, post-feminism, post-Marxism and postmodernism, collapsing in the process the old disciplinary borders of philosophy, science, literature, politics and history, so to arrive at an original and seminal position that can be described as an anti-foundationalist, anti-epistemological, ironic, rhetorical, conversationalist type of philosophy. Rorty therefore seems to me to be the embodiment of the contemporary, a barometer, perhaps, of intellectual pressures across so many discourses, all of which (like history) have the construction of meaning and the problems of representation in focus. In that sense Rorty – moving as he does with such ease across the entire intellectual terrain – expresses some of the arguably most vibrant areas of contemporary intellectual life, areas which I have tried to summarise through an examination of aspects of his philosophy. My aim in using Rorty is therefore two-fold: to introduce historians to his own personal 'take' on these wider concerns, and to provide a guide to that wider intellectual milieu against which Carr and Elton's views on history are just no longer credible, whilst Hayden White's very clearly are.

I came across White's work before that of Rorty through a reading in the mid-1970s of his *Metahistory* (1973) and, since then, I have tried to keep up with the steady stream of his more theoretical books and articles. In 1978, White published a collection of essays entitled *Tropics of Discourse* and followed this in 1987 with *The Content of the Form: Narrative Discourse and Historical Representation*, whilst more recently he has, for example, written on Proust and penned an incisive *Afterword* to a collection of essays edited by H. A. Veeser, *The New Historicism*.[8] Together, in these and other pieces, White has ranged across a host of historians, history theorists and cultural critics – Marx, Michelet, Carlyle, Burckhardt, Droyson, Jacobson, Lévi-Strauss, Kristeva, Foucault, Ricoeur, Derrida, Kenneth Burke, Barthes, Wellek, Auerbach, Frye *et al.* – whilst his footnotes read like compilations of some of the more important debates in contemporary thought: deconstructionism, narratology, linguistics, post-structuralism, and so on, White applying these and other aspects of thought directly to historiography, historical method and wider historical discussions in thought-provoking ways. Even so – and one says this with an enormous amount of regret – because of what can only be described as the chronic, anti-theoretical nature of mainstream 'history culture' in this country, relatively few students, and indeed relatively few teachers and historians, have actually read much White, whilst to some he remains effectively unknown. And it is because I think White should be known and should be discussed that I offer here a sort of 'rough guide to Hayden White', a guide which I hope might be useful for aspiring historians and which might encourage them to read for themselves one of the most stimulating theorists writing today, writing which takes us far beyond the old shibboleths of Carr and Elton both 'in themselves' and certainly beyond the parameters of their 'debate'.

That is not all, however. For it is interesting – and it encourages in this area a polemical tone that I have taken advantage of – that in his 1990 essays on the nature of history (in his backward-looking and backward-entitled *Return to Essentials*) Elton signals all that is wrong with current 'theorising' via a savage critique of post-structuralist, deconstructionist and other postmodern 'fads', picking out Hayden White as the arch-exponent of what might be termed 'this regrettable rubbish' and spending several dismissive pages of a slim text attending to his malign approaches and influence. Accordingly, in this way the old 'Carr–Elton debate' becomes explicitly enmeshed within those discursive practices that Rorty and White are both obviously engaged in so that, at this point, these 'first level'-type reasons for affecting the movement of this introductory text on the question of what is history become embodied in its very title: *On 'What is History?': From Carr and Elton to Rorty and White*.

So to the second level argument as to why move on, an argument that goes beyond the reasons I have just considered by incorporating and contextualising them within the broad thesis that informs this text and which offers me an explicatory frame of reference which I have constantly alluded to with regard to my comments on Carr, Elton, Rorty and White.

Here, my argument is that those general changes which have occurred over the last twenty to thirty years, and which I have already suggested have reorganised the recent/current intellectual landscape, are not unconnected to a whole series of socio-economic, political and cultural changes that have infused them with life. And in order to hold these interconnected material/theoretical actualities together, I have drawn on both the concept of *postmodernity* (as the most useful concept available under which to signify our socio-economic, political and cultural condition) and on the concept of *postmodernism* (as signifying the best way of making sense of various 'expressive' intellectual changes at the level of theory), these concepts enabling me to argue that in this *postmodern world* (and despite their 'differences') the works of Carr and Elton are unmistakably *modernist* and are thus, in that sense, generally irrelevant to an understanding of what history is in our 'new times', a disadvantage that the 'postist' Rorty and White do not suffer from. Let me at this point, then, lightly sketch out in a preliminary and skeletal form (I shall have occasion to revisit it) the understanding I have of our postmodern condition and history and its relevance to Carr, Elton, Rorty and White: let me sketch out the *second level*.

Today we live within the general condition of *postmodernity*. We do not have a choice about this. For postmodernity is not an 'ideology' or a position we can choose to subscribe to or not; postmodernity is precisely our condition: it is our fate. And this condition has arguably been caused by the general failure – a general failure which can now be picked out very clearly as the dust settles over the twentieth century – of that experiment in social living which we call *modernity*. It is a general failure, as measured in its own terms, of the attempt, from around the eighteenth century in Europe, to bring about through the application of reason, science and technology, a level of personal and social wellbeing within social formations which, legislating for an increasingly generous emancipation of their citizens/subjects, we might characterise by saying that they were trying, at best, to become 'human rights communities'.

Of course this general failure has not been total or unrelieved; there have been many substantial successes. But notwithstanding these, I think that it is now possible to see that the two socio–economic–

political–ideological variants set to provide the vehicles for the emancipations of modernity – a bourgeois version of a liberal market capitalism, which, in the very structure and primacy of its economic imperatives was in contradiction to its universalistic 'formal', emancipatory rhetoric – and a proletarian version as articulated most cogently by (as it has turned out) various total(itarian) Marxisms, have by now either faded enough for us to have had to re-think our earlier assumptions, or have disintegrated enough for us to have had to revise our earlier hopes. And it is our own current existence at this disappointing stage (at the stage of being past modernity whilst recognising the unfulfilment of what was promised by it) that here in the West has given rise to either a series of jaded and/or nostalgic re-assessments that can be recuperated back into a now thoroughly sceptical capitalism as apologetics, or to a range of sometime radical critiques which still hold out the vague promise of an emancipatory future beyond the modern. And it is arguably in the variously articulated and tense interconnections of such re-appraisals as to what has gone wrong, that have led various theorists to a detailed consideration and critique of the foundations of modernity, re-appraisals which, historically unique in their intensity and extent as they trip across the whole discursive field, have reached the general 'conclusion' that there are not – and nor have there ever been – any 'real' foundations of the kind alleged to underpin the experiment of the modern; that we now just have to understand that we live amidst social formations which have no legitimising ontological or epistemological or ethical grounds for our beliefs or actions beyond the status of an ultimately self-referencing (rhetorical) conversation. The recognition of this, variously expressed at the level of theory from the actualities of living in the condition of post-modernity, is what I would want to call postmodernism. And here there is a type of choice available. For, although we cannot pick and choose whether we want to live in postmodernity or not, we can (and many of us still do) exercise a bit of picking and choosing between the remaining residues of old 'certaintist' modernisms (objectivity, disinterestedness, the 'facts', unbiasedness, truth) and rhetorical, 'postist' discourses (readings, positionings, perspectives, constructions, verisimilitude) rather than going totally for one or the other. Consequently it is here, between old certainties and rhetorical postist discourses, that the current debates over what constitutes history and how historical knowledge is effectively constructed, live.

The detailed reasons for this are complicated, but to give an introductory generalisation, the argument for saying that this is where history is located today rests not least on the ideological importance given to history in modernist projects. For both bourgeois and proletarian versions of modernity (their obvious differences notwithstanding) articulated as key elements in their respective ideologies, a shared view of history as a movement with a direction immanent within it – a history which was purposefully going somewhere – differing only in the selection of 'its' ultimate destination and the 'essentialist' dynamics (the entrepreneurial individual, the class struggle, etc.) which would get 'it' there. Both bourgeois and proletarian ideologies therefore expressed their historical trajectories in versions of the past articulated in the upper case, as History; that is, a way of looking at the past in terms that assigned to contingent events and situations an objective significance by identifying their place and function within a general schema of historical development usually construed as appropriately 'progressive'.[9] And today, with the capsizal of the optimism of the modernist project in ways which, metaphorically speaking, sink right down to its once ostensible roots, so we have witnessed the attendant collapse of history in the upper case; I mean, nobody really believes in that particular fantasy any more.

But that is not all. It is not only that we now realise that an upper-case history is a formal and thus empty mechanism to be filled according to taste (of History as if it was progressing towards the formal freedoms of a liberal market economy; of History as if it was what Marxists said it was). For whilst these metaphorical/allegorical versions of the past were one crucial element of modernist ideologies, another way of reading the past was also being developed within the bourgeois version. This version was just as ideological as any upper case history ever was, but, expressive of the more conservative elements of the bourgeoisie and already establishing or established interests (of those who did not, as it were, want to 'develop' too much or too fast any more in case such 'progress' proved disadvantageous to them), this variant became increasingly cultivated until, as the need for a future-orientated upper case past lost its urgency as more and more of the bourgeoisie 'made it', it became dominant. This version of history is, of course, history in the lower case, as plain, commonsense, humble 'history'; that is to say, history construed in 'academic' and 'particularistic', not worldly and universal, forms which, whilst insisting with as much force as any upper case history ever did that it was *proper* history, modestly eschewed metanarrative claims that it was discovering in the past meaningful trajectories, purposes and teleologies. Within increasingly bourgeois social formations that were able to undercut and thus marginalise the no longer needed upper case, this more servile version of history has become to such an extent *the* version that today, ensconced within the universities and other academic institutions, this way of looking at the past – as the study of the past 'for its own sake' as distinct from the study of the past explicitly for the sake of the bourgeoisie or the proletariat – has become almost natural.

But only almost. For the attempt to pass off lower case bourgeois history as though it is identical to history itself, as though the study of history in the form of the disinterested scholarship of academics studying the past 'objectively and for its own sake' (own-sakism) really is 'proper' history, is now unsustainable. For, as history in the upper case has been undercut by theorists for reasons to do with their own re-thinking of the modernist project, so the argumentative means to do this fundamental re-evaluation of the foundations of these relative failures has impacted upon the 'foundational' verities of lower case history too, the result being the problematicisation of both 'History' and 'history'. Consequently, we recognise today that there never has been, and that there never will be, any such thing as a past which is expressive of some sort of essence, whilst the idea that the proper study of history is actually 'own-sakism' is recognised as just the mystifying way in which a bourgeoisie conveniently articulates its own interests as if they belonged to the past itself. Because of the way in which upper case claims have been undercut, not only do upper case claims to be in the business of having a 'real' knowledge of the past look comic, but so do lower case claims as well. Consequently the whole 'modernist' History/history ensemble now appears as a self-referential, problematic expression of 'interests', an ideological–interpretive discourse without any 'real' access to the past as such; unable to engage in any dialogue with 'reality'. In fact, 'history' now appears to be just one more 'expression' in a world of postmodern expressions: which of course is what it is.

It is at this moment of *postmodernity* as a socio–economic–political–cultural condition, and of *postmodernism* as a pervasive theoretical presence, then, that we can begin to locate individual historians and types of history. For what current historians make of the present situation – whether they radically and variously welcome the new opportunities it affords in order to work in the cracks opened up in old upper/lower case orthodoxies, or fearfully see in

it the end of, if not the best of, all possible worlds, at least the end of
theirs – determines where they stand with regard to what they think
history now is. My argument will therefore be that those who will
be the best guides to history today are those who not only know all
about the collapse of both upper and lower case versions into
uncertainty, but who like it and can accept it. As Roland Barthes
explained in *The Discourse of History*, whilst the past can be
represented in many historians' modes, some are less mystifying than
others in as much as they overtly call attention to their own processes
of production, clearly flag their own assumptions, and indicate
explicitly and repeatedly the constituted rather than the found nature
of their referent, 'the historicised past'.

If we accept this, then it seems fairly clear to me that Carr and
Elton are, in their 'modernisms', just too certaintist, just too
mystifying, just too committed to the pretence that they can engage
in a 'real' dialogue with the 'reality' of a (somehow) non-historio-
graphically-constituted-past-as-history, to be reflexive enough
guides to the question of what is history today. No, what are needed
today are guides who realise that, modernist histories being sired
and developed within modernity, then with the end of modernity so
its ways of conceptualising history have also ended, and that within
our own postmodern times, modernist renditions are now naive:
their historical moment has passed. What are therefore required
today are guides who, accepting not so much the 'end of history' *per
se* but the 'end of modernist renditions of history', can face this with
equanimity and even optimism. In other words, guides such as
Richard Rorty and Hayden White.[10]

These, then, are my 'two levelled' reasons for choosing to move
on from Carr and Elton to Rorty and White. What I want to do
now is to explain briefly how I have organised the text in which
I have expanded these arguments in order to help the reader 'get
through it'.

I begin with a first chapter entitled 'History today'. In it I
summarise the 'nature of history' today under the impact of
postmodernism, and sketch in a few more particular aspects against
which I have then positioned Carr, Elton, Rorty and White. In
Chapters 2 to 5 I examine the four of them in more detail, detail
which I will explain when I reach the relevant chapters. But I think
that at this juncture it is useful to make just a few preliminary
observations with regard to the way they will be considered. I have
four points to make.

First, it is not my intention to go in for some kind of introductory survey or potted overview of the 'lives and works' of Carr, Elton, Rorty and White; there are, for example, no biographical details in what follows. Rather, in keeping with my general thesis that in order to understand history today we need to move on from Carr and Elton, I have simply posed to the three historians under consideration two questions; namely, what do each of them think history is (i.e., what are their views on the question of 'what is history?') and second, I have asked what possible use are the answers they give to this question to students coming to the study of what is history today in what might be termed its more 'reflexive' ways. And I have posed to Rorty a different question; namely, what does he have to say in his philosophy that 'reflects' our general intellectual condition and its consequences that will help students, from the vantage point of his position, to understand what is happening in the narrower discursive field of history.

Second, I think that by now it will be rather obvious that Carr and Elton will not come out of this particular exercise as well as Rorty and White. To which some readers may well object that my whole approach is seriously flawed because my questions are so weighted against the answers Carr and Elton give. It may be objected, for example, that it is unfair on Carr and Elton to judge their answers and their usefulness against criteria they perhaps did not know very well or rejected. However, I do not think objections of this kind have much force. For if – and this is my argument – history today is best understood in terms which Carr and Elton are, for various reasons, outside of, antithetical to or dismissive of, then this is precisely why they should no longer be used in the 'Steve Reeves meets Godzilla' approach they still so commonly are. I am certainly not arguing – and I want to make this point very clear – that Carr and Elton ought not to be discussed intensely alongside as many other historians/ theorists as can be coped with within, say, any given learning–teaching situation. Of course they should. My argument is only that their still preeminent status as the historians to raise (and possibly exhaust) the issues should be re-thought. For I think the 'issues' have now moved on, and I hope that my more favourable treatment of Rorty and White may indicate where many have moved on to.

Third, the fact that I am less critical of Rorty and White than Carr and Elton, does not mean that the former duo have escaped critiques by many other people. Indeed, in the case of Rorty, 'Rorty-bashing' has almost become an intellectual sport, and for those who would like to get a possibly more 'rounded' view of him, then they could well turn to the substantial criticisms to be found in, say, Norris, Bhaskar or Bernstein, and to the collection of critical essays edited by Malachowski – as I do myself on occasion.[11] But on the whole I have tended to write favourably on Rorty because: (a) I like a lot of what I think he says; and (b) I can use him for my own purposes. Quite fittingly I suppose, my treatment of Rorty has been pragmatic. So has my use of White. Like Rorty, White has some vociferous opponents and I am not unaware of some of the charges levelled against him.[12] But although I have taken some of these on board, and whilst I cannot say I have ever found White an 'easy' or unproblematical read, I have invariably found him immensely stimulating and provocative. It is because of both of these qualities in White – that he is both difficult and yet extremely worthwhile – that I have written about him in the manner I have: in a way which I hope is not too simplistic or 'vulgar' but certainly popularising, leaving it open to readers to go on to the detailed critiques if they wish.

All this is not to say – and this is the last comment I want to make in this third section – that I regard Rorty and White as having the last word on anything, or believe they have just about got things right. Because that is not my view. Nor, of course, are Rorty and White the most 'revolutionary' theorists writing today, not least because they are effectively 'radical/left liberals', and I am particularly conscious of critiques of Rorty and White that come from further along the political left; in that sense they hardly offer 'the last word' either. But as I have already explained, I think that at this specific postmodern juncture Rorty and White do make the sort of radical and broad interventions that both encapsulate the condition of postmodernity and offer starting points to move on from. Rorty and White are not to be read as 'endings', then, but as potential beginnings; theorists to be used as possible starting points, whether positively or negatively it must be for those using them to decide. But I am positive about them.

Fourth, I want to say something about the length of this book and the 'personal' way in which it has been written. I have tried to keep the book fairly short simply because it is something of a polemic as well as an expository exercise. Thus, whilst it is perfectly possible and legitimate for readers to dip into the book in order to get out of it what they want (so that, for example, someone thinking they may be able to get a quick crib on Carr may go just to his chapter) and whilst the individual chapters on Carr, Elton, Rorty and White might be read as fairly autonomous 'interpretations' of their subject as such, I hope that most readers will read the book in the way in which it has been sequenced and in its entirety in order to get the full argument. Hence its relative shortness, which might make it manageable to be read in four or five sittings. At the same time, of course, one of the consequences of writing both a short and a relatively polemical text, is that it increases the risk of both under- and overstatement, whilst the occasional resultant exaggeration or reduction in order to make a point visible and different enough to be noted – especially in the more critical Carr and Elton chapters – is a recurrent risk. However, I think that such risks are worth taking given the possible (if by no means certain) benefits, and here I would draw support from Dominick LaCapra's note in the concluding chapter of what he regards as his own polemical book, *History and Criticism*, wherein he writes:

> This book is obviously polemical in its attempt to rethink certain assumptions and procedures of the historical craft. It is intended as a critical intervention in a profession where debates about self-understanding and practice are not as prevalent as I think they should be. . . . In spite of the difficulties of ever finding convincing proofs of large-scale judgements, I would contend that I do not simply set up 'straw men'. I think the exaggerations bring into relief prevalent features of current historiography that are indeed open to question.[13]

Finally, a further comment not unconnected to LaCapra's. Which is to say that despite all I have previously argued, some readers may still think that when surveying aspects of a discursive field for introductory and expository purposes as well as polemical ones, then I really ought to have been more neutral, objective, balanced and disinterested in my respective treatments of Carr, Elton, Rorty and White. To which my reply is that I think that by now we should all have learned that this particular stricture must go unheeded. For today we know of no such things as neutral/objective 'interpretation', as 'innocent' surveys, as 'unpositioned positions'. Rather, we should all know by now that the best we can do is to alert and keep on alerting 'readers' to the position we are interpreting from, rather than imagining that interpretations not only might spring from nowhere, but that some interpretations are not interpretive at all but 'the truth'. As Dean MacCannell has observed:

Everything written in the 'objective style' . . . now risks being read as a kind of political cover-up; hidden complicity. . . . Interestingly, the one path that still leads in the direction of scholarly objectivity, detachment, and neutrality is exactly the one originally thought to lead away from these classic virtues: that is, an openly autobiographical style in which the subjective position of the author, especially on political matters, is presented in a clear and straightforward fashion. At least this enables the reader to review his or her own position to make the adjustments necessary for dialogue.[14]

Chapter 1

History today

No discourse – and therefore no contribution to, and/or comment on, aspects of an existing discourse – is of 'a natural kind'. You cannot find a historical or geographical or scientific or literary discourse just out there, just growing wild. Discourses are cultural, cultivated, fabricated and thus ultimately arbitrary, ways of carving up what comes to constitute their 'field', so that like any approach in any other discursive practice an introductory discussion about 'history today' could begin from innumerable starting points and be developed in various ways: in these matters one always has to make a start (and come to an end) somewhere. Accordingly, what follows is just my own way of introducing a little of what I think is going on in debates about history today, just one way of trying to locate Carr, Elton, Rorty and White in relation to them, and just one way of helping me to reach the conclusion I want to reach and which I hope might appear plausible; namely, that Carr and Elton, unlike Rorty and White, are, in their modernisms, not much to the point when now discussing the question of 'what is history?'

My approach has four parts. First, in Section One of this chapter, an examination of how aspects of history are now being considered and problematised from textualist and 'postist' viewpoints will be carried out. To get into this area I start from the premise that there is a radical distinction to be drawn between 'the past' and 'history', going on to look at how this distinction has been 'worked' by three historians/theorists (Tony Bennett, F. R. Ankersmit and Hayden White himself) so as to arrive at some early and general understanding of what history today arguably is. Second, I look at just four 'representative' implications for 'traditional' histories as occasioned by such workings of the past–history distinction; implications involving the areas of ideology, historicism, historical truth and empiricism. Third, because these (and similar) implications have given rise to understandable resistances from traditional historians right across the intellectual and ideological spectrum, I give some indication of the sorts of debates that are currently taking place with regard to the impact of such textualist/postist discourses and my own position in relation to them so that I will then be able to contextualise and locate (and this constitutes the fourth and last section) Carr, Elton, Rorty and White, before going on to look at each of them in detail.

SECTION ONE: WORKING THE PAST-HISTORY DISTINCTION

Let us start, then, from the assumption that historical theory today can best be accessed by drawing a radical distinction between 'the past' and 'history', rendering the idea of history – as the various accounts constructed about the past by historians and those acting as if they were historians – by the term historiography. Let us assume that we do not just want to recognise this past–historiography difference and then pass on quickly to 'do' some history, but that 'we' want to dwell on it, to make it the centre of our concerns so that we might understand history via some of today's most important debates. And let us say that the best entrée into these debates is via some general ideas about historiography as articulated by Bennett, Ankersmit and White.

Thus, for Tony Bennett, it would appear that characterising history as historiography (as writing, as texts different to the past which, whilst not itself a literal text, can only be 'read' through its remaining textual traces, its once actuality being inaccessible simply by virtue of it no longer existing) *theorises* both the notion of 'the past' and the 'writing-up' of it.[1] For, given that the past exists by definition only in the modality of its current historiographical representations, then this means that the issues involved in 'traditional' debates about the nature of historical scholarship can be rethought in a manner that allows a break with the ways in which they have been posed as part of a general epistemological problem concerning the nature of our access to the past as such. For, as Bennett says, that 'is not the point at issue in historical inquiry, and never has been'.[2] For historians, of course, never access the past *as such*, so that the problems formulated along the traditional lines of, 'how can historians truly/accurately know the past?', or, 'if historians cannot access the "real past", then how can we have checks on historians' accounts that are "real" checks as opposed to being "just interpretations"?', are beside the point. For what is at issue in historiography – and indeed what can only ever be at issue – is what can be derived and constructed from the *historicised* record or archive. It is the 'historicised' nature of the records/archives that historians access which must be stressed here. For such records and archives are, as Bennett explains, only too clearly highly volatile and mutable products of complex historical processes in that, apart from the considerable amount of organised labour (librarians, archivists, archaeologists, curators) which goes into their production (preserving, cataloguing, indexing, 'weeding out'), the composition and potential of such traces/records vary considerably in terms of their potential use over time witness, says Bennett, 'the influence of feminist historiography in expanding the range of what now counts as the historical record.'[3] In this way, then, we can think of 'the past as such' as being an absent object of inquiry, its presence (its *absent presence*) being signified by its remaining traces, which is the only 'real past' we have, such traces functioning not as the historian's referent in the sense of actually being some kind of extra-discursive reality, but as if they were such a referent in that they constitute the last court of appeal for historical disputes, 'the point at which, so to speak, they hit base – but a base within discourse.'[4]

On this account history is therefore simply the (itself historicised) discipline through which historians working at the level of what Bennett has called the *public historical sphere* (e.g. salaried workers in higher education) come into contact with the historicised record or archive as currently existing in order to 'intervene' in it (to interpret it) so that from this perspective historiography may be regarded as a

> specific discursive regime, governed by distinctive procedures, through which the maintenance/transformation of the past as a set of currently existing realities is regulated. It constitutes a disciplined means for the production of a 'historical past' which exercises a regulatory function in relation to the 'public past'. Its role in this regard is enormously important. [for] While their effects may not be immediately apparent in the short term, the conduct of historical debates and their (always provisional) resolution decisively influence the public face of the past over the long term ... such debates requir[ing] as a condition of their

intelligibility, the sense of a distinction between past and present and an orientation to historical records *as if* they comprised a referent. That this referent proves to be intra-discursive and so mutable does not disable the historical enterprise. To the contrary: the discipline's social productivity consists precisely in its capacity to reorganise its referent and thus transform 'the past' – not as it was but as it is. Understood in this way, the cogency and productivity of historical enquiry may be admitted without the question of its relations to 'the real past' ever arising.[5]

This is not to doubt for a moment that the past actually existed, of course, but rather that in respect of what is at issue in historiographical disputes and the manner in which they are conducted, 'it may be allowed to go its own way – as it surely has'. In this perfectly straightforward way of seeing things, then, the 'real past' doesn't actually enter into historiography except rhetorically – except theoretically – so that in this sense we can understand in quite a matter of fact way some of what Derrida is driving at in his (in)famous remark that 'there is nothing outside of the text', that there is no 'extra text'.[6]

Now, Bennett's own way of putting his argument is more nuanced and developed than the brief reading offered here, but pulling things together as they have been described, Bennett's point might be summarised by saying that 'the past as constituted by its existing traces' is always apprehended and appropriated textually through the sedimented layers of previous interpretations and through the reading habits and categories developed by previous/current methodological practices. Consequently, the status of historical knowledge is not based for its truth/accuracy on its correspondence with the past *per se* but on the various historicisations of it, so that historiography always 'stands in for' the past, the only medium it has to affect a 'historical' presence. Accordingly, such arguments as these go some considerable length towards undercutting traditional historiography insofar as it seems to depend upon that correspondence as actually being between historiography and a separate, non-historiographically constituted past. Here, some interesting arguments by White and Ankersmit develop what is meant by such 'undercuttings'.

Although, as we shall see, White occasionally articulates his definition of what he thinks history is in different ways, the understanding which I think he usually works with is that the historical work is a verbal artifact, a narrative prose discourse, the content of which is as much invented – or as much imagined – as found.[7] It is White's stress on the invented/imagined element that I want to explain and develop at this point: what does he arguably mean?

I think White means at least two things. First, that in order to make sense of events or sets of events in the past, in order to make 'the facts' of the past 'significant', such events/facts always have to be related to a context, to some sort of 'whole' or 'totality' or 'background', or even to the notion of 'the past itself'. Here the problem is that whilst the historian can certainly 'find' the traces of past events in the historicised records/archive and thus (selectively) establish (some of) 'the facts' about them in, say, a chronicle-type form, no historian can ever find the context or the totality or the background or 'the past as such' against which the facts can become truly significant and meaningful. What this means is that any such 'context' which is constructed to contextualise the facts has to be ultimately imagined or invented; unlike facts, the contexts can never be definitively found. Therefore, because to be meaningful all historical accounts have to involve part-to-whole or whole-to-part relationships (that is, as we shall see White put it later, accounts to be meaningful involve metonymic or synecdochal 'tropes'),[8] then at least three conclusions can be drawn at this early point. First, that all interpretations of the past are indeed as much invented (the contexts) as found (the facts) so that, on this first argument alone, White's definition seems plausible. Second, because of this imagined (fictive) element in all histories (i.e. histories of both the upper and lower case) then no history can be literally 'factual' or completely 'found' or absolutely 'true'. Third, that because of the inevitable troping of parts-to-whole and whole-to-parts, then all historical accounts are ultimately metaphorical and thus – because of their inescapable troping – metahistorical.

This is the first thing that White seems to mean by his understanding that the historical work is as much invented as found. The second is this. White thinks that most historians consider that the characteristic form in which they represent their accounts of the past to their audience – that is, the narrative form – is the actual content of the past (namely narrativity) then go on mistakenly to treat such narrativity as an essence shared by both the historical representation and the sets of events in the past. Now, this is perhaps a difficult point to grasp when stated baldly, so it might be useful to take a few sentences to spell it out. Accordingly, White's explanation might be said to go roughly as follows.

Since its invention by Herodotus, traditional historiography has predominantly featured the belief that history consists of congeries of lived stories, individual and collective, and that the principal task of the historian is to discover these stories and retell them in narrative form, the truth/accuracy of which would reside in the degree of correspondence of the story told to the story lived. However, says White, the point to be made here is that, unfortunately for this traditional view, it has recently been realised that people in the past *did not actually live stories* either individually (at the level of 'real-life' stories) or collectively (at the level of, say, metanarratives which give purpose and meaning to the past as, for example, in Marxist or Whig theories of history) so that to see people in the past or the past 'as such' in story form, is to give to it an imaginary series of narrative structures and coherences it actually never had. To see the *content* of the past (i.e. what actually occurred) as if it were a series of stories (of great men, of wars and treaties, of the rise of labour, the emancipation of women, of 'Our Island Story', of the ultimate victory of the proletariat and so forth) is therefore a piece of 'fiction', caused by mistaking the narrative *form* in which historians construct and communicate their knowledge of the past as actually being the past's own. Accordingly, the traditional idea that the truth/accuracy of history as told in narrative is evidenced by its degree of correspondence to stories once lived is 'undercut' when it is recognised that there are *no stories in the past to correspond to*: that the only stories the past has are those conferred on it by historians' interpretative emplotments. Thus, any theory of correspondence that goes beyond the level of the statement and/or the chronicle – *and by definition historiography always goes beyond the statement and the chronicle* – is ultimately self-referencing. Ultimately, any such alleged correspondence is not between the historian's story and the story the past itself would – if only it could – tell, but between the historian's story and the past's story as put into narrative form 'in the past tense' by historians themselves.

This point is reinforced a little differently by Ankersmit. For him,[9] the history text consists of many individual statements. Most of these claim to give an accurate description of some state of affairs in the past. Historians formulate these statements on the basis of the sources they work on in archives, etc., and it is these sources when used as 'evidence' that will decide the truth or falsity of the statements in question. But – and this is Ankersmit's argument – because the sources available to most historians will enable them to write many more 'true' statements than are actually to be found in their texts, then out of all the statements the historian could have made, the ones actually made are carefully selected, distributed and weighted, the result being that a certain 'picture of the past' (an icon) is fabricated. Consequently, says Ankersmit, we can make two points about the texts' statements: (1) that *individually* they refer to, and describe, a fragment of the past and can either be true or false; and (2) they *collectively* define a 'picture of the past' which cannot be said to be either true or false but simply an 'iconic' impression/reading. For – and this is where Ankersmit and White come closely together – the significant point is that whilst it is generally the case that individual discrete statements (facts) can indeed be checked against the discrete source to see if the historian's account corresponds to it, the 'picture of the past' cannot be so checked, simply because the statements as put together by the historian to form such a picture do not have a picture of their own prior to this assembly for that assembly to then be checked against. And since, argues Ankersmit, what is essential in the writing of historians is not to be found at the level of the individual statement but rather at the level of the picture of the past (in that it is these pictures which, for example, most stimulate historiographical debate and thus determine the way we 'see' the past), then historiography is again as much invented/imagined as found. Saying true things about the past at the level of the statement is easy – anybody can do that – but saying the right things, getting the picture straight, that is not only another story but an impossible one: you can always get another picture, you can always get another context.[10]

SECTION TWO: FOUR IMPLICATIONS OF BENNETT, ANKERSMIT AND WHITE

Now, as has already been suggested, these ways of theorising and working the past–historiography difference have some serious implications, especially for traditional history, in that once the impossibility of any literal representation of the traces of the past as the past *per se* is seen, then all such representations, being ultimately as much imagined/invented as found, mean that historiography ultimately becomes a series of ideas (theories) that historians have about making the past into 'history', all of which are problematic.

At this point, then, it might be useful to consider briefly four examples of what such problematicisations of traditional historiography might be, not least because it is against them that some 'traditional' historians have recently reacted, it being this 'engagement' that provides the basis for many of the debates on what is history today, within and against which Carr, Elton, Rorty and White might be located.

The *first* problem is ideological and again takes cognisance of some of White's arguments as a point of entry. For, White knows very well that at the level of historical meaning (as opposed to the level of the statement/chronicle), the conviction that the past has some sort of comprehensible meaning *in it* stands, in these postmodern days, on the same level of conviction that it has not; that is to say, the matter is undecidable. Consequently, any claims which suggest that history *has* to be considered in a specific way because such a way embodies, or reflects, or is expressive of what the past and/or historiography really are, are ideological. Such claims are equally ideological whether they are made at the level of the upper case, as 'History', or at the level of the lower, as 'history', the lower case being seen by White as effectively 'bourgeois'. For having had their own use of history in the upper case (for example in Whiggism) the bourgeoisie, having nothing else to 'become' in so far as they now live in their once future, have no need for a historical trajectory that has not yet reached its destination. Consequently, what could be more 'natural' (i.e. ideological) than understanding 'proper' history as a non-worldly, academic discipline ostensibly above politics? The conclusion to be drawn, therefore, is that all histories (that is, historiography as such) are suasive. History is always history for someone, and that someone cannot be the past itself for the past does not have a self, so that any history which considers its particular type of discourse (its *species* type) as identical to history *per se* (its *genus*) is not only ideological, but ideological nonsense.

The *second* problem is related to the first, and again it draws on White. For White sees all histories, in whichever case, as equally *historicist*. He rejects the dichotomous view, held especially by 'bourgeois' historians, that historicism is an improper use of the past in so far as it uses it 'illegitimately' to illuminate present-day problems and/or, worse still, predict future events, on the basis that every representation, 'however particularizing, narrativist, self-consciously perspectival, and fixated on its subject matter "for its own sake", contains most of the elements of . . . historicism.' All historians have to shape their materials somehow *vis-à-vis* the present imperatives of narrative in general, and White argues that in the very language historians use, they subject the past to the kinds of 'distortions' that historicists impose upon their materials in a more explicit way, for

How else can any past, which by definition comprises events, processes, structures and so forth, considered to be no longer perceivable, be represented in either consciousness or discourse except in an 'imaginary' way?[11]

In that sense, those old dichotomies (so beloved of the seminar room) between 'proper' history and 'historicism', and between 'proper' history and 'ideological' history, obscure more than they illuminate about historical representation, the only difference between these oppositions being that in 'proper' history the element of overt construction is displaced into the interior of the narrative, whilst the element of 'found' data is permitted to occupy the position of prominence in the imagined story-line itself, in upper case history the reverse being the case: these are two sides of the same coin.

That is not all. For, at this particular conjuncture of the post-modern condition, the remarks made earlier (especially in the Introduction) are pertinent. To argue, in this context, that the study of history should have nothing to do with projecting 'a past into the future', is precisely as present-centred and ideological (historicist) as the argument that it should. That is, whereas upper case history is generally quite explicit that it is present-centred in its use of the past as a basis for a trajectory into a different future, the fact that the bourgeoisie doesn't want a different future, and therefore doesn't want a past-based 'future orientated trajectory' (the fact that at this point the past can be neutralised and studied not for 'our sake' but its own) is precisely what is needed in the present. Thus to pretend not to be present-centred is what actually constitutes the present-centredness of lower case history. Consequently, both upper and lower case histories serve – by the way they situate themselves in the present – their own present-centred (historicist) needs.

Third, the above two arguments (and indeed perhaps all the remarks made already) underline the point that all history is interpretive and never literally true (besides anything else, a 'true interpretation' is an oxymoron). For, as already argued après Ankersmit and White, in history discourse historians transform into ultimately imagined narratives a list of past events that would otherwise be only a collection of singular statements and/or a chronicle. Consequently, to effect this transformation, to give disparate facts some 'unity of significance', then the events, dates, agents, etc. represented in the statements/chronicle must be encoded. The obvious point to be made here is that this encoding is not of the type which means that the narrative explains more fully or more correctly the statements/chronicle, but rather that narration produces a meaning quite different from them, as it emplots the events which serve as its primary referent into patterns of meaning no literal representation of them as facts could ever produce. This means that, since no given set of events are, say, intrinsically tragic, heroic, or farcical, but can only be constituted as such relative to a given story-type that endows them with a meaningful form, then precisely insofar as the narrative endows real events with the kind of meaning found otherwise only in myth and literature, we are justified in regarding such a construct as an *allegory*. Indeed, says White, a 'narrative account is always a figurative account, an allegory', it being only a modern empirical prejudice 'in favour of literalism that obscures this fact to many modern analysts of historical narrative'. And certainly all this is well known to those who work on the margins – say in hermeneutics – where historiography is seen less as a decipherment than as a 'translation' and a 'carrying over' of meanings from one discursive community to another.[12] In other words, history as a discourse is not an 'epistemology'.

Fourth and *finally*, because an iconic/narrative account is always a figurative account, an allegory, then history cannot have a 'true' correspondence in ways traditionally seen as *mimetic* or *empirical*. For, as White again argues against the idea of mimesis, even in the most chaste prose (that is, history texts intended to represent things as they are without any rhetorical adornment)

> every mimetic text can be shown to have left something out of the description of its object or to have put something into it that is inessential to what *some* reader, with more or less authority, will regard as an adequate description.[13]

On analysis, then, every mimesis can serve as an occasion for yet another description of the same phenomenon, one claiming to be more 'faithful to the facts'. And so on *ad infinitum* – this is a world of endless deferments – Derrida's world. Thus, by extension from mimesis, empiricism, with its obsession for getting the facts (and getting them right), along with its attendant fetishising of the sources wherein they are to be found, succumbs also to the critique of deferral. For empiricism is most flawed, White argues, when it refuses to see how narrative *constitutes* the grounds whereon one decides what shall count as a 'fact' in the matters under consideration in the first place. Again, this is not to say that 'facts' do not exist, rather that the most they can offer (and here White draws on Collingwood) are the *elements* that can be made into a story by emplotment. This means that how a given past situation is to be plausibly configured depends on the historian's skill in matching up a specific plot structure with the set of events/facts he or she wishes to endow with meanings of a certain kind, the plausibility of the result(s) being matched up not only to the 'now' constituted and worked facts, but intertextually *vis-à-vis* the condition of the history culture of any given social formation.

SECTION THREE: SOME REACTIONS AND SOME RESPONSES

If these are just some of the implications to be drawn from just a few of the current debates, then these various undercuttings of the correspondence-type realist/empirical 'foundations' upon which traditional historians have defined their own brands of history as if theirs was history as such (this being one of the means whereby they have tried to prevent 'history' from falling to the possibility of it being defined as 'whatever anybody wants it to be') have given rise to understandable anxiety. For, as more and more people have come to see that there is no such thing as a history 'of a natural kind' (and that what predominantly passes for history is only the definition of those who have previously had the power to define it and that 'others' may now wish to define it 'other'-wise), then traditionalists have been forced onto the defensive. They have been made to assert that, in a curious sort of way, their definitions of history are more or less 'of a natural kind' type – and that history effectively has a 'properness' which they have captured – in order to prevent what they see as the establishment of a dangerous 'relativism' or even some sort of anarchic nihilism. Hence the rallying cries that have recently been heard from various traditionalist positions, that not only 'their' histories but in fact history 'as such' is in mortal danger, this ringing of the alarm bells against the common dangers emanating from a general 'textual' postmodernism of the sort just described being seen as something which is not restricted to those traditionalists on, say, the political right, but includes all those who might be termed traditionalists within ideological positions. That is to say, opposition to postmodernism is today coming from traditionalists within the Marxist left, from traditionalists within the liberal centre, and from traditionalists within the conservative right. To make this a little more complicated, it can also be seen that the postmodernists who are attacked are not neatly located in some clearly identified and hence easily targeted 'party', but rather – as embodiments of a general condition – are to be found right across the political spectrum and thus *within* each of the broad ideological positions mentioned.

And it is not only that. For, to make all of this even more complicated, many of the traditionalists across the political spectrum are convinced that, although some of their fellow-travellers are indeed inclined to postmodernism, nevertheless, such weak spirits have only deviated from the general party line because they do not see how much postmodernism derives from, and thus benefits, rival ideological positions. Thus, there are those on the left who, whilst appreciating that their number includes postmodernists, still want to say that postmodernism is essentially an expression of a stage of late-capitalism and so is especially advantageous to (and even the property of) the centre and/or the right. Similarly, there are some on the right who, whilst conscious of their own Young Turks, insist that postmodernism is a radical, deconstructive (i.e. destructive) force particularly emanating from the left, and intent upon abolishing all (i.e. their) values. Similarly, there are those in the liberal centre who, whilst recognising the liberal sentiments of anti-foundational pragmatists and the like, are fearful of that type of anti-foundationalist radical who says that his/her postmodernism is a necessary clearing away of the accumulated impediments that have grown up to prevent a freer and more emancipated liberal utopia, interpreting this extension of freedom as an invitation to types of unnatural licence that will further threaten the stability of liberal social formations already problematicised by the individualistic practices of its normative hero, *homo economicus*.

Accordingly, in order to gain a further understanding of the impact of postmodern tendencies on traditional histories/historians across the spectrum, and to locate within it Carr, Elton, Rorty and White, I think it might be useful to give a brief account of just some of the 'controversies' with regard to the question of 'what is history?' which postmodernists are causing, as coming from the traditional centre, the traditional right and the traditional left, and how these criticisms might be met and rebutted. What then, to begin with, are some 'traditionalist' objections to the impact of postmodernism on history like? I start with a typical example drawn from what might best be regarded as the traditional centre.

Thus, in a recent series of exchanges in the journal *Past and Present*, Lawrence Stone and Gabrielle Spiegel have raised a call to arms against the inroads into history made by a 'textualising' postmodernism.[14] According to Stone, what 'historians' ought to object to is when postmodern types say such 'textualist' things as 'reality is defined *purely* as language', or when they declare, 'not that truth is unknowable, but that there is no reality out there which is anything but a subjective creation of the historian; in other words, that it is language that creates meaning which in turn creates our image of the real'. For clearly this is a threat to history *per se* because, 'if there is nothing outside the text, then history as we [sic] have known it collapses altogether, and fact and fiction become indistinguishable from one another'. Only so long as it stays on the right side of this breakpoint does Stone concede that the 'linguistic turn' in history might have some merit.[15] This is a similar position to that taken by Spiegel:

> As a language-based conception of reality, [a textualist] post-structuralism has disrupted traditional ... historical modes of interpretation by its denial of a referential and material world. ... Until recently the writing of history depended on a concept of language which, as Nancy Partner puts it, 'unhesitatingly asserts the external reality of the world, its intelligibility in the form of ideas, concepts, phenomena or other mental things and a direct connection between mental things and verbal signs'. But post-structuralism has shattered this confident assumption of the relation between words and things, language and extra-linguistic reality, on the grounds, as she states, that language is the 'very structure of mental life, and no meta-language can ever stand outside itself to observe a reality external to itself.' This dissolution of the materiality of the verbal sign, its ruptured relation to extra-linguistic reality, entails the dissolution of history, since it denies the ability of language to 'relate' to (or account for) any reality other than itself. Such a view of the closed reflexivity of language ... necessarily jeopardizes historical study as normally understood ... If texts – documents, literary works, whatever – do not transparently reflect reality, but only other texts, then historical study can scarcely be distinguished from literary study, and the 'past' dissolves into literature.[16]

Meanwhile, from the traditional wing of the conservative right, Elton has attacked postmodern exponents of this so-called linguistic/narrative turn as 'obtrusive theoreticians' and as 'prophets of uncertainty, relativism and individual self-love, to the point where history is said to have no independent reality at all', it being this 'nihilist conclusion that a proper training – a professional training – in the treatment of the historical evidence will eliminate: real and informed contact with the relics of the past ought to cure people of those philosophical vapours'.[17]

On the traditional left, there are those (Christopher Norris, Terry Eagleton, Alex Callinicos, Fredric Jameson, Raphael Samuel *et al.*)[18] who see in textualism/postmodernism not only its radical potential to undercut any remaining bourgeois certainties, but also its ability to be used by enemies of the left to do the same to theirs. Here is a passage from Elizabeth Fox-Genovese wherein she articulates rather typically the ambivalence felt by the left for a postmodernism it cannot ignore but which apparently threatens its own political cogency and power:

> We still use history to refer, however imprecisely, to what we like to think really happened in the past and to the ways in which specific authors have written about it. Contemporary critics [however] tend to insist disproportionately on history as the ways in which specific authors have written about the past at the expense of what might actually have happened [and] insist that history consists primarily of a body of texts and a strategy of reading or interpreting them. Yet history also consists, in a very old-fashioned sense, in a body of knowledge – in the sum of reliable information about the past that historians have discovered and assembled. And beyond that knowledge, history must also be recognized as what did happen in the past – of the social relations and, yes, 'events' of which our records offer only imperfect clues.
>
> History cannot [therefore] simply be reduced – or elevated – to a collection, theory, and practice of reading texts. . . . It is possible to classify price series or coin deposits or hog weights or railroad lines as texts – possible, but ultimately useful only as an abstraction that flattens historically and theoretically significant distinctions. . . . For historians, the text exists as a function, or articulation, of context. In this sense historians work at the juncture of the symbiosis between text and context, with context understood to mean the very conditions of textual production and dissemination.

... History [therefore] at least good history ... is inescapably structural. Not reductionist, not present minded, not teleological: structural. ... By structural, I mean that history must disclose and reconstruct the conditions of consciousness and action, with conditions understood as systems of social relations. ... I further mean that, at any given moment, systems of relations operate in relation to a dominant tendency ... what Marxists call a mode of production – that endows them with a structure. Both in the past and in the interpretation of the past history follows a pattern or structure, according to which some systems of relations and some events possess greater significance than others. Structure, in this sense, governs the writing and reading of texts.[19]

Now, how might these not untypical objections to a 'textualist', postmodern approach to history of the type recommended by Bennett, Ankersmit and White et al. be met? Well, it is clear that engagement with the details of Spiegel or Fox-Genovese would take some time and, besides, there are points in their arguments where one may be in some agreeement. But having said that, the sorts of critique offered by Spiegel et al. seem to rest at a *general* level either on misunderstandings of what 'textualism' is, as used, for example, by Bennett and Ankersmit and White, or they hark back to a way of thinking about types of 'grounds' for historical knowledge that have, in actual fact, *never* been available to them. What follows are therefore four lightly sketched in responses to Stone et al.[20]

First, it is no part of any postmodernist argument that I know – not Bennett's nor Ankersmit's nor White's nor Rorty's nor Derrida's, nor even Baudrillard's – to deny the material existence of the past or the present. Not for a moment do they not take it as 'given' that there is indeed an actual world 'out there' which has been out there for a long time, which has a past. Nor do they deny that that world is the effects of causes which do not include as causes their current mental states. In other words, postmodernists are not idealists.

Second, whilst there is thus no assumption at work within postmodernism about there not being an actual past, there *is* a strong insistence that that once actual past is, après Bennett, only accessible to us through texts and thus as a 'reading'. Thus, the point to be made against Stone et al., is that Stone would be identifying a problem within the idea of the past as textuality, only if the past had ever been accessed (or could logically ever be accessed) outside of textuality. For, if the past had ever been, or could ever be, accessed/appropriated/

expressed directly, then textuality would indeed deform and distort it. But given that such direct access has never been possible (presumably for the past to 'express itself' it would have to 're-enact itself'); given, that is, that the only past that historians have ever had access to is precisely Bennett's historicised records/archive, and given that in practice historians have pretty much to a woman and man had no problems whatsoever in accepting this *as if* this was exactly what, at a minimalist level, 'studying the past historically' meant (i.e. going to the record office, surveying a site, reading other historians, accepting a structural metaphor if one felt like it), then the objections to textuality by Stone *et al.* are taken on behalf of a practice no historian has ever achieved or is ever likely to.

Third, this is not of course to deny the point implied and/or variously made by Stone *et al.*, that if the historian's interpretation of the past cannot be checked against the past as such (i.e. if the stories historians tell cannot, après White, be checked out with reference to the past's own historical rendering of itself; or, if the pictures constructed – après Ankersmit – cannot be checked out with reference to the past's own historical iconography) then it follows that over and above the statement and the chronicle there can be no fully independent check on historians' accounts save by other historians' accounts; that is to say, intertextually by recourse to 'peer appraisal'. But of course this would only be a problem for historiography *now*; would only signal the end of historiography *now*, if historiography's continued existence depended on this having not always been the case (i.e. if, in effect, 'peer review' was not the generally accepted bottom line with regard to the plausibility of any historian's interpretation; if, in effect, an historian's reputation was not ultimately dependent upon 'peer conversations'). But it has to be, for the events and situations of the past cannot judge the interpretations conferred upon them precisely because they are the phenomena about which the interpretations are being made. So what is going on here, what might Stone and the others be worried about? I think there are possibly two things: (a) that Stone *et al.* fear that the 'peers' who may be increasingly called upon to do the reviewing of 'proper' historians' practices may find them intellectually unconvincing; and (b) that such new peers might accordingly open up historiography far more generously than hitherto so as to include historians currently marginalised, so relativising (by taking away their ostensible 'real' foundations) traditional practices and thus indeed endangering 'history as "we" have known it'.

Similarly, the crucial argument from Spiegel that the 'dissolution of the materiality of the verbal sign means the dissolution of history', would only have any weight if Spiegel could show that history as a 'discipline' had ever rested on a verbal sign whose materiality had never been 'undissolved'. But given that this has never been the case, then it is difficult to see what has changed by 'textualising historiography', except that we now know that history just is, and always has been, textual, so making us suspicious of the motives of those who see this recognition of what has always been the case ('nothing has changed') as something of a crisis, rather than, say, a celebration and an opportunity for increasingly reflexive work. Here ideology and mystification are at work. Of course this last point can be applied directly to Elton's fear of 'postist' tendencies as leading towards nihilism. For it seems reasonable to suggest that it is only because Elton thinks that his version of history (as a lower case phenomenon) is really 'proper' history that he can fear – as a result of his own view of history coming to an end – that this signals the end of 'things' themselves, i.e. nihilism (and what, one might ask, could be more full of self-love than that?) For, if this was not the case, if Elton did not identify his particular *species* of history with its *genus*, then it is difficult to understand why he cannot relax and enjoy the rich plurality of the different ways of reading the past which postmodernism suggests (not least because Elton is at pains to point out that he is himself a pluralist – the generally anti-Eltonist McLennan agreeing that this constitutes a major part of Elton's ideological position).[21] The only conclusion to be drawn, then, is not that Elton doesn't like pluralism, but that he likes only the sort of pluralism he likes, i.e. a pluralism which doesn't have the generosity to include, say, Hayden White within it.

Fourth, and finally, with regard to the sort of objections to textualism raised by Elizabeth Fox-Genovese from the vantage point of a Marxist (structural) methodological appropriation of the past, it would be useful here simply to juxtapose against her position the claims for textuality made by Hayden White himself. For, it would appear that if Fox-Genovese thinks textualism *prevents* her from doing the 'structural' history she wants to do (and if Stone or Spiegel *et al.* think it prevents them from using the kind of historical method they like; or if they think it stops them from not being able to continue in the same way as they have been doing if they wish) then she (and they) have just not realised that textualism *is not a way of 'doing' history at all*. This is the crucial, but, it would seem overlooked, point. For what textualism does is to draw attention to the 'textual conditions' under which *all* historical work is done and *all* historical knowledge is produced. What textualism does is to allow all the various methodological approaches, be they Marxist, or empiricist, or phenomenological, or whatever, to continue just as before, but with the proviso that none of them can continue to think that they gain direct access to, or 'ground' their textuality in, a 'reality' appropriated plain, that they have an epistemology. What textualism does is to add a heightened sense of reflexivity as to the limits and possibilities of historical understanding. Textuality, then, is the condition operating in *everybody's* histories; it is impossible to conceive of a history that is not textual; textuality, as they say, 'is the only game in town'. Here then is White pulling all of this together, after which I want to summarise my own defence of textualism/ postmodernism before proceeding – in the light of what will by then have been said – to the fairly straightforward (but essential if they are to be easily understood *vis-à-vis* the 'history question') ideological positionings of Carr, Elton, Rorty and White. And here is White now:

> First, it should be said that every approach to the study of the past presupposes or entails some version of a textualist theory of historical reality of some kind. This is because, primarily, the historical past is, as Fredric Jameson has argued, accessible to study 'only by way of its prior textualisations', whether these be in the form of the documentary record or in the form of accounts of what happened in the past written up by historians themselves on the basis of their research into the record. Secondly, historical accounts of the past are themselves based upon the presumed adequacy of a written representation or textualisation of the events of the past to the reality of those events themselves. Historical events, whatever else they may be, are events which really happened or are believed really to have happened, but which are no longer directly accessible to perception. As such, in order to be constituted as objects of reflection, they must be described ... in some kind of natural or technical language. The analysis or explanation ... that is subsequently provided of the events is [therefore] always an analysis or explanation of the events as previously *described*. The description is a product of processes of linguistic condensation, displacement, symbolization, and second-ary revision of the kind that inform the production of texts. On this basis alone, one is justified in speaking of history as a text.

This is, to be sure, a metaphor, but it is no more metaphorical than Marx's statement that 'all previous history is the history of class struggle' or the statement by Fox-Genovese that 'History, at least good history, is inescapably structural'. More importantly, the statement 'History is a text' is in no way inconsistent with [all] . . . other statements about the nature of history. On the contrary, it is or at least can be so considered for methodological purposes . . . qualification of these . . . [methods]. As thus envisaged . . . textualism . . . has the advantage of making explicit and therefore subject to criticism the textualist element in any approach to the study of history.[22]

What, I wonder, would Fox-Genovese's response to this be?

These, then, are some typical 'traditional' critiques of a textualist, 'postist' type of historical understanding and some responses to them – critiques and responses that are indicative of the sorts of debate now taking place over the question of what is history and which Carr and Elton are, at best, marginal to. Accordingly, it is now possible to pull together the sorts of 'defences' that have been considered so far, my position on what I take to be a textualist approach to history being summarised (with a little help from Stanley Fish and Hayden White) as follows.

(a) The generally implicit, but occasionally explicit, claim of 'proper' historians to be more immediately in touch with the actualities of the past (and in more disinterested ways) than 'textualists', cannot be maintained because *all* accounts of the past (and, of course, the present) always come to us textually through some kind of 'natural or technical language'.[23]

(b) That because the past cannot carve itself up and/or articulate itself, but always needs to be 'spoken for' and constructed, then every approach to the study of history presupposes 'some model for construing its object of study, for the simple reason that since "history" comprises everything that ever happened in "the past", it requires some *tertium comparationis* by which to distinguish between what is "historical" and what is not and, beyond that, between what is "significant" and what is relatively insignificant, within this "past"'.[24]

(c) Consequently, this means that the various theoretical conflicts between textualists and their anti-textualist 'proper historian' critics are not actually disputes between textualists and 'proper' historians at all, but because everybody's historical knowledge is textual – because textuality is indeed 'the only game in town' – between 'different theories of textuality', i.e. between different conceptions of what history is, and how historical knowledge is produced, and to what end. As Stanley Fish has put it, 'one can always lodge objection to the histories offered by one's opponents, one cannot (at least legitimately) label them as non-historical . . .'.[25]

(d) For, as White has himself argued, whilst anti-textualists may not like the implications of textuality for their sort of understanding of what they think history is, given that whether 'history' is considered simply as 'the past', the documentary record of this past, or the body of reliable information about the past, 'there is no such thing as a distinctively "historical" method by which to study this "history"'. Therefore, for anti-textualists to accuse textualists (notwithstanding the fact that they are actually 'unreflexive' textualists themselves) of being non-historians and/or 'theorists' (for all historians – including Elton – are 'theorists' given that historical knowledge is not of a natural kind) is an accusation which cannot stand. Consequently – and this is why White does not see textualism as preventing any sort of methodological approach to the past – White thinks (and I agree) that historical study will always be *formally* taking place irrespective of the *substantive* method employed if

it takes as its object of study any aspect of 'the past', distinguishes between that object and its various [imagined] contexts, periodizes the processes of change governing the relationships between them, posits specific causal forces as governing these processes, and represents the part of history thus marked out for study as a complex structure of relationships at once integrated at any given moment and developing and changing across any sequence of such moments.[26]

(e) Thus, whilst I think we need to be very much aware of why Stone *et al.* are ideologically committed to their own ways of doing history, what they cannot do – or are remarkably unreflexive if they *do* do it – is to define their preferred version of what constitutes history as resting on some kind of foundation beyond textuality and beyond 'the status of a conversation'. For history 'as *we* have known it' therefore, read history 'as *they* have known it'; for '*history* is in danger', substitute '*their* history is in danger'. I mean, why not?

These are some of the conclusions I want to draw from some of the debates around the postmodern impact on historiography, all of which suggest to me that the better way of thinking about the question of what is history today is well and truly in the grip of a textualist/rhetoricist/conversationalist style of postmodernism: that we have reached the end of modernist versions of what history is. I think that as historians we should be aware of these types of argument simply because they now saturate the general intellectual culture in which we all operate. In particular, I think that we might all begin to take on board the ideas of someone like Stanley Fish, Fish being of the view – as articulated at considerable length in his *Doing What Comes Naturally*[27] – that we live today in an unmistakably rhetorical world which has given rise to a whole series of *turns* (the 'linguistic turn', the 'semiotic turn', the 'discursive turn', the 'deconstructionist turn', etc.) all of which have replaced *literalism*, and all of which have problematicised the old foundational attitudes of both the 'Western Tradition' in general and, more recently, its modernist manifestations. I think it might therefore be useful at this point to briefly link up by way of a conclusion the sort of textual/rhetorical/narratological history discussed so far to the recognition of what is a general phenomenon in our present cultural condition; namely, that of the problematical textualising and narrativising of knowledge *per se*; that of the ubiquity of the problematical *story* as such. To link the history I have discussed so far to this general phenomenon, and to summarise quickly and draw a line under the discussion in this section, let me briefly present Brian McHale on the impact of the 'narrative turn' in general, and Raphael Samuel on the impact of the 'deconstructive turn' on history in particular. Thus McHale:

> Story, in one form or another, whether as object *of* theory or as the alternative *to* theory, seems to be everywhere. Historiography (LaCapra ... White ...) psychology (Spence ... Bruner ...) philosophy (Rorty ...) sociology (Brown ...) economics (McCloskey ...), and many other fields and disciplines of the human sciences – all have recently been affected by what Christopher Norris... has called the 'narrative turn' of theory. It is [thus] indicative that the editors of a recent volume of conference papers on 'Objectivity and Science' ... would choose to use 'stories' in titles where once they would have used 'theories': 'Stories about Science', 'Stories about Truth', 'Stories about Representation', even (what else?) 'Stories about Stories'.

The narrative turn would [therefore] seem to be one of the contemporary responses to the loss of metaphysical 'grounding' or 'foundations' for our theorizing. We are no longer confident that we can build intellectual structures upward from firm epistemological and ontological foundations. We suspect ... that, whilst there may well be somewhere a 'world' underlying all our disparate versions of it, that world is finally inaccessible, and all we have are the versions; but that [that] hardly matters, since it is only the versions that are of any use to us anyway, and [that] the putative world-before-all-versions [like the putative history-before-all-historiography] is, as Rorty ... says, 'well lost'.[28]

And thus Samuel, bringing (not all that approvingly) all this back home to history:

The deconstructive turn in contemporary thought, even if its influence has only been felt at second and third remove, or ... by osmosis, puts all of history's taken-for-granted procedures into question, both as an intellectual discipline and as a literary (or writerly) mode. By placing inverted commas, metaphorically speaking, around the notion of the real, it invites us to see history not as a record of the past, more or less faithful to the facts, nor yet as an interpretation answerable to the evidence even if it does not start from it, but as an invention, or fiction, of historians themselves, an inscription on the past rather than a reflection of it, an act of designation masquerading as a true-life story. It asks us to consider history as a literary form, on a par with, or at any rate exhibiting affinities to, other kinds of imaginative writing – narrative or descriptive, comic or realist, as the case may be. Our continuities are [therefore] storytellers' devices to give order and progression to the plot; the periodisation, by which we set such store, is a strategy for narrative closure. Events are singled out for attention not because of their intrinsic interest, but because of the logic of the text; they are not material realities but the organising units of historical discourse, 'highly coded tropes that "read" or allegorize the past.'[29]

LOCATING CARR, ELTON, RORTY AND WHITE

If these are the sorts of debate constituting some of the more 'advanced' rhetorical/textual/postmodern ways of regarding history, all that remains to do now before looking in detail at Carr, Elton, Rorty and White is to position them *vis-à-vis* history today. How can this positioning be done?

The first thing to note is that none of the four being discussed can be positioned in the sort of old-fashioned way Elton likes; that is, on the basis of whether they are 'proper' historians or not (for on this basis Rorty and White would certainly not – and perhaps Carr would not – qualify). Nor, in the light of my previous comments, can we put Carr on the left, Rorty and White in the centre, Elton on the right, and just leave it at that. For, whilst that is where they roughly belong, it has already been noted that the left, the centre and the right, are divided internally. For – to recall briefly these divisions – whilst Carr is indeed on the left, his old Marxist/modernist attitude is very different from the post-Marxism of, say, Tony Bennett, Ernesto Laclau, Chantel Mouffe, Dick Hebdige, and so on.[30] Although Rorty and White are more iconoclastic and rigorously critical of the centre and right than Carr ever was, Rorty and White are not so much on the left as in the liberal centre, a centre broad enough to contain Stone *et al.* Again, whilst Elton is certainly on the right, this is a location his Toryism shares with such 'radicals' as Jonathan Clark who can readily accept that the struggle for hegemony exposed by post-modernism is a game anybody can play – and who plays it. Again, Elton's Toryism may not suit, say, Arthur Marwick or Lawrence Stone, but his hard professionalism finds echoes in their own versions of 'proper' history. So, how can Carr and Elton and Rorty and White be fairly easily located against/within the postmodern?

Well, I think the best way to do it is simply to recall that postmodernism is a complex re-assessment of the modernist project, and that what makes a person like (or, at least, not fear that re-assessment) is whether or not he or she can see a *future* without any nostalgic longings for the old traditions, certainties, foundations and accumulated mental furniture of modernity. Thus, it would seem that what makes historians respond favourably to the postmodern condition – *irrespective of their left, centre or right ideological positions* – is whether they are happy with, for example, an understanding of the past as a historiography which asserts that such an understanding is always positioned, is always fabricated, is always ultimately self-referencing and is never true beyond peradventure; that history has no intrinsic meaning, that there is no way of privileging one variant over another by neutral criteria, and which sees histories located at the centre, or on the margins, not necessarily by virtue of their historiographical rigour and/or sophistication – for brilliant histories can be variously marginalised – but by their relationship to those that have the power to put them there. Further, that historians respond favourably to the postmodern condition if they have no yearning for, or feelings of despair for, the loss of either 'reality' or 'the reality of things past', accepting that what traditionalists might regard as a 'crisis' is more of an opportunity to carry on working with an increased reflexivity in all types of 'different' and 'other' areas. Historians respond favourably to the postmodern condition if they care nought for the foundational certainties of modernity, feeling that they can effectively construct something on the 'basis' of nothing (for when – in fact – was it ever different?). Postmodern historians think that human beings can live ironic, reflexive, historicised lives, without the magic, incantations, mythologisations and mystifications spun by certaintist historians from across the board in both upper and lower cases. Postmodern historians see their own histories as being made not for 'the past itself' but for themselves and for people whom they like (for when, they ask, was that ever not the case?). Postmodernism is thus about history all right, but not, as Brenda Marshall puts it, of the kind of history that

> lets us think we can know the past. [No] History in the postmodern moment becomes histories and questions. It asks: Whose history gets told? In whose name? For what purpose? Postmodernism is about histories not told, retold, untold. History as it never was. Histories forgotten, hidden, invisible, considered unimportant, changed, eradicated. It's about the refusal to see history as linear, as leading straight up to today in some recognisable pattern – all set for us to make sense of. It's about chance. It's about power. It's about information. . . . And that's just a little bit about what postmodernism [is].[31]

But it's enough to see why Carr and Elton are not postmodernists and why Rorty and White effectively are.

Carr belongs to that part of the left, then, which is suspicious of postmodernism, seeing it as emerging primarily from the exigencies of late-capital, a response to the fragmentation of the social into the commodity forms that underwrite it and which allows for umpteen differences to be recuperated back into it via both consumerism and a contrived, fakey, political pluralism. From this perspective, tainted by capital, postmodernism cannot really be embraced. For whilst, as already noted, this part of the left does not hesitate to use postmodernism's ironic rhetoric to deconstruct any lingering bourgeois certainties, it would still like to retain a few of its own: a basic rationality, some contact with a reality which is not hyper-reality and, so far as history is concerned, some knowledge of the past that would be useful to it because it would be, to all intents and purposes, *true*. To this element of the left – to Fox-Genovese *et al.* – the attitude taken towards postmodernism is therefore an ambivalent one, an attitude Carr shares.

For although Carr is of an older generation than Fox-Genovese and company, it is within the sort of ambivalence just mentioned that Carr should be located as an historian who, while sceptically discounting any claims for a type of historical knowledge which prioritised an empirical/positivistic concern for facts that could be meaningful without the intervention of the constitutive historian, still hankered for a leftist interpretation that was not just interpretative. The circle that Carr tried to square was that, whilst he knew all historiography was interpretive 'all the way down', he still wanted his own interpretation to be somehow exempt; that in some way the history which he interpreted as 'progressing' really was progressing in exactly the way his interpretation suggested, and would have been doing so whether he had spotted it or not. That is to say, historical progress really was objectively 'there' and not just created by Carr: whether by luck or by judgement his interpretation had, in fact, come up trumps.

Carr was no pessimist then – indeed his optimism about the continuation of progress was what he felt distinguished him from the sceptics and cynics he saw all around him – but what sets his optimism apart from a postmodern type is clearly his desire for some real foundations upon which to base his historical analyses and knowledge. Thus, in the end (and despite his sometime carefully controlled scepticism) it is Carr's modernist yoking together – in precisely the immanent ways of nineteenth-century certaintists – of the past to the present and to the future, which provides him with the far from sceptical answer he eventually gives to his famous question: 'What is History?'.

Elton is a man who holds Tory principles and talks about them openly and frankly. And, as a Tory, there must therefore be within his position that typical combination of scepticism (which comes from having an ideology that holds to the idea of the imperfectability of man, the imperfectability of politics, and hence the imperfectability of knowledge) and absolute, even authoritarian, values: of the 'real' capacity to be able to tell good from bad, right from wrong, the proper from the improper, the professional from the amateur, the true from the false, so as not to let imperfectability gain the upper hand. Predictably, both scepticism and certainty are held in a balanced (organic) way; the scepticism measured and controlled when applied professionally to history in the lower case (leaving room for the possibility of 'objectivity' and various degrees of 'truth'), unrelenting and savage when applied to those enthusiasts who might think that objectivity and truth (as, for example, in Carr and his lefty fellow-travellers) was a possibility in the upper. In these ways Elton's approach as to what constitutes proper history and the correct attitudes to bring to it mirrors his ideological position.

Of course, Elton may well have objected to this, holding pretty much to the view that his politics and his historical work are not mixed. Moreover, there is perhaps no one on record who more strongly believed that the proper study of the past is the study of it 'for its own sake' and that the cardinal, 'treasonable' crime, is to prostitute oneself to the siren songs of a present which would ask its historians to give it the past it wants; for Elton, (his) history is above (his) politics.

But what doesn't seem to have occurred to Elton – or if it did he never discussed it at length – is that the lower case history he pursues as if in his hands it was apolitical, just is modernist/bourgeois ideology, just is ideology *tout court*. In fact, Elton's views on history are steeped in the ideological combination of pessimism on the one hand and a stubborn (if wearily held) hope on the other, it being symptomatic of such a position that Elton's first sentences in the first chapter of what he has called his modest manual for professional, lower case historians (*The Practice of History*) reads in a most unprofessional and non-lower case way:

> The future is dark, the present burdensome; only the past, dead and finished, bears contemplation. Those who look upon it have survived it: they are its product and its victors. No wonder, therefore, that men [sic] concern themselves with history.[32]

Rorty and White are in that (smallish) part of the liberal centre that goes along with the postmodern without any nostalgia for a foundational fix. For, unlike the majority of historians in the centre (which means – because the centre is so large – the majority of historians of whom Stone and Spiegel are typical), Rorty and White's 'scepticism' goes all the way down, applying to both upper and lower cases. The reason why Rorty can be so 'laid back' about his undercutting of metanarratives, western foundationalism, traditional epistemology, orthodox ontology and so on, is because he doesn't at all see liberal social formations, North Atlantic style, as either terrible, or in crisis, or threatened by the capsizal of philosophical values. For Rorty, it is precisely anti-foundationalism and anti-representationalism that will clear the decks of all that metaphysical clutter which the first modernist project got caught up in. No, what liberals needed then (but what they could not quite get for understandable historical reasons) they can have now: *irony*;

> the citizens of my liberal utopia would be people who had a sense of the contingency of their language of moral deliberation, and thus of their consciences, and thus of their community. They would be liberal ironists – people who met Schumpeter's criterion of civilization, people who combined commitment with a sense of the contingency of their own commitment. ... I use 'ironist' to name the sort of person who [therefore] faces up to the contingency of his or her own most central beliefs and desires – someone sufficiently historicist and nominalist to have abandoned the idea that those central beliefs and desires refer back to something beyond the reach of time and chance.[33]

From this position, Rorty therefore has no fears about the end of certainties – for it is precisely old certainties (in the form of various total(itarian) closures) that have caused problems for 'freedom' in the first place. And for those who think that an ironic, nominalist, anti-foundational attitude towards life cannot be a strong enough cement to hold social formations together, Rorty suggests that they think again:

> If you tell someone whose life is given meaning by [the] ... hope that life will eventually be freer, less cruel, more leisured, richer in goods and experiences, not just for our descendants but for everybody's descendants ... that philosophers are waxing ironic over real essence, the objectivity of truth, and the existence of an ahistorical human nature, you are unlikely to arouse much interest, much less do any damage. The idea that liberal societies are bound together by philosophical beliefs seems to me ludicrous. What binds societies together are common vocabularies and common hopes. ... To retain social hope, members of such a society need to be able to tell themselves a story [stories] about how things

might get better, and to see no insuperable obstacles to this story's coming true. If [such] social hope has become harder lately, this is not because the [philosophers] . . . have been committing treason but because, since the end of World War II, the course of events has made it harder to tell a convincing story of this sort.[34]

And hence the need to unravel and re-weave the unfinished project of modernity in postmodern type structures; to re-articulate in those radical historicist and nominalist ways offered by postmodernism the hope of actualising more fully emancipated 'human rights communities'.

It would be wrong to present White as some pale reflection of Rorty, not least because White occupies a political position which I think he himself regards as somewhat more radical than the 'civility' typical of Rorty's discourse. Nor has White been silent (as opposed to being detailed) about his own political preferences, his historical work leading him towards a reading that embraces an ironic disposition whilst reflexively offering a position beyond it, and which optimistically holds out a promise of a post-ironic culture. In the end, White agrees with Kant that we are free to conceive of history as we please, just as we are free to make of it 'what we will'; free to construct accounts of the past consistent with 'whatever modality of consciousness is most consistent with [our] . . . own moral and aesthetic aspirations'.[35] Those aspirations seem to be, for White, individually emancipatory and empowering, especially for those whose discourses are on the margins and/or barely audible. White's view on history allows for those 'creative, interpretive distortions' which, optimistically, go beyond orthodox ways of reading the past the present and the future in *utopian* ways.

For White then, if you are going to go to the past, to help in the present, to get the future you want (which is indeed why he thinks we go to history) then, as he puts it, you had better 'have an address [a purpose] in mind', rather than go wandering around the streets of that past like a *flâneur*. To be sure, says White, 'Historical *flâneur-isme* is undeniably enjoyable, but the history we are living today is no place for tourists.' Thus if, he writes, you are indeed 'going to "go to history"', you had better have a clear idea of which history, and you had better have a pretty good notion as to whether it is [or can be made to be] hospitable to the values you carry into it.'[36] And as we shall see, I think that White has got both of these things.

Chapter 2

On E. H. Carr

Although I have argued that much of the continued use of Carr and Elton to represent the 'alternatives in the self-understanding of the discipline' has been through the popularity of the 'Carr–Elton debate', that debate is not the subject of this study. It is not a question of taking sides on this 'controversy'. Nevertheless, *à propos* my earlier remarks on the nuances contained in left, centre and right positions with regard to postmodernism, I think it is clear that both Carr and Elton have rather more complicated positions than their debate often suggests, such that the common view of Carr as simply the radical sceptic and relativist, and Elton simply as the truth-seeker and objectivist, may, in some ways, be misleading. In case readers are thinking that I am saying this just in order to make my somewhat more qualified reading of Carr and Elton 'original', it might be worth spending a couple of paragraphs to point out that the popular view of Carr as the unalloyed relativist and Elton as the unalloyed certaintist are not characterisations I am inventing for effect but do constitute much of the conventional wisdom.

Thus, for example, in his popular, introductory text, *The Pursuit of History*, John Tosh not only still thinks (in 1991) that 'the controversy between Carr ... and Elton ... is the best starting point for the debate about the standing of historical knowledge' (and that Carr's *What is History?* is still 'probably the finest reflection by a historian on the nature of his subject in our time'), but that Carr is best located on the sceptical and relativistic side of the 'Carr–Elton debate'.[1] Similarly, Gregor McLennan in his *Marxism and the Methodologies of History* pigeonholes Carr (considered by McLennan to have produced perhaps 'the most sustained critique of British empiricist historiography') as a sceptical relativist, whilst even Dominick LaCapra argues that if one wishes to rebut Elton's 'documentary objectivism', one need not necessarily be 'forced to line up with E. H. Carr and the relativists'.[2] And although these and other similar views[3] on Carr and Elton are sometimes qualified (though often in the small print of the footnotes) there is little doubt in my own mind that because of such characterisations as the above, few students are aware that Carr's final answer to the question of what is history is neither sceptical nor relativistic, but is expressed explicitly as a belief in objectivity, in real historical progress and in truth, whilst Elton goes out of his way to insist that 'our' attitude toward 'proper' history should include a healthy (if carefully directed) dose of scepticism. Accordingly, it is this slightly more complex Carr and Elton which I want to discuss here, offering my reading not only as a 'correction' to some of the simplicities of the 'Carr–Elton debate' as popularly construed but, more importantly perhaps, as an interpretation which will serve to show up their shortcomings – and thus *pace* Tosh *et al.* – their lack of relevance to the question of what is the nature of history/historiography today. So, these preliminaries being completed, my reading of Carr can begin, a reading that has three sections: 'On Carr Being Sceptical', 'On Carr Being Positive', and 'Carr Today'.

ON CARR BEING SCEPTICAL

Carr begins *What is History?* by saying what he thinks history is not; by being negative. What history 'is not', is a way of constructing accounts about the past that are obsessed with, and indeed fetishise, both 'the facts' and 'the documents' which are said to contain them, as a consequence of which the crucially important shaping power of the historian is massively downplayed.[4] Carr goes on to argue – in the early pages of his first chapter – that this fetishisation and downgrading arose because mainstream historians combined three things: first, Ranke's simple but all pervasive (lower case) dictum that the proper function of the historian was to slough off his or her partisan views and show the past as 'it really was'; second, a positivist stress on inductive method (first ascertain the facts and then draw conclusions from them) and third (and this especially in England) a dominant empiricist ethos. Together these constituted for Carr what still passed for the commonsense view of history:

> The empirical theory of knowledge presupposes a complete separation between subject and object. Facts, like sense-

impressions, impinge on the observer from outside and are independent of his consciousness. The process of reception is passive: having received the data, he then acts on them. ... This is what may be called the commonsense view of history. History consists of a corpus of ascertained facts. ... First get your facts straight, then plunge at your peril into the shifting sands of interpretation – that is the ultimate wisdom of the [dominant] empirical, commonsense school of history.[5]

Clearly this will not do for Carr. This is precisely the view one has to reject. So how does he do it? Well, this is where things begin to get a little complicated. For, whilst Carr has actually got three ways of going about this (one epistemological, two overtly ideological) it is normally only the first epistemological rejection that is found in most of the literature, it being this which effectively constitutes much of the Carr element in the 'Carr–Elton debate' as it is popularly rendered. However, because it is this prioritising of the epistemological over the ideological that is largely responsible for those readings of Carr as the unalloyed relativist, although I myself want to outline this argument first, I shall be quickly following it with the other two.

So, what is Carr's first epistemological argument? It is simply this. He thinks that not all the 'facts of the past' are actually 'historical facts'; that there are crucial distinctions to be drawn between the 'events' of the past, the 'facts' of the past, and 'historical' facts. That 'historical facts' only become so by being historicised by positioned historians. Carr develops this argument as follows:

What is a historical fact? ... According to the commonsense view, there are certain basic facts which are the same for all historians and which form, so to speak, the backbone of history – the fact, for example, that the Battle of Hastings was fought in 1066. But this view calls for two observations. In the first place, it is not with facts like these that the historian is primarily concerned. It is no doubt important to know that the great battle was fought in 1066 and not 1065 or 1067. ... The historian must not get these things wrong. But when points of this kind are raised, I am reminded of Housman's remark that 'accuracy is a duty, not a virtue'. To praise a historian for his accuracy is like praising an architect for using well-seasoned timber. ... It is a necessary condition of his work, but not his essential [sic] function. It is precisely for matters of this kind that the historian is entitled to rely on what have been called the 'auxiliary sciences' of history – archaeology, epigraphy, numismatics, chronology, and so forth.[6]

From which it follows, thinks Carr, that the insertion of such facts into an historical account and the significance which they will have relative to other selected facts, depends not on any quality intrinsic to the facts 'in and for themselves' (for obviously some historians put different facts into their explanatory accounts of the same events from other historians), but on the reading of events the historian chooses to give:

> It used to be said that facts speak for themselves. This is, of course, untrue. The facts speak only when the historian calls on them: it is he who decides to which facts to give the floor, and in what order or context. ... The only reason why we are interested to know that the battle was fought at Hastings in 1066 is that historians regard it as a major historical event. It is the historian who has decided for his own reasons that Caesar's crossing of that petty stream, the Rubicon, is a fact of history, whereas the crossings of the Rubicon by millions of other people ... interests nobody at all. ... The historian is [therefore] necessarily selective. The belief in a hard core of historical facts existing objectively and independently of the historian is a preposterous fallacy, but one which it is very hard to eradicate.[7]

Following on from this, Carr rounds off his argument with his now famous illustration of the process by which a mere event/fact from the past is transformed into a 'historical fact'. Thus, at Stalybridge Wakes in 1850, Carr tells us, a gingerbread seller was beaten to death by an angry mob; this is a well documented and authentic 'fact from the past'. But for it to become a 'historical fact', Carr argues that it needed to be taken up by historians and inserted by them into their interpretations, thence becoming part of our historical memory. In other words concludes Carr:

> Its status as a historical fact will turn on a question of interpretation. This element of interpretation enters into every fact of history.[8]

This, then, is the substance of Carr's (actually extremely slight) first argument and, as I say, this is the 'position' that students generally take away with them from Carr to then juxtapose against the 'objectivist' Elton (so that one hears them saying things like: 'Carr thinks that all history is just interpretation and there are really no such things as facts') which, whilst it has an element of accuracy about it, is far from being the whole story. For this is precisely the misleading conclusion (as based on a partial reading of only a part of Carr's first chapter) that we need to go beyond. For, if the interpretation of Carr stops at this point, then not only are we left with a strong impression that his whole argument about the nature of history and the status of historical knowledge is effectively epistemological and sceptical/ relativist, but we are also not in a good position to see why, only a few pages after the Stalybridge example has been given, Carr rejects as too sceptical the relativism of Collingwood, and why he begins a few pages after that to reinstate 'the facts' in rather unproblematical ways himself, ways eventually leading him towards his own version of objectivity, truth and so on. Carr's other two arguments are therefore crucial to follow, not least because they are, as noted, explicitly ideological. The first of the two arguments is a perfectly reasonable one; namely, that Carr is opposed to the fetishisation of facts, etc., because of the way in which Rankeanism, positivism and empiricism were yoked together and lived under the auspices of nineteenth and twentieth century liberalism; in other words, because the resultant common sense view of history was/is an ideological expression of liberalism.

Carr's argument runs as follows. The classical, liberal idea of progress was that, left to their own devices, individuals – and by extension, left to their own devices the economic, the social, the national and international spheres – would, in exercising their freedom in ways which took 'account' of the competing claims of others, somehow and without too much external intervention, move towards a harmony of interests resulting in a greater (freer) harmony for all. Carr thinks that this idea was then extended into the argument for a sort of general intellectual *laissez-faire* (that is, that from the free expression of competing ideas there would emerge a harmonious acceptance of the best argument for everyone; the real truth), and thence more particularly into history. For Carr, the fundamental idea underpinning liberal historiography was that historians all going about their work in different ways but cognisant (and appreciative) of the ways of others, would be able to collect the facts and then, pretty much without their explicit intervention, allow the 'free-play' of such facts – as though guided by their own 'hidden hand' – to effectively 'speak for themselves', thus ensuring that they were in harmony with the events of the past which were now truthfully represented. As Carr puts this:

> The nineteenth century was, for the intellectuals of western Europe, a comfortable period exuding confidence and optimism. The facts were on the whole satisfactory; and the inclination to ask and answer awkward questions about them was correspondingly weak. ... The liberal ... view of history [therefore] had a close affinity with the economic doctrine of laissez-faire – also the product of a serene and self-confident outlook on the world. Let everyone get on with his particular job, and the hidden hand would take care of the universal harmony. The facts of history were themselves a demonstration of the supreme fact of a beneficent and apparently infinite progress towards higher things.[9]

Carr's second argument is thus both straightforward and straightforwardly ideological. His point is that the idea of the freedom of the facts to speak for themselves arose from the happy coincidence that they just happened to speak liberal. But of course Carr did not. Therefore, knowing that in the history he wrote the facts had to be made to speak in a way other than liberal (i.e. in a Marxist type of way) then his own experience of making 'the facts' *his* facts is universalised to become everyone's experience. *All* historians, including liberals, have to transform the 'facts of the past' into 'historical facts' by their positioned intervention. And so Carr's second argument against 'commonsense' history is not epistemological at all, but, as stated, ideological.

And so is the third. But if the second of Carr's arguments is easy to see, his third and final one is not. This argument needs a little teasing-out; it needs to be approached by way of a few preliminaries.

In the first two critiques of 'commonsense' history, Carr has effectively argued that the facts (and the documents, etc., wherein they were held to be inscribed) have no *intrinsic* value (i.e. they have no fixed/necessary place within any historian's account) but that they only gained their *relative* value (their 'use' value) when inserted by historians into their accounts *vis-à-vis* all the other fact(or)s under consideration, the conclusion Carr drew being that the facts only speak when the historian calls upon them to do so. However, it was part of Carr's position – again as already noted – that liberals had not recognised the shaping power of the historian because of the 'cult of the fact' and that, because of the dominance of liberal ideology, their view had become common sense not only for themselves but for practically all historiography. It appeared to Carr that historians seemed to subscribe to the position that they ought to act as the conduit through which 'the facts of the past for their own sake' were allowed self-expression.

So far so good. But then Carr switches his attention to the 1950s and 1960s and, in his later preface to *What Is History?* to the 1970s and early 1980s. And here Carr writes that he senses that liberal and other expressions of a general optimism (the accumulation and distribution of wealth in increasingly progressive ways, the accumulation of a knowledge of the world through an incremental inductivism, etc.) were being undermined – and undermined, ironically, precisely by 'the facts' of the 1960s and beyond. Thus, in 1960 when Carr completed the first draft of *What Is History?*, he thought that things were pretty bad but not impossible. On the one hand, he tells us that the western world was still reeling from the aftermath of two world wars and major revolutions, that the Victorian age of innocence and self-confidence had dissipated, and that an 'automatic' belief in progress lay behind us. Nevertheless, on the other hand, the predicted world economic crisis had not occurred, the British Empire had been effectively disposed of, and the Kennedy era promised at least the possibility of a new dawn. Accordingly, and grasping at these rather mixed straws, Carr opined that these 'conditions provided, at any rate, a superficial justification for the expression of optimism and belief in the future with which I ended my lectures in 1961.'[10]

From the vantage point of his later Preface, however, Carr admits that he thinks things had worsened. The 'new facts' were dismal. The Cold War had been resumed and intensified. The delayed economic crisis had set in with a vengeance, spreading 'the cancer of unemployment throughout western society'. The third world had been transformed from a passive into a disturbing factor in world affairs. Things looked bleak:

> In these conditions any expression of optimism has come to seem absurd. The prophets of woe have everything on their side. . . . Not for centuries has the once popular predication of the end of the world seemed so apposite.[11]

And yet Carr remained stubbornly optimistic, for two reasons. First, Carr considered that the diagnoses of hopelessness that he thought he detected in most of his fellow intellectuals, though they purported to rest their case on 'the facts', were, of course, just giving vent to their own opinions given that 'the facts' had no 'intrinsic' meaning (i.e. there is no fact-value entailment). Second, Carr thought that their sense of hopelessness was confined to the conditions they saw in the West, whereas he himself thought there was no reason to think optimism did not hold sway elsewhere in the world.

Consequently – and drawing his own conclusion from these 'facts' – Carr was of the opinion that 'the current wave of scepticism and despair which looked ahead to nothing but destruction and decay and dismissed as absurd any belief in progress, was a form of élitism, the product of social groups whose security and privileges had been most conspicuously eroded by the crisis, and of élite countries whose once undisputed domination over the rest of the world had been shattered.'[12] And it was such intellectuals, the purveyors of the ideas of 'the ruling social group which they served ("the ideas of a society are the ideas of its ruling class")', who were the standard bearers of such gloom. Accordingly, whilst Carr certainly considered himself an intellectual, the idea that he was that kind of an intellectual was anathema to him, seeing himself, and indeed styling himself, as an 'intellectual dissident', and thereby distancing himself from such pessimists by a re-affirmation of his faith in progress. For, as he put it, in the end he was an intellectual who had grown up,

> not in the high noon, but in the afterglow of the great Victorian age of faith and optimism, and it is difficult for me even today to think in terms of a world in permanent and irretrievable decline[13]

Consequently, all this being the case, in *What Is History?* Carr has thus got this very specific ideological reason (that he must not go along with the pessimists and their facts/interpretations and so renounce progress) to add to his earlier expressed opinion that one must not fetishise the 'facts' nor succumb to the intellectual bleatings about the demise of the experience of modernity; not at all:

> In the following pages I shall try to distance myself from prevailing trends among Western intellectuals ... to show how and why I think they have gone astray and to stake out a claim, if not for an optimistic, at any rate for a saner and more balanced outlook on the future.[14]

It is thus this very clearly flagged position which stands behind and gives much, if not all, of the *raison d'être* for Carr's writing of *What is History?* For his text is profoundly misunderstood if it is seen as some kind of disinterested study of historical epistemology. Rather,

Carr himself seems to be quite clear that the real impetus behind his text was the ideological necessity to re-think and re-articulate the idea of continued historical progress amidst the 'conditions' and the doubting-Thomases of his own 'sceptical days': Carr's 'real' concern was 'the fact' that he thought the future of the whole modern world/ experiment was at stake.

But – and this is my point in running this third argument – as Carr's text unfolds, what might be called the 'epistemological problem' continually returns to trouble him. For, despite his own epistemological scepticism as outlined in his first argument Carr will still try to find some proper *grounds* for his own personal belief in progress and to suggest that his own particular reading is not just his but is actually 'the case'. Now we can immediately and very clearly see the problem that Carr's epistemological scepticism and his dismissal of the facts and 'intrinsic' meaning has got him into. Because if, as Carr says, the various diagnoses of hopelessness purportedly held by most of the intellectuals around him are not really based on 'the facts' in some sort of necessary (entailed) way, but are simply their 'value judgements' as based on a careful selection of those facts that suit them; and if the same goes for all those nineteenth-century liberals whose optimism was (unwittingly) based on a similar selection; in other words, if there are no factual grounds *per se* for either pessimism or optimism given the fact that 'past facts' have to become 'historical facts' by the historian's selective practices, then Carr is hoisted with his own petard. For, given that there is no fact–value entailment, then Carr's own optimism cannot be incorrigibly supported by 'the facts', so that his own position is just his opinion, as equally without foundation as those held by old optimistic liberals and by their contemporary, pessimistic counterparts. Consequently, the only conclusion that can arguably be drawn – and here we are back with the position of Bennett *et al.* – is that 'the past' doesn't actually enter into historiography – except rhetorically.

Now, one might suppose that if Carr was not the modernist he so clearly is, then he might well have embraced this extremely obvious and 'correct' conclusion. And if he had done so, nothing would actually have changed. For Carr might still have argued his own value position as he most plausibly could and left it on the table along with everyone else's; here his reading could jostle for 'hegemony' with other equally 'groundless' ideological positions. But because of his modernism Carr won't do this. Instead, he will try to show that there really are some foundations which privilege his own position over others both in terms of what constitutes history as a discipline and in terms of the past considered as history. That is, *Carr will be driven back from the epistemological scepticism he has outlined in the first twenty pages of his book and for which he is best known, precisely so that he can embrace a more certaintist position for politically overt reasons.* To be sure, Carr cannot, and will not, go all the way. The days of absolutes are gone. But, as his text unfolds, so he will do his best to claw back his early critical scepticism so that he can move towards an answer to the question of what is history that is compatible with the task he has actually set himself so clearly: to underwrite his faith in progress.

This clawing back takes place in several stages: (a) a rejection of Collingwood's too sceptical idealism; (b) a reinstatement of 'the facts' in an attempt to join the previously asundered fact and value; and (c) an attempt to link the past into a dialogue not only with the present but also with the future in ways reminiscent of, if not identical to, old teleologies, thereby trying to derive a sense of history that is effectively objective and even, perhaps, true. Accordingly, it is to these positive arguments that I now turn.

ON CARR BEING POSITIVE

Carr begins his examination of Collingwood by placing him amongst those philosophers of history who, since the late nineteenth century, had worked seriously on the question of what is history. According to Carr, the Germans had started this ('the country which was to do so much to upset the comfortable reign of nineteenth-century liberalism')[15] citing Dilthey as one of those who had challenged the primacy of facts in history, the sceptical torch then being passed on to Italy in the early twentieth century when Croce declared that 'all history is contemporary history', and thence to America where, in 1910, Carl Becker argued that 'the facts of history do not exist for any historian till he creates them'.[16] From 1910 Carr then jumps to 1945 and England where, in that year, R. G. Collingwood's *The Idea of History* was published posthumously.

Collingwood is then summarised by Carr as follows. Collingwood's philosophy of history is concerned neither with 'the past by itself', nor with the historian's 'thought about it by itself', but rather is about these two things in their mutual relationship: 'the past which a historian studies is not a dead past, but a past which in some sense is still living in the present'. But a past act is dead (i.e. meaningless to the historian) unless he/she can understand the thoughts which lay behind it and thus infused it with life; hence 'all history is the history of thought . . . the re-enactment in the historian's mind of the thought whose history he is studying'.[17] This reconstitution of the past in the historian's mind is dependent on empirical evidence but is not itself an empirical process, and cannot thus consist in a 'mere recital of facts'. On the contrary, the process of reconstitution governs the selection of the facts and their interpretation, and this is precisely what transforms them into historical facts. At this point Carr draws support for Collingwood's argument from the sceptical, conservative historian/philosopher, Michael Oakeshott, for whom history, as he puts it, is simply the historian's experience. It is 'made' by nobody save the historian: 'to write history is the only way of making it'.[18]

From this potted résumé of Collingwood, Carr is then able to extract three oft-neglected 'truths' which he thinks support his own sort of scepticism (i.e. the scepticism he is soon to rein back from the 'extremes'). First, that past facts never come to us pure; they are always refracted through the mind of the recorder. Therefore, it follows that when we read a history, 'our first concern should be not with the facts which it contains but with the historian who wrote it'.[19] Second, Carr advocates a sort of empathy; the need for an 'imaginative understanding for the minds of the people [the historian] is dealing with'. And third, Carr advocates that we recognise, with Croce, that we can only ever understand the past through the eyes of the present. And from these three points, Carr is thus able to conclude that 'the function of the historian is neither to love the past nor to emancipate himself from the past, but to master and understand it as the key to the understanding of the present'.[20]

But if these are valuable nuggets to be gleaned from Collingwood's work, Carr sees some attendant dangers. And it is therefore at this point that Carr begins to draw back from the radical scepticism he has so far professed. Pressed to its logical conclusion, he warns, Collingwood's emphasis on the power of the creative historian rules out any objectivity at all. Indeed, says Carr, in his reading, Collingwood comes [21] perilously close to saying that history/historiography is something spun out of human brains with as many histories as brains, so that here we are offered 'the theory of an infinity of meanings, none any more right than any other'.[22] And this is not on. Just because, argues Carr, a mountain takes on different shapes from different angles, we cannot conclude that it has either no shape at all or that it is an infinity of shapes; nor does it follow that just because interpretation plays a necessary part in establishing historical facts (and because no interpretation is absolutely objective) that one interpretation is as good as another or that 'the facts of history are in principle not amenable to objective interpretation' (Carr adding immediately at this point that he will 'consider at a later stage what exactly is meant by objectivity in history').

This is not all, however, for a 'still greater danger lurks in the Collingwood hypothesis'. For, if the historian necessarily looks at his/her period of history through present-centred eyes; and if he/she studies history as a key to an understanding of the present – both of which we have seen Carr regarding as advantages stemming from Collingwood – then there arises the awful prospect that he/she may 'fall into a purely pragmatic view of the facts, and maintain that the criteria of a right interpretation is its suitability to some present purpose' (for which we might have been forgiven for thinking up until this point that this was precisely Carr's purpose). But apparently not, for now Carr sees the shadow of Nietzsche (and other fellow Germans not so useful now to Carr's anti-empiricist liking as Dilthey had been earlier) looming on the horizon. For what if, after all, might is right?; what if, worries Carr, objective history is just what those with the power to define it as do define it as? Accordingly, Carr considers that it is time to get away from these dangerous bits of Collingwood and re-instate 'the facts' (i.e. his facts).

Carr is explicit about this re-instatement: 'How then, in the middle of the twentieth century, are we to define the obligation of the historian to his facts?'[23] And Carr's answer – the mood of which is indicated by the notion that the historian has an obligation to his facts (thus introducing into the argument the ethical vocabulary of duty and its cognates) is that the 'proper' historian has indeed 'a duty' to respect the facts; that he is 'obliged' to see that all the facts are accurate; that he 'must' include all the relevant facts, and that he 'must' be balanced; for example, including in his description of the Victorian Englishman as a moral and rational being, the murder of the Stalybridge gingerbread vendor. Of course, all this cannot eliminate interpretation, but for Carr the position of the historian balanced between what he now refers to as the two 'extremes' of one untenable theory of history (as the unqualified primacy of fact over interpretation) and another (of history as the subjective product of the mind of the historian) is not so precarious as it may seem. For the proper historian (i.e. Carr himself) is finally able to rely on that essentially British characteristic: common sense. Here Carr begins to move towards his first (partial) stab at defining what history is. Carr's argument runs as follows. In 'making history', the historian begins with a provisional selection of facts and a provisional interpretation in the light of which that selection has been made – by other historians working in the field as well as by himself/herself. As the historian works on, and as new information (both 'primary' and 'secondary') is processed, so both the interpretation and the selection and ordering of facts undergoes subtle changes through the reciprocal action of the one on the other. This reciprocal action also involves a reciprocity between the present and the past. Thus facts and interpretation, past and present, intermingle in a unity of scholarly duty such that Carr's preliminary answer to the question of what is history can, at this point, roll off his tongue with ease; history, says Carr, 'is a continuous process of interaction between the historian and his facts, an unending dialogue between the present and the past'.[24]

So, Collingwoodian-type excesses having been shed and the facts having been put in their proper place, Carr's next task is to try to claw back his earlier, rather rash, dismissal of 'the facts' in favour of the primacy of the historian. For, now that the facts and the historian have been brought together in a mutual dependency – and now that he needs to have the facts to 'objectively' support his belief in progress – so Carr will also have to try and reunite in a mutual dependency that which he had previously put asunder; namely, facts and values. Because if this cannot be done, if facts and values cannot be conjoined, then any 'values' Carr draws will still only be a 'loose' interpretation. Thus, Carr thinks that he will just have to try and solve the old fact–value problem.

It cannot be said that his attempt is a very good one. It consists of little more than a compilation of historians who have acted as if fact and value could be unproblematically entailed. But we are now in a position to see why Carr thinks that he must try to follow them, and thus we might follow him as he attempts to square this particular circle. He begins by arguing that for the last two hundred years most historians had assumed that there was a direction in which the past was moving, that it was moving in the right direction, and that this right direction consisted of a movement from 'the worse to the better, from the lower to the higher', a movement historians not only recognised but endorsed so that, in this way, the alleged dichotomy between the is and the ought, between fact and value, was restored.

This resolution was thus an 'optimistic' one, and was the view actually held, in various articulations, by those who were sometimes confident in the future – by Whigs and Liberals, Hegelians and Marxists, theologians and rationalists – so that, for two hundred years, Carr argues that a view of history as progress could be described 'without much exaggeration as the accepted and implicit answer to the question, "What is history?".' But against this view – a view which represents the golden age of the upper case – has come the current mood of apprehension and pessimism. And Carr knows who to blame: disillusioned liberals (Bury, Fisher), French existentialists (Sartre) and Germans such as Meinecke, all of whom have come to insist on the pointlessness of history and the significance of chance and accident, the importance of which Carr dates from a growth of uncertainty which set in in 'the present century and became marked after 1914'. Here Carr will no longer have any need for the similarly 'uncertain' Dilthey and the wedge he and others drove between the human and the natural sciences at the end of the nineteenth century (and which helped prise history from the grip of the old certaintists and located it firmly in the contingency category); rather, in his now positive mood, Carr rejects – and this expression is typical of his positive attitude throughout the later stages of his book – all such sceptics. For today, says Carr, the field has been left open

> for the theologians who seek the meaning of history outside history, and for the sceptics who find no meaning in history at all.[25]

Consequently, and in no way a sceptic in those senses, Carr sees himself as necessarily having to re-yoke the historical facts to the value of progress in some detail. So, what sorts of detail does he come up with?

As already indicated, his detailed argument is of little validity. Carr's main method is just to go through a list of historians who have effectively yoked together facts and values as if there was no problem. As Carr casually comments: 'Let us see how a few historians, or writers about history, chosen more or less at random, have felt about this [fact–value] question'. And sure enough, those who appear on his actually far from random list (why not put Dilthey and Nietzsche on it?) namely, Gibbon, Tawney, Carlyle, Berlin and Marx, have all felt fine. But of course the problem remains. For it is obvious from his argument that Carr does not understand what the fact–value question is. Carr puts his own argument this way:

> Let us now take another look at this alleged dichotomy between fact and value. Values cannot be derived from facts. This statement is partly true, but partly false. You have only to examine the system of values prevailing in any period or in any country to realise how much of it is moulded by the facts of the environment. . . . Or take the Christian church as an institution largely concerned with the propagation of moral values. Contrast the values of primitive Christianity with those of the medieval papacy. . . . These differences in values spring from differences of historical fact. Or consider the historical facts which . . . have caused slavery . . . to be generally regarded as immoral. The proposition that values cannot be derived from facts is [thus] to say the least, one-sided and misleading . . . [26]

Of course none of this is to the point. For the fact–value problem doesn't for one moment refuse to recognise that all of us, everyday, link facts to values all the time. Rather the fact–value argument hinges on whether or not it is logically demonstrable that one, and only one, value can be derived from one, or one set of, facts in terms of a strict, unambiguous, incorrigible, absolute entailment. And despite centuries of attempts to prove such an entailment (recent 'famous' examples being by John Searle, Alistair MacIntyre and Roy Bhaskar) in the light of reading, say, Fish, Foucault, Lyotard and Rorty, such an alleged entailment seems unconvincing to me. Besides, if facts and values were entailed in the way Carr suggests, that is, by people just going around doing it, then Carr would be unable to argue – as he had done earlier in his text when it suited him – that those contemporaneous intellectuals who surrounded him and who drew the value of pessimism from the facts of the 1950s and 1960s and 1970s were 'wrong' to do so, and that the pessimistic readings of, say, Bury or Fisher, were 'wrong' also. No, what we have here is simply all sorts of people drawing all sorts of values from either the same or differently constituted facts. And this is simply because the past – not having in it any purpose or meaning that it itself can 'arrange' and/ or communicate to us – is simply waiting for meanings and purposes to be ascribed to it; to be conferred upon it. In that sense the past can be described as an utterly 'promiscuous past', a past which will, as it were, go with anybody; a sort of loose past which we can all have; the sort of past that is, arguably, not much use having in the first place. Carr's argument, then, cannot possibly succeed but, as already indicated, it is easy to see why he so badly wanted it to. Because without it his own view of history remains just that; his own view. And this is exactly what he does not want to accept. Finally for Carr, progress really is written not just in his own positioned 'mind', but in the actuality of the past:

> Progress in history is achieved through the interdependence and interaction of facts and values. The objective historian is the historian who penetrates most deeply into this reciprocal process.[27]

Not only that. For Carr will now start to push this particular line much further, not least because in this direction lies objectivity and, yes, even truth:

> Somewhere between these two poles – the north pole of valueless facts and the south pole of value judgements still struggling to transform themselves into facts – lies the realm of historical truth. The historian ... is balanced between fact and interpretation, between fact and value. He cannot separate them. It may be that, in a static world, you are obliged to pronounce a divorce between fact and value. But history is meaningless in a static world. History in its essence [sic] is change, movement, or – if you do not cavil at the old-fashioned word – progress.[28]

Well, one may of course cavil. There are a lot of oughts and certainties here, whilst the fact–value difference is unlikely to be due to the notion of a 'static world'. There is, moreover, that old recourse to essentialism in that when Carr says history is progressive then it really is. That is to say, by now Carr effectively thinks that history and progress are two words for the same thing: they are identical. History is progress, progress is history:

> History properly so-called can be written only [sic] by those who find and accept a sense of direction in history itself. The belief that we have come from somewhere is closely linked with the belief that we are going somewhere.[29]

From which position follows Carr's enlarged definition of what history is. For now history is no longer a dialogue between the present and the past, but the present and the past and the future:

> When ... I spoke of history ... as a dialogue between past and present, I should rather have called it a dialogue between the events

of the past and progressively emerging future ends. The historian's interpretation of the past, his selection of the significant and the relevant, evolves with the progressive emergence of new goals.[30]

And this is what Carr means by *objectivity*. For, only the future

> can provide the key to the interpretation of the past; and it is only in this sense that we can speak of an ultimate objectivity in history. It is at once the justification and the explanation of history that the past throws light on the future, and the future throws light on the past.[31]

What then, asks Carr, do we mean when we praise a historian for being objective? Or when we say that one historian is more objective than another? Well, it is not just that he/she gets his/her facts correct – although this is important. No. What makes one historian better than another – what makes Carr a better historian than another – and what prevents any old history being equally as good as any other (for Carr is, in this important sense, no relativist) is very clear. It is whether or not the historian chooses the right facts. It is whether or not he/she chooses and applies the right 'standard of significance'. So that when 'we' call an historian objective we mean, says Carr, two things:

> First of all, we mean that he has a capacity to rise above the limited vision of his own situation in society and in history – a capacity which . . . is partly dependent on his capacity to recognise the extent of his involvement in that situation, to recognise, that is to say, the impossibility of total objectivity. Secondly, we mean that he has the capacity to project his vision into the future in such a way as to give him a more profound and more lasting insight into the past than can be attained by those historians whose outlook is entirely bounded by their own immediate situation. No historian today will echo Acton's confidence in the prospect of 'ultimate history'. But some historians write history which is more durable, and has more of this ultimate and objective character, than others; and these are the historians who have . . . a long-term vision over the past and over the future. The historian of the past can make an approach towards objectivity only as he approaches towards the understanding of the future.[32]

Such objectivity is not 100 per cent then. The 'facts of history' cannot be ultimately correct. The concept of absolute truth cannot be appropriate to the historian. But insofar as historians can approximate to objectivity and truth about the past, the touchstone by which to do so is the future. In this, the last quotation I will be taking from Carr, he just about says it all:

> The absolute in history is not something in the past from which we start; it is not something in the present, since all present thinking is necessarily relative. It is something still incomplete and in the process of becoming – something in the future towards which we move, which begins to take shape only as we move towards it, and in the light of which, as we move forward, we gradually shape our interpretation of the past. . . . Our criterion is not an absolute in the static sense of something that is the same yesterday, today, and for ever: such an absolute is incompatible with the nature of history. But it is an absolute in respect to our interpretation of the past. It rejects the relativist view that one interpretation is as good as another, or that every interpretation is true in its own time and place, and it provides the touchstone by which our interpretation of the past will ultimately be judged. It is this sense of direction in history which alone enables us to order and interpret the events of the past – the task of the historian – and to liberate and organise human energies in the present with a view to the future – the task of the statesman, the economist, and the social reformer ... I now come back to my starting point by declaring my faith in the future of society and in the future of history.[33]

This concludes my reading of Carr. It goes without saying (or at least without much saying) that Carr's notion of objectivity and historical truth as resting on the picking out of the significant from the insignificant relative to a putative future according to which historical changes as expressed in historiography – the only useable past/history there is – is, of course, still relative with regard to other ways of putting the past 'under a description'; you can always get another description. Carr may have thought he had pretty much escaped relativism, but of course in that sense he hadn't done so (and privately as it were, R. W. Davies tells us that 'The problem of objectivity in history evidently continued to trouble him long after he had completed *What Is History?*').[34] For simply change what you think the future ought to be and you change the perspective from which you read the past; shift the end point of the narrative slightly, and you change the criterion for significance. This is not to say that

Carr is not correct to think that histories are written with a desired future in mind; we do indeed always have the past we want because of the future we desire. We saw this in the Introduction and in Chapter 1; that all histories, including postmodern ones, are future-orientated. However, on the reading that has been given here, the point is not that Carr's solution to the problem of relativism ultimately failed, but that what is central to his history is that he tried to be an objectivist; that he tried to get to the truth, and that what scepticism he had was reserved for those historians who did not see history in the upper case terms that he himself certainly did. [35]

Here lies Carr's weakness, then, if we wish to use him to gain an understanding of what is history today. This weakness is not that he did not understand what is involved in, say, the fact–value debate (though he didn't) or that his epistemological scepticism is slight and underdeveloped (though it is) but that he thought that objectivity and even truth – no matter how well qualified – were still items on an agenda drawn up in the 'old style'. Carr's self-conscious, stubborn decision to stick with a proclaimed Victorian optimism of a Marxist type can therefore be seen as being just too certaintist, too earnest, too unreflexive and so, in a way, too naive to be taken seriously today. And it is not only that. In Carr – and as we will see in Elton too – there is an air of besieged defensiveness as he recognises that he is running an old-fashioned argument against the tide: he is an embattled optimist. What makes Carr the old modernist he is is thus precisely that he will not, or cannot, change.

CARR TODAY

A few concluding thoughts. In the last few sentences I think I have given the answer to why Carr is not a good enough guide for students as they pick their way through the labyrinths of history today. Nor is there anything in Carr's later Preface or his Notes towards a new edition of *What Is History?* to suggest that he had picked up on all those 'postist' debates which were embryonic or fully fledged well before his death and which would have indicated to him the 'end of modernist history'. For the briefest of examinations of the Index of the latest edition of Carr's text – which includes items from his later Notes – shows few references to the debates of the 1960s, 1970s, and early 1980s, or to theories then being developed by theorists with an increasingly high public/intellectual profile. Thus there are no references to, say, Foucault or Barthes or Derrida or Lyotard or

Auerbach; no mention of feminism, hermeneutics, phenomenology, narratology, post-structuralism or postmodernism, whilst existentialism or structuralism are written off, generally in one-liners. Nor, within the broadly Marxist framework within which Carr works, is there really any mention of those sophisticated revisions that took place within 'Western Marxism' from the 1920s onwards; certainly there is no serious analysis of them. Thus, Lukacs gets only a sentence in the Notes, the Frankfurt School (of Horkheimer, Adorno, Marcuse *et al.*) gets no mention (Adorno gets a single entry in the Notes), nor do, say, Gramsci, Della Volpe, Benjamin, Althusser, Jameson, and so on. Nor is there any reference to that whole gamut of intellectual movements drawn on by Hayden White in the making of his *Metahistory* and which was published as early as 1973, nor any mention, of course, of either White or his work despite the fact that it received critical attention in the 1970s.

In fact, what Carr draws upon for his discussion of the question of the nature of history are the authors and texts of his youth; of an altogether different generation (or two) of historians/theorists: Acton, Arnold, Barth, Becker, Bloch, Bury, Carlyle, Clark, Collingwood, Dilthey, Eliot, Fisher, Green, Grote. So one can run through Carr's 'reference points' and emerge with a clear understanding of why today Carr is seen to be so unhelpful: he is out of date.

This is not to say, of course, that there are not signs in Carr which suggest he is not totally unaware of certain developments, but only that whenever intimations of familiarity occur, then such 'developments' are either dismissed or recuperated back into older, more familiar contexts, present in his text only as the merest shadows of the substance they actually possess – a substance that has, of course, re-written what now passes as plausible under the question of what is history and reconstituted the *grounds* for the making of historical knowledge. For, whilst Carr may well have learnt the late-modernist notion of perspectivism, he hardly seems to have been ready for the postmodernist lesson that perspectivism 'goes all the way down'; that it includes everything and everybody – including himself. Hence the tension which runs throughout Carr's text caused by him needing to be, on the one hand, sceptical and perspectival *vis-à-vis* his critique of empirical, postivistic, 'commonsense' liberal historiography and, on the other, to be non-sceptical, objectivist and non-relativist about his own alternative. In a nutshell, this is why Carr cannot relax with, or be of much use to, the sort of history which the conditions of postmodernity and postmodernism demand. Carr was of course

immensely interesting and influential in his own time; his critical
sceptism helped enormously to break down some of the old certaintist attitudes, and this can be acknowledged. But times have
moved on and those old debates are precisely 'old debates'. For,
amongst postmodernists, perspectivism and its anti-essentialist,
anti-teleological, anti-foundationalist, anti-representationalist and
anti-realist implications, occasion no fear and trembling but, in their
more radical renditions (the renditions of Rorty and White) usher in
new possibilities; new opportunities. Here there is no nostalgia for
the loss of a 'real' past, no wistful remembrance of more certaintist
times; no panic that there are no foundations for knowledge firmer
than an ultimately rhetorical conversation. Here, few would disagree
with the sentiment, après Rorty, that like the idea of a putative world-
before-all versions, so the idea of a putative history-before-all
historiographical versions is indeed one 'well lost'. Accordingly, it
is for these kinds of reasons that Carr ought no longer to be in a
central/introductory place in our understanding of what history is
nowadays. And neither should Geoffrey Elton.

Chapter 3

On Geoffrey Elton

It is understandable that we should find in a conservative (Tory) historian like Geoffrey Elton, who sees valuable continuities in the past, continuities in his own approach to the question of what is history. Thus, in the first pages of *Return to Essentials* (1991) Elton tells us that whilst the main theme of its early chapters (comprising The Cook Lectures, 1990) will indeed 'revolve around the current debates on the nature of history', his discussions will be neither exhaustive or necessarily appreciative, not least because he will be 'defending what may appear to be very old-fashioned convictions and practices' from those theorists and philosophers of history who he thinks have scarce done a decent day's historical work in their lives.[1] These late sentiments, which fix Elton's area of concern and his attitude towards it, echo those of the Preface to the *Practice of History* written about twenty-five years before. For there the apparently already embattled Elton tells us that his aim will be to defend – on the basis of his practical experience as a professional historian – his 'craft' against a motley collection of history theorists, philosophers and sociologists. For:

> When I read [their] discussions of how historians think ... I marvel at the ingenuity of the writers, for usually they are men who have never apparently themselves tried to do the work, to see the manifestly surviving evidence of past fact and event, or to practice critical judgement on the materials of history rather than the minds of historians.[2]

From these sorts of comment, then, one may well think – and one may well be right – that Elton's long-term hostility towards theory ('I think ... that a philosophic concern with such problems as the reality of historical knowledge or the nature of historical thought

only hinders the practice of history')[3] suggests that he is hardly the
best person to go to if one wants to understand the nature of history
as a discourse at any time let alone a time like today when historians
really cannot any longer bury their heads in the sand. But it is not
only that. For, whilst there are few people more decidedly against
historians taking up 'uncritical positions' towards history than
Elton, he appears remarkably unreflexive about just how far his own
political convictions affect his practices, and how easily these can be
theorised and positioned. Of course, it has been noted already that
Elton may well have objected to this sort of political positioning, for
whilst he is not afraid to tell his readers quite bluntly what history
is and ought to be based on his own experience, he is on occasion
ready to qualify this and become tolerantly pluralistic:

> I know, of course, that my experience has been limited . . . that
> there is a great deal more history than I know about, that there are
> methods of studying it which I have not had occasion to practice,
> and that there never is any single road to success.[4]

There is also a sense in which Elton sometimes appears to be
disarmingly 'laid back' and casual in his defence of his professional
work (The historian's *raison d'être* is that 'it is a pleasant occupation'
for which 'we even get paid – isn't that marvellous').[5] But, overall,
Elton rides high in the conviction stakes ('I can only preach what I
believe, and I do believe in those entrenched positions concerning
the reality of historical studies'),[6] so that in this respect Gregor
McLennan's comments appear to be pretty much to the point when
he says that, although Elton's 'militant stance is at times deceptively
easy going', his theoretical and ideological targets are clear enough:

> Elton takes 'visionaries' in history [such as E. H. Carr] to be a
> 'menace', and abstraction or morality are deemed dangerous
> luxuries. He defends instead the qualities of apprenticeship,
> professionalism, and the authority of the 'man' expertly trained in
> source work. His work is above all the defence of the Oxbridge
> ethic.[7]

Elton's view of history, then, as articulated in his interventions
against various 'charlatans' and 'amateurs', is therefore just as
'interested' and positioned *vis-à-vis* the question of what is history
as everyone else's, and although the absolute certainty of that
position is indeed qualified, at the end of the day one gets the very
strong impression that, as far as Elton is concerned, if history could

speak for 'itself' and disclose the essence of its being, then it would to all intents and purposes speak Eltonian.

So, what does Elton say with regard to the nature of history? My answer on this occasion is one based on a reading of just two texts – *The Practice of History* and *Return to Essentials*[8] and considered under the following sub-headings: Convictions and Prejudices; On Principles; On Ontology, Epistemology, and Method; On Writing History, and, Using Elton Today: The Poverty of Experience.

CONVICTIONS AND PREJUDICES

Like Carr, Elton partly answers the question of what he thinks history is by distinguishing it from what it is not. So, what are 'improper' approaches and who are 'improper' historians: who does Elton dislike? He has a longish list.

First, he doesn't like amateurs; the sort of 'man' who comes to history in a happy spirit of untrained enterprise, and who thinks research means just reading a lot of books rather than 'assimilating into oneself the various and often very tiresome relics of the past'; the sort of man who tends to regard the past, or parts of it, as quaint, who unknowingly makes anachronistic judgements, and who is oft given to sentimentality, romantic love and mordant sympathy. This is the sort of man who pales into insignificance against the professional, a man who has learnt his job on the job and who, even at his most tedious and pedantic cannot fail to add 'to learning, understanding and knowledge; he contributes truth'.[9] For this is a man who knows his evidence almost 'instinctively'; who almost intuits the right questions to ask, and who can construct an argument or a narrative in a clear prose such that, however much 'we may prefer to read the amusing amateur rather than the tedious professional . . . we shall trust the second when we really want to know'.[10] For this man (it is of course Elton himself) is an 'insider'.

Second, given the uniqueness of history, it has been Elton's long-term position that he doesn't want it contaminated by cognate discourses. To be sure, the opening up of new lines of inquiry is a reputable ambition and one should constantly be looking over (whilst retaining) the boundary fences. However, warns Elton, too careful 'an ear cocked for the pronouncements of non-historians is liable to produce disconcerting results'. Besides, 'tastes' in neighbouring discourses change rapidly, so that historians may embrace Freud only to find psychologists (Elton does not register the difference between psychologists and psychoanalysts) poised for a mass flight from him. Similarly, the anthropology which most influenced historians in the 1960s, 'is still too often at the Malinowski and Margaret Murray stage' (one wonders what stage Elton thought it should be at?), whilst Marxist sociology has, of course, long been superseded by more accurate and subtle analyses.[11]

Third, Elton is against the endeavour to make history scientific or 'upper case'. By scientific he seems to mean generalisations of a law-like kind with future prognoses, a quest which, for Elton, the ideographic and contingent nature of the past (let alone 'the evidence') rules out: 'Few practicising historians would probably nowadays fall victim to the search for such laws; the experience of research is enough to cure such ambitions.'[12] From which position Elton is able to develop an argument which holds that, whilst all historians should aim to reach the truth of the past, any ultimate truth, and certainly any metanarrative (any upper case history) is impossible. Of course this is not to say that any historian, himself included, has in fact 'ever treated his subject as though it were entirely without meaning; if he had, he would have been unable to write'. But what is really at issue is 'whether one may discern a larger purpose, whether things produce effects that are continuous and, up to a point predictable'. And for Elton, Carr is just one of a long list of those who have fallen for this ridiculous idea, a list including, variously, Arnold Toynbee, R. H. Tawney, Christopher Hill and other assorted Marxists, all of whom have lost their integrity as historians by falling to a faith or to a vision – secular or religious it matters not – Elton thereby 'defining out' of the categories of proper history/historian those who do not effectively subscribe, as he does, to history in the lower case, a general agnosticism, and a serendipitous conservatism in politics, justifying this attitude on the basis of holding a healthy scepticism towards all theories (as if lower case history was not a theoretical construct).[13] Yet, having said all this, Elton thinks that today there are some 'theorists' around who have apparently got more scepticism than is good for either them or for himself, so that their very different kind of 'deconstructive' enthusiasm must also be rejected.

Thus, *fourth*, Elton makes a move against the postmodernists; against those theorists who not only think that neither they nor anyone else can understand the past in some sort of upper case way, but who deny that it can ever be 'really' known at all; to those, that is, who have absorbed the apparently widespread conviction that certain extravagances current among students of literature render all forms of objective study impossible and therefore disable the historian from ever achieving what for a long time now he has stated to be his ambition. Ideological theories create preconditioned convictions about the historical past; philosophical theories deny that the historical past can ever be reconstituted. The first undermine the [proper] historian's honesty, the second his claims to existence.[14]

Hence Elton's critique, in *Return to Essentials*, of those somewhat unhinged 'continentals' such as Heidegger and Adorno, Saussure and Barthes, Gadamer, Derrida and Foucault; such Americans as 'the daddy of the endeavour to treat historical exposition as a form of literary discourse and no more', Hayden White; such older Americans who should know better like Dominick LaCapra, and a host of such young scholars as David Harlan and Judith Anderson who, sadly misled by the 'theory mongers', justify Elton taking to the barricades once again to defend proper history – his history – from these new dangers. For, as Elton puts it – warming up to the prospect of the fray and getting in the mood:

> Certainly, we are fighting for the lives of innocent young people beset by devilish tempters who claim to offer higher forms of thought and deeper truths and insights – the intellectual equivalent of crack. . . . Any acceptance of those theories – even the most gentle or modest bow in their direction – can prove fatal. . . . Those who preach the virtues of these recent styles of literary criticism, naturally believe themselves to have learned new truths about the manner in which the human mind absorbs and reacts to reality. However, when listening to some quite extraordinarily unreal guides they are in effect only seeking the . . . propagation of their own selves. They come to think that only their own existence is real; everything else exists only in relation to that one central fact. This is an attitude entirely proper to the adolescent mind . . . but it is not a stance that should survive growing up.[15]

Consequently, the solution lies in the proper, adult study of the past. For the professional historian, his central concerns reside in the first place with the people of the past; with *their* experiences, *their* thoughts and *their* actions, and not with the people of the present and, least of all, the historian himself:

This does not mean that I consider it possible for him to exclude himself from the enterprise called studying the past: of course, the history he tells has to be processed through his mind and pen. But . . . that involvement is not equal to dominance; it does not mean that he stands at the centre of the historical reconstruction (Croce and Collingwood were utterly wrong); it does not mean . . . that he cannot escape from his prejudices and preconceptions. That risk he runs only when he obeys the false guides with their destructive message.[16]

These, then, are the sorts of attitude Elton has and which help him, by ruling out certain theories/practices, to rule in his own preferences. So what, more positively now, is history for Elton?

Well, the position in which he says he stands has its own history which he sketches out: Elton sees himself as part of a tradition. And here it has to be said that Elton seems to display a curious blindspot in that it soon becomes clear (in *The Practice of History*) that whilst Elton sees himself as standing in a historiographical tradition which is particular and indeed unique – which in that sense is a *local* tradition – he is soon treating it as nothing of the sort, portraying it as if it were the real embodiment of a slowly emerging universal truth.

Elton begins his historical location by pointing out that whilst the desire to know what went before – the desire to understand the passage down time – is a universal human desire, not all civilisations have been equally concerned to know and write human history 'as it really was'. Whilst in Europe there were precursors, the study of history as a 'proper developed discipline' came late. Only in the nineteenth century, building on the foundations laid down especially by Ranke, did historians began to study the past disinterestedly and by way of 'systematic research'. Accordingly, it was only by the first half of the twentieth century that English historians became convinced 'that the principles of respectable historiography could be reduced to one main precept: to study history for its own sake'. And although since then there have been reactions against this precept – giving rise to sometime healthy and (as now) sometimes juvenile debates – Elton was of the opinion (in 1966/7) that the time was ripe to

> restate some of the truths of practice and experience, to rescue history from its candid friends, and to remind the historical world that there is work to be done . . . that that work must be carried out in a cage set by certain inescapable conditions, and that bright ideas, however seemingly new, are not everything.[17]

Now, what is interesting in all this is, of course, the ahistorical and indeed, Whiggish position Elton has created for himself, as he takes Rankean-type, lower case (bourgeois) 'own-sakism' as not just another *species* of history but as history *per se*. For what Elton has effectively argued is that, once upon a time and especially in Europe, earlier fumbling attempts to understand the past had been made, but that only in the nineteenth century was the bulk of previous mystical, religious and metaphysical approaches sloughed-off, allowing proper history to emerge. In that sense, it looks as though Elton sees himself as standing as the culmination of the history of historiography itself. That is to say: previous attempts to understand what history really was had fallen short, but gradually, in incremental and evolutionary ways things had become better and better until, with lower case, professional, own-sakist 'academic' study, its journey had ended. It therefore seems that Elton regards himself as standing at the end of a process such that we might well wonder what could be more 'Whiggish', what could be more theoretical, indeed, what could be more Hegelian, than that?

Of course as a conservative Elton cannot, and does not, rule out further change entirely. Nevertheless, given the fact that other sorts of development in and around history are, as has been seen, generally viewed negatively (and defensively) by Elton; and given that it does not seem to have crossed his mind to see lower case history in 'real' historical terms (i.e. in terms to do with power, with class and ethnic and gender location, with material exigencies and ideological positions and so on) then perhaps the only conclusion which can be drawn is that insofar as Elton actually seems to identify his *species* of history with its *genus*, then this is a profoundly essentialist and ahistorical thought for a historian to have. Which means that what Elton goes on to call the 'principles of historiography' are not in any sense the principles of historiography as such, but simply the principles Elton likes construed in a universal form. So, what are the principles Elton misleadingly suggests are history's own?

ON PRINCIPLES

In *Return to Essentials*, Elton writes that a knowledge of history has two legitimate uses. First of all, it equips the living 'with a much wider and deeper acquaintance with the possibilities open to human thought and action than people can ever gather from their own limited experience'; and second (and more importantly) 'it demonstrates the magnificent unpredictability of what human beings may think and do'.[18] But of course these two usages which Elton likes and presents (understandably in the light of my remarks in the previous section) as universal truisms, are actually his own value judgements, value judgements which do not and logically cannot follow from any past events or the facts thereof. For obviously one could just as easily (i.e. just as illegitimately) draw from 'the fact' of the 'unpredictability of the past', the normative conclusion that the present and the future *ought* – given the distress and misery such unpredictability could be interpreted as causing – to be organised and planned along, say, Marxist lines, so that such unpredictability could be prevented in the name of greater freedoms, which is precisely the opposite conclusion to that which Elton himself draws. For Elton, what is valuable about history (historiography?) is that it is precisely 'its' unpredictability which embodies something too essential in human beings ever to be snuffed out by organisation and planning; by predictability, free will.

Now, it might have already been seen from the above argument how Elton's views as to what are legitimate uses for history are every bit as 'present-centred' as anyone else's, despite the fact that in Elton's book 'present-centredness' is almost a treasonable offence. For Elton, being present-centred is tantamount to saying that one is not being historical at all, arguing that if 'knowledge of the past is to entitle the historian to speak to his own day, it must not be so organised as to satisfy that day's whim, if it is to teach usefully about mankind and the [imperfectability which apparently constitutes the essence of the] human condition, it must be understood for itself and in all its variety, undetermined by the predilictions of the present'.[19]

But, treasonable or not, Elton cannot resist breaking this self-denying ordinance for long. For we soon find that he is surreptitiously using the two things which I have previously noted and which he thinks the past has taught him, in order to combat two alternative ways of thinking about the past which are, in his lights, definitely present-centred and which he thinks must be defeated if his own 'proper' history is to survive. First, there are those 'strictly ideological' histories which impose an overarching, and thus fixing, interpretation on the past (and future) and, second, there are those philosophical arguments of a postmodern type which question the 'whole concept of the study of the past', a questioning which comes from the attempt to use (in the manner of Hayden White) literary theory to destroy the reality of the past as it had previously emerged from a study of that past's relics; that is to say, a questioning which problematicises the very basis of his own position, resting as it does on his knowledge that history really is what Elton says it is, that is, unpredictable.

The two lessons which Elton seems to think just do derive from *any* proper study of the past – the valorisation of a certain concept of freedom and a suitably conservative *theory* of history as *serendipity* – are thus quite clearly lessons conferred on and not found in the past. But Elton doesn't recognise this point. Accordingly, from this unreflexive position he then argues that not his history but history *per se* has, if it is to be properly understood, three characteristic principles; three methodological approaches which together constitute it. What are these three universal principles/methods?

Elton approaches them by way of three qualifying, preliminary observations. First, whilst he allows that different periods of the past and different questions asked of it by historians have called and still call for the application of different 'techniques', nevertheless, such varying techniques all live under the aegis of a method that is held constant (i.e. which is of a universal type). Second, at the basis of his notion of what constitutes proper history lie the *sources*. These cast a sovereign spell over Elton. For 'we' historians, he says, 'are firmly bound by the authority of our sources (and by no other authority, human or divine), nor must we use fiction to fill in the gaps'.[20] For it is in the sources – and only in the sources – that the *truth* can be found:

> *Ad fontes* remains the necessary war cry. For the historian the reality – yes, the truth – of the past exists in materials of various kinds, produced by that past at the time that it occurred and left behind by it as testimony. Historical evidence is not created by the historian ... which means that ... arguments about the study of 'texts' help hardly at all in our understanding of the tasks undertaken by most historians.[21]

Third, the historical evidence which for Elton comprises 'the extant traces of past events and experiences' needs, if it is to be used correctly, 'properly acquired and applied' professional skills so to work the evidential sources. And, for Elton, it is these professionally tuned skills which allow the historian to 'do his work well'. Hence, via these three preliminary points, he arrives at his three specific principles. They are these.[22]

First: separate your question from your answer. By which is meant that 'the question one puts to the evidence should not be biased towards an answer already in the mind'. Second: 'remember that you have the advantage and burden of hindsight, whereas the people you are talking about lacked this. This is one of the essential points in what I have called studying the past on its own terms.' And third: 'keep an open mind'; that is, allow 'further study and fuller knowledge . . . to modify what you have thought and said'.[23]

It is from these three principles that Elton is ready to answer the question of what he thinks history is and why we ought to study it, an answer he puts as well as anywhere in the following passage:

> History provides the laboratory in which human experience is analysed, distilled and bottled for use. The so-called lessons of history do not teach you to do this or that now; they teach you to think more deeply, more completely, and on the basis of an enormously enlarged experience about what it may be possible or desirable to do now . . . history for ever demonstrates the unexpectedness of the event [i.e. is serendipitous] and so instils a proper scepticism in the face of all those vast and universal claims [of the upper case]. A knowledge of the past should arm a man against surrendering to the panaceas [as opposed to the realistic conservatism] peddled by too many myth-makers. This is known as growing up. . . . Thus I will burden the historian with preserving human freedom, freedom of thought and . . . action. . . . Understand the past in its own terms and convey it in terms designed to be comprehended. And then ask those willing to listen to attend to the real [sic] lessons of the past, the lessons which [presumably being entailed] teach us to behave as [certain types of] adults, experienced in the ways of the world, balanced [sic] in judgement, and sceptical in the face of all the miracle-mongers.[24]

This effectively constitutes Elton's answer to the question of 'what is history?' And so the question I want to comment on very briefly at this point is, what, if anything, is wrong with it? (or, as Michael Stanford has put it: 'These are Elton's principles of historical practice, and who could [possibly] quarrel with them?')[25]

I think that at least two quarrelsome points can be made. First, whilst there is nothing wrong with Elton's view of, and use of, history in the sense that he can legitimately draw from his studies of the past whatever conclusions he likes (I mean, we can all do that), what he cannot do is to present his own deepest 'convictions and practices' (some manifestations of which I have drawn attention to via the brackets in the above passage) as just naturally *flowing from* the ways he studies the past as opposed to him *inserting into* it his preconceptions. For if, as it seems, 'doing history' for Elton is the 'professional' application of technical skills, given that skills are empty mechanisms (i.e. they have no substantive content) then any substantive conclusions are bound to be 'significant' interpretations. If this is so, then Elton would presumably have difficulty in arguing against a feminist, say, who *was* professionally trained, who *did* go back to the sources, who *did* have the skills, etc.; and yet who came up with a piece of research which was unmistakably feminist. Of course, Elton could – and probably would – have claimed that she didn't have an open mind; that she had preconceived ideas; that her research was ideological and thus illegitimate. To which her reply could be simply to ask why the 'open-minded Elton' always seems to come back from the past with a serendipitous history and never a Marxist or a feminist one, especially when Marxists and feminists have no trouble in doing so. *Could it be that Elton had put his reading there?*

Now, clearly these exchanges could go on and on, but the point of interest is whether Elton is doing 'proper history' (ostensibly objective, disinterested and non-present-centred history) if it always seems to enable him to bring back the sorts of lessons he thinks *we now need* and not others, i.e. to grow up (in a certain way), to be balanced (in a certain way), to see history as for ever demonstrating a nature that is unequivocally serendipitous and to claim, somehow, that it is the past 'itself' which suggests that it is properly studied and its nature revealed only if it is approached in the lower case. And my point here is again to say that such lower case 'proper' history is, of course, not proper history at all, but just Elton's way of describing what he himself liked to do.

So to the *second* quarrelsome point, which is this. There is a sense in which, by his stress on the skills of the professional historian, Elton runs the risk of committing what McLennan has called the 'technicist fallacy'; that is, 'the identification of a theoretical discipline with certain parts of its technical instrumentation'.[26] Which is to say that in his emphasis (especially in *The Practice of History*) on the mechanics of 'source work' (i.e. by his stress on internal and external criticisms of documentary evidence) Elton has done two things. First, he has effectively defined history as an empiricist and technical set of applied skills, as though such techniques 'stood in for' and were thus denied as constitutive of history's problematic theories, methodologies and ideologies. Second, Elton has construed the techniques of proper (i.e. his) history as having moral (normative) implications. For, if history as a discourse is actually produced and distributed within complicated power arrangements of ideological/institutional types (which is what I am arguing) then to suggest to young historians that history *is* made above, or beyond, or outside of, those actualities; to suggest, moreover, that it *ought* only to be made by the application of professionally acquired skills above and beyond and outside of those actualities, is not only misleading but can also generate feelings of guilt. For young historians often feel morally guilty – they think they are doing something wrong and bad – if they 'admit' that they actually do have a 'position', that they are not 'objective', and that they do not read history 'for its own sake'. And this is because, as McLennan has pointed out, within the *doxa* of what constitutes 'proper' history the acquisition of skills is often accorded *moral* status:

> For Langlois and Seignobos, in the classic empiricist primer, the mastery of auxiliaries [diplomatics, paleography, numismatics . . .] is seen as a 'serene' achievement. They set 'prudence, patience and accuracy' against 'dilettantism'. In Barzun and Graff's modern equivalent, the personal virtues of the researcher are themselves part of the technical apprenticeship – again, they are love of order, patience, accuracy, and vicarious imagination. V. H. Galbraith, too, puts 'humility and devotion at a high premium in history'.[27]

And so too does Elton:

> The historian fulfills his function properly if, aware of the unsolved and insoluble problems, conscious that he is not a machine and can be moved by love, anger, contempt and vanity, he concentrates on honesty and integrity.[28]

If the historian does not, if for example he/she does not do as he/she ought and practise humility before 'the sovereignty' of the sources and the evidential facts; if he/she has the arrogance to prioritise his/her own purposes, then Elton claims that he/she runs the risk of being, like Carr, 'a traitor to his calling'.[29] Accordingly, for young historians to have the courage to be overtly positioned is morally difficult, but only of course, if one is convinced by Elton's argument that his principles are, in their normative expression, the principles of history as such. And obviously they are not. Elton's principles of history are just his, and so we have no need to succumb to any feelings of guilt when we, like him, use the past 'to please ourselves'.

ON ONTOLOGY, EPISTEMOLOGY AND METHOD

So far I have dealt with Elton's general convictions and principles *vis-à-vis* what is history. But there is more to Elton than this. For Elton is also concerned, much more than Carr is, to underpin his views on proper history by a range of complementary arguments about how historians *ought* to proceed in their efforts to gain historical knowledge. In other words, Elton has an epistemology and a method, and recognises this to be so. But he also has something else which he is less explicit about; namely, an ontology, i.e. a theory of 'being'. For whilst Elton holds to various degrees of scepticism *vis-à-vis* the amount one can actually know about the past dependent upon one's various needs, his insistence that the historian should dedicate himself to the 'search for truth' is a recurrent one, and one which rests on the assumption that an objective knowledge of the past (for that is what the truth would be if it could be gained) is, in principle, achievable. Yet, precisely because of his scepticism, it might be useful to see what Elton means when he uses words like truth and objectivity with regard to getting a 'knowledge of the past'. When we do, it appears that things are more problematic and unsatisfactory than one may have initially thought. Accordingly, I want to look at this area for a few paragraphs. But I also have another reason for spending some time here. For, when I reach my discussion of Hayden White, and when we see the complexities of the formal epistemological and methodological categories/practices that he suggests *all* historians put their materials through before they exist as histories, then the practical advice and epistemological/methodological points raised by Elton pale into insignificance. So, with this thought also in mind, what does Elton says about all this? Let me begin by looking at his understanding of ontology.

As befits Elton's polemical style, when he comes to talk about the possibility of gaining (in principle and practice) some kind of objective historical truth, it seems that he is arguing against those who think that historical knowledge cannot definitively be found either because the place where one would have to look for it – the past *per se* – no longer exists; or against those who argue that because of the shaping power of the historian on his material, then all history is inevitably partial, selective, textual/intertextual and thus ultimately relativistic and self-referential. Elton regards both of these positions as too pessimistic, not least because he seems to think that they both arise from using *science* as the yardstick for 'true' knowledge. He puts this in a straightforward way:

> The problem of whether the past can be known at all – since it is not now here in the presence of the observer and cannot be brought back for study – arises from the attempt to make history seem a science, comparable in purpose and method to the natural sciences. [30]

Of course, Elton is aware that scientists themselves no longer have the confidence of their more optimistic nineteenth-century predecessors; they too have not escaped from the rising marsh gas of a general and potentially debilitating scepticism. Thus, nowadays the

> natural sciences have, it would seem, virtually abandoned the concepts of truth and falsehood; phenomena once regarded as objectively true are now seen to be only a statistical abstraction from random variables, and the accusing finger of the uncertainty principle further insists that, since observation alters a phenomenon, nothing is capable of being studied except after it is changed from the state in which it was meant to have been investigated. . . . This has not [of course] stopped scientists from continuing their efforts . . . and in so far as it has reduced their positivist pride . . . the new philosophy may be thought of as gain. But historians have always been inclined to doubt the value, even the possibility, of their studies; they require not the new humility preached in the wake of Heisenberg, but [rather] some return to the assurance of the nineteenth century that the work they are doing deals with reality. [31]

And Elton will give this 'nineteenth-century' assurance, and give it by the following ontological argument.

In a curious way, says Elton, history is actually concerned with a subject matter – the past – that is more 'objective' and more 'independent' than the objects of the sciences. For, whilst the historian cannot verify his reconstruction of the past by, say, repeating it at will in the manner in which a scientist can repeat his/her experiment, this apparent weakness can be turned into a strength. Although the scientist may obtain his/her problem by asking questions of nature, the scientific method of experimentation allows him/her to 'treat nature wilfully and to compose for himself the argument which he wishes to resolve', such that it is 'not going too far to assert that nearly all scientific study deals with specifically prepared artificial derivatives from what naturally occurs': science is an artificial construct.

But for Elton *history* is not. To be sure, the historian has to ask questions of the past. These questions may be ones he asks to suit himself; he may 'and probably will, include himself in the equation when he explains, interprets, even perhaps distorts'. But the point is this: he cannot invent the experiment; the subject under investigation is outside of the historian's control. Thus, concludes Elton:

> When the problem of truth is under consideration, his essential difference from the natural scientist works in his favour. He cannot escape the first condition of his enterprise, which is that the matter he investigates has a dead reality independent of the enquiry. At some time, these things actually once happened, and it is now impossible to arrange them for the purposes of experiment.[32]

Of course, this is not to say that we can therefore know exactly what, or when, or how, or why everything occurred. No historian 'should suppose that his knowledge can be either total or finite'. But the point is this: it is precisely because the past has gone, is irrecoverable and unrepeatable, that 'its objective reality', its ontological existence, 'is guaranteed'. Of course it must be noted, says Elton,

> that what is in question here is the subject matter of history, the events of the past, not the evidence they have left behind or the product of the historian's labours [historiography]. However biased, prejudiced, incomplete and inadequate that product may be, it embodies an account of events that happened quite independent of the existence of him who now looks at them ... the past ... is commandingly there.[33]

Accordingly, Elton is able to conclude that the historian is concerned with a truth which is more absolute than 'mere truthfulness', that is, more truthful than a verified experiment. Thus, whilst the historian will rarely be able to say

> this is the truth and no other answer is possible [he] ... will always be able to say: this once existed or took place, and there is therefore a truth to be discovered if only we can find it.[34]

Now, whether or not the truth of these past realities is in fact discoverable, is a matter that Elton says he will be going on to consider later (for this is a matter of epistemology and method-ological procedures) and when he does go on, I shall follow him. But for the moment I want to consider the ontological argument that Elton puts in order to ground his notion of objective truth. Thus,

> I have been concerned only to deny the charge that because the past cannot be re-enacted therefore there is, by definition, no such thing as historical truth.[35]

For such a truth is possible for Elton on the basis of the past's once ontological existence: it once was *being*. So, does this argument of Elton's mean anything? It is doubtful.

For, it is not as obvious as Elton thinks that from the objective existence of a given phenomenon – in this case the past – one can derive anything like an objective/truthful explanation of it. There are at least two problems here. The first is that the examples Elton gives of things having an existence may only touch upon the statement and the chronicle and not at all on history. And indeed, he says as much:

> We may not know precisely why William the Conqueror decided to invade England; we do know that he did invade. . . . We may argue over his invasion and its motive. . . . Nine hundred years ago they had existence; and just because they are irrecoverable in the flesh now, they are indestructible in the past reality.[36]

This first objection leads on to a related, but more serious, second one; namely, that the mere existence of a once real past (and recall also that we have already seen that it is no part of the arguments of White or Ankersmit or Rorty or Bennett *et al.* to deny for a moment the once actual existence of the past) does not in the slightest way tell you how to go about making the historical representation of it true and/or objective. Objectivity and truth are not derived in any way from the mere existence of an object of inquiry, but only from (say) the internal mechanisms and coherences of methods of ex-planation that are applied to it. Consequently, if Elton wants to construct an objective historical knowledge of the past beyond the statement and the chronicle, he will need to construct an epis-temology and a method, not suggest that a singular historical explanation can be true/objective (even in principle) just because it has a single object as the focus of its enquiry: you need more than an ontological assertion to give explanations of the whys and where-fores of the ontological.

It is not only that. Elton also tends to give a false impression of what is going on when he talks of objectivity and truth and ontology. Because when he talks of the truths of the once concrete past, or when he says that the past's objectivity is recuperable, it looks as if he is saying that truth and objectivity are in the past waiting to be discovered instead of being extrinsic evaluations waiting to be applied. What he should therefore have said about the once existing past as ontology is simply something like: 'historians like me take as axiomatic that the past did once exist, full stop', and thus not go on to say that such an existence was 'true'. For truth and objectivity are not properties that are *inherent* to the past; are not properties *belonging* to the past, but are terms we use when evaluating the accounts of the past which historians *make*.

So why does Elton not see this? The reason is not clear, but the effects that the regular application of the terms truth and objectivity to the ontological existence of the past are (and perhaps this is the reason why Elton argues as he does) in that the impression is given that from the ontological 'fact' of the past as a singular object that actually and really (truly) existed, one can draw singular(ly) true explanations of the states and the conditions of its existence: that from the ontological facts one can draw normative values (evaluations). But of course this no more works for Elton than it did for Carr. If there is any truth in this area, then, (and this is doubtful because this is the area of evaluative interpretations and we have already commented on the oxymoronic status of a 'true interpretation') they will have to come from epistemology and method, not ontology. And so we might look at Elton's views on these areas now.

Elton's epistemology and method live within the category of empiricism. He did not have to choose this category, but he has and he is a proud champion and defender of it. Of course, other theories and methods have obvious empirical elements, but Elton seems to have gone for the full-blown version: this is the way to proceed. And the point I want to begin to make here is simply that it is a pity that Elton thinks in this way. Because in doing so, what he has embraced is a theory (for empiricism as a method is just a systematised series of thoughts about how to do certain things) which is seriously flawed. And whilst I think that we should have some knowledge of empiricism's shortcomings from my earlier discussions of Bennett and White *et al.* (and my future discussions of Rorty and White will extend these) I would like to spend a little time now discussing the problems of empiricism. To do this – to put a brief but arguably cogent critique of empiricism – I think it might be useful to do so via a short resumé of such a critique as made by P. Q. Hirst in his book, *Marxism and Historical Writing*; to follow this by some complementary points drawn from Roland Barthes and Richard Johnson, and then leave the points which will have been made to be considered in relation to Elton's claims. What, as it were, could an empiricist reply to the critiques of Hirst *et al.* be like?[37]

Hirst begins his critique by saying that historiography is a practice predominantly conducted 'under the sign of empiricist epistemology'. Elton is therefore not alone in his choice, indeed, as Hirst says, most historians – and especially most of those who work professionally in the lower case – subscribe to this doctrine of knowledge production. Yet, as Hirst points out, this is strange, not least because 'empiricism as an epistemology posits an impossible knowledge process'. So, why do most proper historians use it? Hirst is not sure, but he thinks that it is probably because empiricism 'threatens what they actually do least', an empiricism he describes and then critiques as follows.[38]

Historical investigation and writing (historiography) says Hirst, have a dual object; first, certain hitherto existing phenomena (the things and events, etc., which actually existed in the past) and, second, the various historicised traces of such phenomena in documents and other artifacts which 'signify' the existence of the 'once real'. In that sense, history's 'facts' (which are generally just accepted as 'a given') are the materials which the historian works on – records, documents, archives – and it is these which contain those 'significations' which require 'interpretation'. It is through that interpretation that the hitherto existing is reconstructed. As Hirst puts it (after E. P. Thompson):

> historical 'facts' are 'produced' by appropriate discipline from the evidential facts. . . . These disciplines (methods) serve to reveal one order of facts present in another, existential facts are constituted from evidential facts.[39]

It is these existential facts extracted via the evidential traces which then become the 'measure of all the discourses placed upon them, *they* are the judges in the court'.[40] It is these which are the primary elements in the process of knowledge production, and it is these which reveal the falsity of any inappropriate significations which are placed upon them. Consequently, any theories – usually 'disguised' by empiricists as hypotheses or propositions – are then measured against the 'givenness' of the 'now-established' facts as from the evidential traces, the test being whether or not the new hypotheses match the 'evidential significations or patterns of relation between and consistency in the documents' which, as a method of interpreting documents, can only be assessed by its 'results'.[41]

Now, in all this, the theoretical element – from which hypotheses and propositions are derived and which are used to test the significance and consistency of the given materials – are seen as external to those materials and considered as secondary to them. As such, these hypotheses can be dispensed with if disconfirmed with reference to any selected body of evidential materials (though they may be re-used in relation to another such selection). Accordingly, the relationship between theory and evidence is a matter to be decided upon by the historian in each case. What matters, however, as Hirst puts it, is that in every case the 'facts speak in their own voices in the end [and] that the bodies of evidential materials tell all they have to say in the most consistent and intelligible fashion'.[42] Here, *all* theory lies impoverished against the richness and intelligibility of the primary sources.

Consequently, says Hirst, what we have here is the classic historian's prioritisation and valorisation of documents. For it is the documents, it is the sources which in being defined as the real objects of the historian's inquiry, define 'the unity and nature of the practice itself'. And in a way, says Hirst, empirical historians are not mistaken in this prioritisation for, separated 'from the evidentialization of documents as testimonies to hitherto existing phenomena, historiography ceases to have any unity as a practice. As such it is [thus] united by object and method.'[43] But – *and this is the big but* – although empirical history is united by its object and its method, such a unity has *no unity of significance*. For, given that the documents etc. form such an enormously diverse mass of materials which relate to so many practices and to so many activities, then there are potentially as many histories as there are grounds 'for selecting and constructing bodies of evidential testimony' such that, from this unavoidable dispersal, any unity of significance, any form of meaning, any sort of history, could potentially be constructed. Which means that whenever such a proliferation and dispersal is disciplined into some *specific* kind of unity, into some *specific* sort of significance – when it is unified to form a reading which might be of a Marxist, or a liberal, or a feminist, or a post-structural, or a *serendipitous* type – then that unity is not, and cannot be, one which has arisen from the dispersed facts themselves; is not one which has arisen from the sources, but is a unity which is and can only be logically derived from outside of these things – from *theory*; only theory can give history any unity of significance. Consequently, no matter how much the 'evidential materials' or the 'sources' or the 'documents' are prioritised within empiricism at the expense of 'mere' theory, theory ultimately reasserts itself as the inescapable determinant of meaning. Here is Hirst summarising all this:

> [H]istory is theoretically saturated. It finds its unity as object and its value as a practice in concepts which transcend what it can establish by the 'empirical procedures' it sets up as tests of valid knowledge. These procedures or tests are conducted within a theoretical field. This field is [in empiricism] assumed rather than argued for. For all [Elton's] ... insistence on the evidence and 'finding out', the procedures which purport to determine what is signified in bodies of documents rely for their relevance on theoretical arguments as to their contemporary value. There is no 'evidence' as such (as given); evidentialization is a conceptual process. A non-antiquarian history [and Elton's history is certainly not antiquarian] requires a philosophy of history.[44]

The argument from Roland Barthes serves to underline Hirst's point. For Barthes,[45] empirical history in particular performs a sleight of hand insofar as the referent (the object the historian refers to) 'is projected into a realm supposedly beyond signification, from which position it can be thought to precede and determine the discourse which posits it as referent' in the first place.[46] As Barthes puts this:

> The fact can only have a linguistic existence, as a term in a discourse, and yet it is exactly as if this existence were merely the 'copy' ... of another existence situated in the extra-structural domain of the 'real'. This type of discourse is [thus one] ... in which the referent is [ostensibly] aimed for as something external to the discourse without it ever being possible to attain it outside this discourse. [Consequently] the discourse of history is guilty of reducing the three term structure of signification (signifier, signified, referent) to a two term structure (signifier-referent), or rather of smuggling into this ostensibly two-term structure an illicit signified 'the real in itself'.[47]

Finally, underlining both Hirst and Barthes, Richard Johnson makes the point that not only do empiricist canons tend to render the historian invisible as his/her importance as the 'agent of historiographical significance' is played down *vis-à-vis* 'the evidence'; not only does empiricism rubbish theory to the point where it almost becomes a dirty word, but it is also the case that empiricist procedures disguise the culturally constructed character of the sources themselves. Johnson's argument goes as follows.

If we treat historical sources only as bearers of 'facts', says Johnson, we will tend to be mainly interested in certain areas of *facticity* concerning past actions and behaviour and not so interested in the historical and socially constructed values which are the precise medium of this 'information'. And whilst at its most 'banal' level historical practice simply ignores the cultural framing of 'fact', even smart professional empiricists tend to treat sources as if they were a fairly transparent medium. This is not to say that such historians are not aware of notions like 'source production' and 'source generation' and so forth, but it is to say that ambiguities in the sources are treated not – as with postmodernism – as 'differences' to be celebrated, but as 'problems' to be eradicated, so that they are construed as effectively transparent. In other words, even in the more critical professional mode, frameworks of meaning are treated negatively:

> they are a problem, a bias, a distortion. Critical procedure attempts to strip them away revealing the verifiable 'fact' inside. Actually [however] it is very doubtful if empiricism even describes this process accurately, let alone tells us what it should be.[48]

The reason why this is so harks back to empiricism's anti-theoreticism, which scarcely allows empirical historians to understand that, since *all* historical interrogation operates within its own frameworks of meaning, 'the reading of sources is better described as a process of *the competition of theories*'. For,

> Our own explanations are judged not against the pre-given facticity of the source (except in the vulgar sense of its material existence) but against the human constructions of meaning that are found there ... facts only signify, only have human meaning, within explanatory frames [within theories of significance].[49]

So, we are back to Hirst. And here we can leave ontology, epistemology and method, empirical style, with the reminder that the problem for Elton(ists) would be this: what would be a convincing rebuttal to the points made by Hirst and Barthes and Johnson; how viable as an epistemology and methodology is empiricism? And I think that that query might raise another one; namely, what weight might be given to Elton's views on the nature of history and the construction of historical knowledge after all that has been said by Hirst *et al.* about the inescapable presence of theory in historiography? For, if all historians, including empiricists, are inevitably as theoretical as Hirst argues (and Hirst's position seems plausible to me) then when Elton is attacking theorists isn't he actually attacking himself? Isn't he, as we shall see, just like everyone else; a metahistorian in White's sense of the term?

ON WRITING HISTORY

Closely linked to the epistemological and methodological problems of gaining historical knowledge is the equally problematical area of how this 'knowledge' is to be communicated; that is, the whole area of *representation*. Representation is problematic, not least because the major way in which the past has been considered within western historiography has been through the form of narrative discourse, the very form which has been subject to all those post-structuralist, textualist, postmodern debates which have been noted already.

In other words, as White puts it, 'In contemporary historical theory the topic of narrative has been the subject of extraordinarily intense debate.'[50] This debate has implications for Elton not least because he is not only a narrative historian but also one of its champions. Consequently, it would appear that Elton has not seen narrative in the problematic way in which White has:

> To raise the question of the nature of narrative is to invite reflection on the very nature of culture and, possibly, even on the nature of humanity itself. So natural is the impulse to narrate, so inevitable is the form of narrative for any report on the way things really happened, that narrativity could appear problematical only in a culture in which it was absent – or, as in some domains of contemporary Western intellectual and artistic culture, programmatically refused.[51]

Accordingly, not being too concerned with these sorts of things, Elton's chapter on the historiographical representation of the past in *The Practice of History* (and incidentally in chapter 5 of his *Political History: Principles and Practice*) is particularly myopic. For, whilst Elton has something to offer to those who accept his own brand of professional, lower case history (and whilst some of his lower-case advice can be incorporated as necessary into histories carrying with them very different assumptions to Elton's in much the same way as non-empiricist historians may partake in the use of 'the empirical') I think he has little to say to those who might actually like to understand what they are doing when they are writing/constructing history. For whilst Elton's chapter is dedicated to advising young historians on how they ought to proceed, in effect this is little more than a series of comments on how – within a relatively unproblematicised narrative ordering – one can express 'the truths of the past'.

Elton's advice can be grouped into three types. *First*, he is aware that historical representation is a process of ordering and shaping the evidence of the past, revealing (in what might be termed a 'ideologically symptomatic' comment) that 'what we call history is the mess we call life reduced to some order, pattern and possibly purpose'.[52] But (and here Johnson's comments are directly to the point) this is not registered as a significant problem, rather Elton uses it (and other related 'issues') to simply flag the dangers it can lead to (grandiose versions of the past as in, say, Marxism), dangers his own common-sense homilies will enable his sort of 'man' to steer clear of. For, whilst allowing for the inescapable fact that the historian's 'position' and 'psyche' will always intrude into his interpretation to some extent (an extent Elton thinks can sometimes turn to good effect – as in his comment that the vice of 'bias' can become a virtue in so far as it can, if 'controlled', enable the historian to look 'afresh' at the 'facts of the past' and so generate debates and controversies), nevertheless, his 'man' must always do his best to 'minimize his intrusion into the story'. Besides, the historian can worry unnecessarily about mere 'philosophical' problems in this area:

> The business of shaping the pattern and the explanation is beset, it seems, by serious philosophical problems involving the very question whether historical explanation . . . is possible at all. This need not concern us. . . . From the point of view of understanding the past, the many learned discussions concerning the sense in which historians explain it are quite remarkably barren and irrelevant.[53]

Second, such 'problems' filed away, Elton can then concentrate on the practices of writing. Here he gives his detailed advice freely: one must always write clearly, must always avoid unnecessary technicalities, must always outlaw jargon, must always write at the appropriate length and in an appropriate style and register relative to one's subject matter and one's audience, and so on. In effect, *one must copy*

Elton and preferably mix with the sort of people Elton revealingly sees history as being for. For, in an extremely interesting and élitist passage, Elton claims that

> No problem of historical study that I have come across . . . has seemed to me to be incapable of being explained with full clarity to any person of reasonable intelligence, and no person of insufficient intelligence will anyhow be in the way of reading or hearing historical analysis or description. If the historian has really explained things to himself, he can explain them to others [like himself]. . . . In all writing, three dignities must be observed: . . . of the historian . . . of the audience . . . and above all the dignity of the matter treated.[54]

Third, towards the end of his 'writing' chapter, Elton tries to underpin his various injunctions to good practice with the expected moral urgency we expect him to show. For, although Elton agrees that there are some problems which must be seriously considered when representing the past, in the end these matters *must* be set aside if the point of it all – the finding of historical truth – is to be achieved:

> It should be plain by now that though I believe in the . . . possibility of discovering a right truth by the techniques of scholarship, I do not hold that these facts result in historical writing independent of the writer. . . . Add the uncertainties of historical writing – the gaps in the evidence, the frequent obscurity of what does survive, the need to read and interpret with a controlled imagination, the demands of order and sense – and it is plain enough that no work is free of the tentative, the doubtful, the correctable.[55]

Yet, goes on Elton, what of it? Why should this limit the historian's desire to know and to write and to be listened to? No, the historian fulfills his proper function if he is a man of honesty and integrity; a scholarly man of a measured scepticism who wants to get to the truth:

> All the deficiencies of knowledge and writer notwithstanding, the historian can rest assured that he can fulfil his ambition to know and tell about the past. His can never be the last word . . . but he can establish new footholds in the territory of truth.[56]

Here is the voice of authentic, lower case orthodoxy; here, it might be said, is *the* 'mission statement'.

What, in a way, is so wrong with it? Well, nothing so far as it goes, except that it does not go far enough; it does not alert the young historian to the fact that, 'out there', there are many other histories each with their own slightly different (and legitimate) mission statements. And it does not alert us to the fact that many of these are rather more complex and, in that sense, rather more 'thorough' attempts to try and fathom out the problems of historical representation especially in narrative form. It does not tell us, either, that whilst Elton's views may well constitute the *doxa* amongst professional/academic historians, that *doxa* is, of course, ideologically positioned.

Now, these are complex and perhaps slightly controversial comments which might benefit from some further contextualisation. And here White is able to again come to the rescue, in one of his essays in *The Content of the Form*, fixing Elton's type of history against four other recent ways of thinking about representation in ways that suggest certain Eltonian shortcomings.

In *The Question of Narrative in Contemporary Historical Theory*[57] White begins by asking what, for narrative historians of the traditional empirical type, does historical method basically consist of and what is wrong with it, answering as follows:

> For the narrative historian, the historical method consists in investigating the documents in order to determine what is the true or most plausible story that can be told about the events of which they are evidence. A true narrative . . . is less a product of the historian's poetic talents . . . than it is a necessary result of a proper application of historical 'method'. The form of the discourse, the narrative, adds nothing to the content of the representation; rather it is a simulacrum of the structure and processes of real events. And insofar as this representation resembles the events . . . it can be taken as a true account.[58]

Now, in terms of what is wrong with this, the answers – hopefully familiar ones by now – are twofold. First, that the sought-for correspondence between the stories of the past and the historian's narrative breaks down given that there are no stories in the past to correspond to. Second, the continued insistence that somehow there is a correspondence, is not only to misunderstand but to misunderstand in ways which have obvious ideological affects so far as the *doxa* of the profession – of which Elton is supremely representative – define their way of doing history as proper history:

> For if ideology is the treatment of the form of a thing as a content

or essence ... [narrative] historiography is ideological precisely insofar as it takes the characteristic form of its discourse, the narrative, as a content, namely, narrativity, and treats 'narrativity' as an essence shared by both discourses and sets of events alike.[59]

And so White can come to fix Elton's notion of historical narrative/ writing as a misunderstanding of how narrative representation works, and as having ideological effects. And to contextualise Elton's type of typical misunderstanding and show its reflexive poverty, White juxtaposes it against four recent developments in narrative theory. Briefly, his account goes as follows.

Over the last few decades, four principle strains in discussions about narrative have taken place. First, there is a strain represented by certain Anglo-American analytical philosophers (Walsh, Gardiner, Dray, Danto *et al.*) who tried to establish narrative as a sort of explanation especially appropriate 'to the explication of historical, as against natural, events and processes' (a strand which, insofar as there is in England a 'respectable' if old fashioned philosophy of history, constituted and still pretty much constitutes it). Second, White points to the French Annales school (Braudel, Furet, Le Roy-Ladurie *et al.*), a group who have tended to regard narrative historiography 'as a non-scientific, even ideological representational strategy, the extirpation of which was necessary for the transformation of historical studies into a genuine science'.[60] Third, White argues that there developed a semiologically orientated group of theorists – on whom White himself has drawn – for example Barthes, Foucault, Derrida, Genette, *et al.* – theorists who have viewed narrative as simply one more discursive 'code' among others. Finally, there is a fourth group associated with Gadamer and Ricouer who have, as White puts it, 'viewed narrative as the manifestation in discourse of a specific kind of time-consciousness or structure of time'.[61]

Now, White's list is not exhaustive – for example it misses out Machery and Benjamin[62] – but two points can be made with regard to Elton; namely, that all of the strands mentioned by White have reached levels of sophistication with regard to historical representation that students ought to be aware of but which they could hardly be aware of from reading Elton and, second, that White is now able to put Elton 'in his place'. For, White argues that it might have been possible to add a fifth category to the other four; namely,

that of certain historians who can be said to belong to no particular philosophical or methodological persuasion but speak from the standpoint of the *doxa* of the profession, as defenders of a craft notion of historical studies, and who view narrative as a perfectly respectable way of 'doing' history (as J. H. Hexter puts it) or 'practicing' it (as Geoffrey Elton would have it).[63]

But as White goes on to explain, this 'fifth' possibility does not so much represent

> a theoretical position as incarnate a traditional attitude of eclecticism in historical studies – an eclecticism that is a manifestation of a certain suspicion of theory itself as an impediment to the proper practice of historical inquiry, conceived as empirical inquiry. For this group, narrative representation poses no significant theoretical problem. We need, therefore, only register this position as the *doxa* against which a genuinely theoretical inquiry must take its rise and pass on to a consideration of those for whom narrative is a problem and an occasion for theoretical reflection.[64]

And I think that we would be wise to pass on too.

USING ELTON TODAY: THE POVERTY OF EXPERIENCE

The above, then, are some of the main views Elton has on the nature of history, views which seem to me to be problematic across the board, ranging from his identification of that peculiar lower case history which emerged in nineteenth-century Europe as effectively identical to history as such, to his embracing of an empiricist epistemology/method and a communication-type approach to representation that are all unreflexively held insofar as Elton spurns theory in favour of the common-sense verities of the experienced professional. For this is not good enough today. Given that today history just is in the grip of various 'post' formulations, then the answer to the question, what have Elton's views on the nature of history *per se* (though not his views on the nature of lower case history as ideology, for clearly with regard to this *species* he is its embodiment and champion), got to offer us, the answer has to be – not very much.

There is a sense in which I think Elton recognises this too, stating at the beginning of *Return to Essentials* not only (as we have seen) that he thinks he will be defending 'what may appear to be very old-fashioned convictions and practices', but that in some people's eyes he may well appear ossified.[65] Yet reluctant to hand over the field to young upstarts and 'wiseacres', Elton adds that he still passionately believes in the 'entrenched' positions he holds on 'the reality of historical studies', and that there is still some virtue left in 'tackling the champions of innovation and new fashion from a position of mere experience'.[66]

Now, although defending a position one has faith in may well be virtuous, one has to wonder about the wisdom of doing so on the basis of 'mere experience'. For, it seems to me that experience provides no basis at all (and certainly no basis from which to engage in philosophical argument) on which to take on the 'champions of innovation', so it is inevitable that Elton should lose out when such innovators discuss the nature of history and the status of historical knowledge theoretically. And in this respect Elton is put into a similar situation as that which befell E. P. Thompson's famous (and similarly failed) attempt to get the better of the French 'philosopher' Louis Althusser in his The Poverty of Theory.[67] For in that text, Thompson recognises from the start that he is at a disadvantage. To be sure, in Thompson's laconic and ironic style, he uses this knowledge in a self-deprecating way in the hope that his own 'mere experience' will see him through, writing disarmingly:

> I commence my argument at a manifest disadvantage. Few spectacles could be more ludicrous than that of an English historian – and, moreover, one manifestly self-incriminated of empirical practice – attempting to offer epistemological correction to a rigorous Parisian philosopher.[68]

And at this early point in his essay – and espying the 'shadowy faces of an expectant audience, scarcely able to conceal their rising mirth' – Thompson really should have given up. For, as already stated, discussions about the status of historical knowledge – an epistemological problem – can only be dealt with epistemologically, the question of how can we know anything about what happened in the past being subsumed under the general philosophical problem of how can we *know* anything at all. Of course Elton (a little like Thompson in this respect) may object to this, running one of his favourite arguments that, in fact, philosophers cannot know anything about historical knowledge because they do not actually do the work of producing it. But as R. F. Atkinson pointed out many years ago (in 1978) in direct response to Elton's argument, philosophers of history are not trying to do, and have no need to do, any historical work at all in order to comment on the theoretical problems of historical knowledge production, and that it is of absolutely no concern to them that their 'activities help, hinder or otherwise bear upon the practice of history'.[69] In looking at the nature of history then, Elton (if he is to win in the ways winning is set up by him) has to meet any philosophical points (for instance, points relating to empiricism) by articulating his own ideas philosophically if they are to have any force. Yet this is precisely what Elton seems incapable of doing, having deliberately set himself in opposition to theory in favour of – as it has turned out – 'the poverty of experience'.

It is therefore for these reasons that Elton's criticisms of postmodern type 'theories' in *Return to Essentials* cut no ice, and why his desire to get back to essentials would be a return to 'essentialism' without foundations. Taking his critiques of postmodernists first, whilst in the old days Elton may well have got a lot of justifiable mileage from taking on such believers in upper case history as 'unreconstructed' Marxists – and whilst he may have scored heavily and deservedly against R.H. Tawney, Christopher Hill and, on occasion, E. H. Carr – there is no way he can have the same sort of 'success' against 'postist' theorists. For taking on the likes of Derrida, Foucault, Barthes, Rorty and White, is not like taking on a few old Marxists (as distinct from post-Marxists) for these are theorists who have themselves variously taken on the entire tradition of Western foundationalism – *and won*. Consequently, it hardly seems likely – and it doesn't happen – that a few pithy comments by Elton on the basis of his experience as a sixteenth-century historian, accompanied by a restatement of principles now profoundly problematicised, are going to have much effect on postmodernist positions. And if his critiques do not work, neither does his attempt to find some real basis for his essential convictions and desires: too much undercutting has gone on for that.

In this context, perhaps nowhere is the poverty of Elton's notion of experience, his disdain for theory and his impotent modernism, better illustrated than in chapters 2 and 3 of *Return to Essentials*. For there it is clear that, having had his usual success in chapter 1 against his old sparring partners, R. H. Tawney *et al.*, he has no effective arguments to deploy against postmodern theories. Instead, Elton's approach is composed of little more than *ad hominem* attacks on Foucault, Derrida, White *et al.*, and the reduction of complex and rigorous arguments to a few well-honed (and generally sarcastically delivered) phrases.

Thus, with regard to Elton's *ad hominem* approach, for him postmodernist-type theories have the character of a *virus*, the victims of which acquire a dangerous sense of *cocooned contentment*. The roots of the postmodern are fixed in German philosophy (Heidegger *et al.*) and French *ésprit*, a 'dangerous cocktail because whilst the former may be incomprehensible it looks wise, and the latter demonstrates that the absurd always sounds better in French'.[70] Again, Elton thinks that young historians should be shielded against that 'cancerous radiation that comes from the foreheads of Derrida and Foucault', whilst Hayden White's ideas are 'altogether meaningless verbiage'. The history of ideas – a well-known refuge for scoundrels – has been 'infected' by the latest fashions; whilst those feminists who go along with Foucault's power/knowledge arguments are variously 'fanatical' (thus, the 'reasonably fanatic Joan Wallach Scott' manages to marry deconstructionism and Marxism which is like spiking 'vodka with LSD'). And so it goes on, pages of *ad hominem* attack after *ad hominem* attack on the 'theory-mongers'.

If *ad hominem* attack often stands in for argument, then, on those few occasions when an argument is deployed, Elton doesn't seem to be too aware of what he is getting himself into. This point might be demonstrated by looking at Elton's critique of deconstructionism, the general thrust of which, he tells us, is that 'nothing written can be read as meaning what it seems to say: it always needs decoding in some way or other'.[71]

Now, for Elton, deconstructionism as thus understood does two things. First, it egotistically privileges the decoder over the author being decoded (the implication for history being that this improperly privileges 'the historian as decoder' over the sources/the past being decoded), and second, deconstruction has an ideological purpose, which is to try and do what Marxism has failed to do; namely, 'demolish the smug assumptions of the bourgeoisie' whose domination depends in part upon agreed and stable meanings and hierarchies/distinctions (of values and people), such that the capsizal of 'literal' or intrinsic meaning, of semantic consistency and unambiguity, ushers in a Humpty-Dumpty world where words (and things) mean what one 'chooses them to mean – neither more nor less'. Deconstructionism, then, as well as being ideologically tainted, is treated by Elton as a bit of a joke, and to illustrate this he defends literalism and unambiguousness by asking, rhetorically, that since nothing is supposed to mean what it says, then what would happen 'when a deconstructionist, serving in a bakery, is asked for a loaf of bread?'[72]

It is clear that for Elton this 'smart' comment makes the point and he passes on. But what if one dwelt on this remark for a while and did a little deconstruction on it of one's own? What if one starts off from Elton's throwaway remark and uses it to deconstruct much of his position? And to bring this chapter on Elton to a close this I intend to do, hinting, via a bit of amateur deconstruction, at the sort of power 'proper' deconstructionism has and how uninformed Elton is when being dismissive of it.

So, to the question of what would the deconstructionist serving in a bakery say when asked for a loaf of bread, the answer is unlikely to be 'Yes, here it is', but rather (on the assumption he/she has some bread and wants to sell it) 'What sort of bread do you want? Do you want a brown, white, granary, sliced, unsliced, small, medium or large loaf – or what?' It's no good the customer saying, 'I just want a loaf', because they're all loaves. And it's no good the customer then saying, 'I want a proper loaf', because they're all proper loaves. Similarly, to the question of what would the deconstructionist purveyor of history say if he/she was asked for a history, the answer is not likely to be, 'Yes, here it is' (although that would be the reply Elton is 'logically' expecting because it is only on the assumption that there is one real history that he has assumed there would be one real loaf), but rather, 'What sort of history would you like? Would you like a Marxist, Tory, feminist, black, empirical, local, post-structural, scientific, military, sixteenth-century history – or what?' And it's no good replying, 'I just want history', because they are all history. And it's no good saying, 'I want the proper history', because they are all proper history (if they meet, for example, White's formal definition given earlier).

Therefore, to establish what Elton arguably wants to establish by way of his joke, namely, that when someone asks for a history (or a loaf) they will be given the real thing ('no question about it') on the basis that both the buyer and the seller actually *know*, unambiguously, the difference between the genuine article and the fake, Elton will have to show that there is a genuine and proper history (i.e. *his own*) that is clearly distinguishable from inferior brands. That is, once Elton's assumption – the assumption behind his joke – can be shown not to be an assumption he can hold just by assertion, then if Elton wants to win in the 'certaintist' way he arguably does, then he has to do the hard work of demonstrating that his history is proper history, otherwise he will be in no position to hand out the sort of criticisms he wants to.

So, how might Elton try to show this? It would seem there are only two ways. Either he must show that he has a better knowledge of the past and of history *per se* because he has a better epistemology/method/theory, or, that his experience as a practicing historian gives him an edge over his rivals.

The problems attached to both of these options are easy to see. In the case of epistemology and method, I have already argued with Hirst *et al.* that Elton's anti-theoretical empiricism is seriously flawed. Accordingly, experience is the only thing he has left. But, again as already noted, this really is a useless basis for any position to stand on. For, what happens when Elton disagrees about the nature of history and the status of historical knowledge with someone who has an *equal* but *different* experience; say, E. P. Thompson, or Braudel, or Hobsbawm or Christopher Hill or Hayden White? Well, in such circumstances all that Elton could presumably do is to say and repeat – and when challenged keep on repeating – that, in *his* experience, *his* experience just is better. And Thompson *et al.* could only reply that, in *their* experience, *theirs* is. Stalemate. And it is difficult to see how it could be broken.

Now, one can of course distinguish between histories; some are better than others. But what would count as better at this present juncture would have to be argued for in terms of, say, theoretical frames of reference and method and social use; that is, in terms of the very things Elton's anti-theoreticism and (ostensible) anti-present-centredness hardly equips him to argue about.

It would therefore appear that both the options Elton has are effectively closed for him. So, is there nothing else? In fact there isn't, but one way which Elton tried – this being linked up to his experience option – was to 'put down' the experiences of others by way of his oft-used *ad hominem* attacks. And we have seen that this is exactly what he does: Tawney, Hill, White, Foucault, Derrida, La Capra, umpteen Marxists and feminists guilty by association, and so on; all have been on the receiving end of this mode of attack. But the point is this. Elton is arguably doing this not because it is an *incidental* feature of his personality; Elton's sometime swingeing critiques are not just Elton being grumpy. Not at all. Elton's *ad hominem* attacks are the only way he has left to try and privilege his experience – and hence his history – over other people's. By casting aspersions on others, Elton can privilege his own professional, proper, moral high-ground history. In other words, taken together, through his *ad hominem* attacks, Elton is creating a *demonology*, a demonology composed of *what he sees as theorists*. In this demonology individual differences between theorists do not count, what does is that they (and not he) are all 'theory-mongers'; 'devilish tempters' as Elton puts it, from the proper study of the past.

One could go on like this, but perhaps at this point we can stop. For I hope I have shown how one can take a throwaway remark – a joke – that Elton just assumes to be undercutting of decon-structionism, to be a way into an undercutting of, and an under-standing of, the assumptions which Elton holds from whence he uttered the remark in the first place. For me, Elton's dismissal of deconstructionism is as ill-informed as it is understandable, and signifies, yet again, why he can hardly help us to understand history nowadays. Accordingly, to get into what I think constitutes that history, it is now time to leave Elton (and Carr) and move on; move on to Richard Rorty and Hayden White.

Chapter 4

On Richard Rorty

To read Richard Rorty is to enter an intellectual world Carr never really knew and which Elton, insofar as he was aware of it, rejected. How does one get into this world, this perspective?

On the face of it, it does not look easy. A list of Rorty's books and articles as given at the end of Malachowski's *Reading Rorty* (which includes work from 1959 to 1989 to which he has since added) covers some eight densely packed pages. Yet, if this means that there is an awful lot of Rorty to consider, and whilst there is clearly no 'essential Rorty', it seems possible to identify a limited number of concerns – or indeed 'a' concern – to which he constantly attends. What might this be?

In an essay in *Consequences of Pragmatism* I think that Rorty's concern is capable of being identified (or at least this supposition will act as the basis for my entire reading). For there Rorty seems to agree with John Dewey that perhaps the most important purpose for 'philosophy' is to free mankind from remaining in thrall to what Nietzsche called 'the longest lie'; that is, to release mankind from the idea that

> outside the haphazard and perilous experiments we perform there lies something (God, Science, Knowledge, Rationality, or Truth) which will, if only we perform the correct rituals, step in to save us[1]

that behind appearances and the everyday contingencies of time and chance there lies a solid, foundational, 'Real World', a sort of perpetual reality which supports us and which we can somehow gain access to and so grasp it true and so grasp it plain. And Rorty thinks that this particular fantasy – which has effectively constituted/legitimised 'The Western Tradition' – is now just about played out. And he is glad.

Consequently, I argue here that Rorty's main task is to erase any lingering traces of that longest lie in order to put something else – not something true but something metaphorical and attractive – in its place: an ironic, anti-foundational, freedom-orientated, conversational style of discourse. It will also be suggested that this replacement is not intended to be made for the good of philosophy 'itself', but is meant to explicitly serve the politics Rorty likes best; a bourgeois, postmodern, North Atlantic-type politics which he hopes might increasingly provide – as it develops *beyond* its current condition – the sort of liberal environment his ironist can live in. At best the aim is therefore to project imaginatively the idea of a developing polity where those holding to Rorty's notion of the liberal ironist would feel increasingly 'at home'; a polity of Rorties.

Now, how can this 'reading' be put into a 'plan of action'; how are we to proceed here? My exposition of Rorty has *six* parts to it.

First, I want to give a close reading as to why Rorty thinks that upper case truth – a truth that is true because it is in some sort of knowing correspondence with 'the Real' – is an absurd notion, and how this suggests to him the sort of non-argumentative style his own philosophy will have to try and adopt. *Second*, I look at how Rorty defines the lower case truth he is left with in two ways (a) as a tautology and (b) through a working of William James' idea that truth is 'the name of whatever proves itself to be good in the way of belief, and good, too, for definite, assignable reasons';[2] going on to look at how he uses such truth-effects to undercut any remaining upper-case notions which still have some vestiges of life in them: Epistemology, Science, Method and so on. I conclude that as a result of Rorty's anti-essentialist critiques there are no certaintist traces left in these areas. *Third*, I examine how – given the collapse of any notion of a meaningful real world existing outside of the ways we humans variously constitute it – the idea of language as an effectively transparent medium for representing this ostensible world to us becomes redundant, Rorty replacing it with the idea that language is just a convenient tool which is 'instrumental' in getting us some of the things we want – and *ought* to want. And this last phrase can be seen to allow Rorty to argue that such a conception of language is at its most creative when used metaphorically, the point being that the metaphorical creation of new words/concepts leads to the possibility of creating new worlds, alternative actualities, the most desirable of which would be a polity happily inhabited by Rorties. *Fourth*, I sketch in some aspects of such a polity. And here, because of the way

Rorty sees his desired polity as destined to start off from – if not finish up in – the rich, bourgeois, North Atlantic democracies – I consider briefly why he has received so much criticism (especially from the left) in terms of being characterised as an apologist for the American way of life, for American imperialism, and so on. Section *five* ('Debating Rorty') thus contains something of a defence of Rorty from what might be termed a representative member of the anti-American left, Christopher Norris. *Sixth*, in a section entitled 'On History – From Rorty to White', some of the implications for historians and historiography today of Rorty's 'postmodern' position as described in sections one to five will be summarised both in general terms and more particularly in relation to Hayden White. For, if Rorty's philosophy embodies the sort of intellectual credibility that is representative of postmodernism, this means that the sort of modernists' answers given to the question of what is history by Carr and Elton doesn't. In today's climate, then, for history to be credible it must therefore partake of the postmodern; it must fit into the sort of intellectual debates Rorty exemplifies, the point being, of course, that if Carr and Elton do not fit into these then White very clearly does.

SECTION ONE: ON TRUTH

Rorty makes the points he wants to make about truth in many different ways, but perhaps the most useful entrée into this area on this occasion is to follow him closely when he says that, about two hundred years ago, the idea that truth was made (was invented and imagined) rather than found, began to take hold of the imagination of Europe,[3] a change which, argues Rorty, rested in part on the recognition of the linguistic nature of the meanings we ourselves give (ascribe/confer) to the world as opposed to the view of the world as having meanings of its own to which our vocabularies correspond. For what was effectively being articulated here were two ideas; namely, the repudiation of the view that anything – mind or matter, self or world – had an intrinsic nature to be expressed or represented, and the drawing of a radical distinction between the claim that the world 'is out there' and the claim that truth 'is out there':

> To say that the world is out there, that it is not our creation, is to say, with common sense, that most things in space and time are the effects of causes which do not include human mental states. To

say that truth is not out there is simply to say that where there are no sentences there is no truth. . . . Truth cannot be out there – cannot exist independently of the human mind – because sentences cannot so exist, or be out there. The world is out there, but descriptions of the world are not. Only descriptions of the world can be true or false. The world on its own – unaided by the describing activities of human beings – cannot.[4]

Consequently, Rorty says that the idea that both truth and the world are actually 'out there' is a legacy of a mythological age in which the world was seen as a creation of a Being who had a language (a Word) of his own – an age whose time had now passed. Thus,

If we cease to make sense of the idea of such a non-human language, we shall not be tempted to confuse the platitude that the world may cause us to be justified in believing a sentence true with the claim that the world splits itself up, on its own initiative, into sentence-shaped chunks called 'facts'.[5]

Of course this mistake is still made – it still casts its shadow – not least because we have got used to the habit of confining ourselves to single sentences as opposed to whole vocabularies when talking about the existence of worldly facts and then extrapolating from the sometime veracity of the former to the inferred veracity of the latter. What Rorty is referring to here is the epistemological/method-ological mistake that historians also often make – a mistake previously commented on by Ankersmit and White – that from the fact that it might be possible at the level of the statement/chronicle to know that discrete facts are 'true' because they correspond to the evidential record and thence by inference to the existential, then we can also know the 'truth of the past' on the basis of such facts when conjoined in an icon or a narrative. For, as we saw then, and as Rorty is arguing now, that conflation of the *known* particular with the *imagined* whole, breaks down precisely when one moves from parts to wholes or, as Rorty puts it, when one moves from single sentences to whole vocabularies. For, whilst we often do apparently let the world 'decide' between competing sentences – between 'whether the butler or the doctor did it' – this is not possible with whole vocabularies:

When we consider examples of alternative language games – the vocabulary of ancient Athenian politics versus Jefferson's . . . the jargon of Newton versus that of Aristotle . . . it is difficult to think of the world as making one of these better than another, of the world as deciding between them. When the notion of 'description of the world' is moved from the level of criterion-governed sentences within language games to language games as wholes, games which we do not choose between by reference to criteria, the idea that the world decides which descriptions are true can no longer be given a clear sense.[6]

Accordingly, attention paid to the way whole vocabularies are formed brings home to us the crucially important point that 'the fact that Newton's vocabulary lets us predict the world better than Aristotle's does not mean that the world speaks Newtonian'.[7] Of course, adds Rorty, the fact that the world does not tell us which language game to play should not lead us to think that the decision about which game to play is arbitrary, and that just any langugage game will 'work', nor that it is the 'expression of something deep within us':

> The moral is not that objective criteria for choice of vocabulary are to be replaced with subjective criteria, reason with will or feeling. It is rather that the notions of criteria and choice ... are no longer in point when it comes to changes from one language game to another. Europe did not *decide* to accept the idiom of Romantic poetry, or of socialist politics. ... Rather, Europe gradually lost the habit of using certain words and gradually acquired the habit of using others.[8]

And on this basis Rorty hopes that eventually 'we' might get used to thinking in his vocabulary; the vocabulary of the liberal ironist.

Having said all this, Rorty believes that he is now in a position to summarise what he thinks the revolutionaries and poets of two centuries ago were getting at when they dropped the notion of intrinsic nature (and value). For what was

> glimpsed at the end of the eighteenth century was that anything could be made to look good or bad ... useful or useless, by being re-described. ... What political utopians since the French Revolution have sensed is not that an enduring, substratal human nature has been suppressed ... by 'unnatural' or 'irrational' social institutions but rather that changing languages and other social practices may produce human beings of a sort that had never before existed.[9]

And Rorty sees himself in their tradition.

Yet immediately he has a caveat to add. For Rorty is not the sort of philosopher who wants to hint that 'now' he is getting all these sorts of things right; that his sort of philosophy 'corresponds to the way things really are'. Not at all:

> On the view of philosophy which I am offering, philosophers should not be asked for arguments against, for example, the correspondence theory of truth or the idea of the 'intrinsic nature of reality'. . . . Interesting philosophy is rarely an examination of the pro's and con's of a thesis. Usually it is . . . a contest between an entrenched vocabulary which has become a nuisance and a half-formed new vocabulary which vaguely promises great things.[10]

Therefore, says Rorty (and associating himself with those who have had or have such a new vocabulary 'which promises great things') Rorty's 'method' brings together the philosophical and the political into a pragmatic unity as his task – the eradication of the longest lie and its replacement by a philosophy embodied in the liberal ironist – opens up:

> The latter 'method' of philosophy [i.e. the philosophy that promises great things] is the same as the 'method' of utopian politics or revolutionary science (as opposed to parliamentary politics, or normal science). The method is to redescribe lots and lots of things in new ways, until you have created a pattern of linguistic behaviour which will tempt the rising generation to adopt it, thereby causing them to look for appropriate new forms of non linguistic behaviour, for example . . . new social institutions. This sort of philosophy does not work piece by piece, analyzing concept after concept, or testing thesis after thesis. Rather, it works holistically and pragmatically. It says things like 'try thinking of it this way' – or more specifically, 'try to ignore the apparently futile traditional questions by substituting the following new and possibly interesting questions'. It does not pretend to have a better candidate for doing the same old things which we did when we spoke in the old way. Rather, it suggests that we might want to stop doing those things and do something else. . . . Conforming to my own precepts, I am [therefore] not going to offer arguments about the vocabulary I want to replace. Instead, I am going to try and make the vocabulary I favour look attractive by showing how it may be used to describe a variety of topics.[11]

SECTION TWO: ON DEFINING AND USING 'TRUTH'

By now I think we should have no problem in understanding why Rorty is able to formulate the only plausible concept of truth which there arguably is, in two short definitions: that for him truth is (within a reading of the world which has always already 'been brought under a description') first of all a tautology – 'the name of a property all true statements share' – and second, 'the name we give to whatever proves itself to be good in the way of belief, and good, too, for definitive, assignable reasons'. Rorty is happy to define truth in these ways because they serve at least three purposes.

First (and on the one hand) his definitions enable him to 'close down' the whole of the Western Tradition insofar as that tradition rested (and rests) on upper case foundations: on 'real' foundations. For if there is no 'Real World'; indeed, if that very idea is a lie, then clearly we cannot ever discover its Essence, know when we have done so Epistemologically and Methodologically, construct Theories about it, Represent it accurately, make sure its imminent Teleology is captured, and so on, simply because 'it' doesn't exist. Consequently, we can forget all about that Western Tradition which runs down from Plato via Descartes and Kant to us, can forget all about that tradition's 'central problems of philosophy' construed as if they were philosophy's own; indeed, can forget all about that sort of philosophy full stop. That sort of philosophy has now reached its dead end:

> Pragmatists think that the history of attempts to isolate the True or the Good, or to define the word 'true' or 'good', supports their suspicion that there is no interesting work to be done in this area. It might, of course, have turned out otherwise. People have, oddly enough, found something interesting to say about the essence of Force and the definition of 'number'. They might have found something interesting to say about the essence of truth. But in fact they haven't. The history of attempts to do so, and of criticisms of such attempts, is roughly co-extensive with the history of that literary genre we call 'philosophy' – a genre founded by Plato. So pragmatists see the Platonic tradition as having outlived its usefulness. This does not mean that they have a new, non-Platonic set of answers to Platonic questions to offer, but rather that they do not think we should ask those questions anymore. . . . They would simply like to change the subject.[12]

Second (and on the other hand) this doesn't mean that 'we' cannot keep using the concepts truth, epistemology, method, theory and so on. It means only that when we do so we always restrict them to the lower case, the advantage of this being, that if this distinction between the upper and lower case is always kept, then students should not have the problem – as students sometimes do – of being able to say without any kind of contradiction both that for example, 'there is no such thing as truth', and be able to answer the question, 'Is it true or false that it is now 10.30 p.m. by the clock?' by saying (if it is 10.30 p.m. by the clock) 'Yes, it's true.' For here you just keep the two categories distinct. For, whilst there is no such thing as a knowable upper case time (so that it makes no sense to ask if it is 'true' that it is 10.30 p.m. in the universe), nevertheless, once we humans have set up clocks that are understood in hours and minutes, then we can say – relative to the way time has been conceptualised and brought under a description – that it truly is, or is not, 10.30 p.m.; that this sort of truth *is good by way of belief for definite, assignable reasons*. Of course, this is actually an elementary point to make, and who could forget it? Well, as will be seen, it appears that Christopher Norris does in part of his critique of Rorty.[13]

And so to the *third* benefit derived from the twofold nature of truth, which is that it allows Rorty to link the eradication of the upper case and its replacement by pragmatic-type language games quite explicitly to his politics: to arguments for forms of human solidarity purged of any reference to the transcendental or Truth. For as Rorty puts it in his essay, *Solidarity or Objectivity?*[14] there are two principal ways in which reflective human beings can try – by placing their own lives in a larger context – to make sense of those lives. One is to tell a story about how they see their contribution to a human community either actual or imagined. The other is to describe themselves relative to a non-human reality – to Reality as such. Rorty calls stories of the former kind examples of the desire for solidarity, stories of the latter as examples of objectivity, adding that, in his understanding, the tradition in Western culture which centres around the notion of the search for Truth, a tradition which runs – as we have seen – from the Greeks through the Enlightenment until today, is the 'closest example of the attempt to find a sense of one's existence by turning away from solidarity to objectivity'.[15] Today he thinks – as we might by now expect him to think – that the sorts of argument (call them 'realist') which try to ground solidarity in some form of objective way by construing Truth as correspondence to Reality, are simply untenable.[16] For we now no longer require such a methaphysics of 'presence' or epistemology.[17] Viewing truth from the vantage point of James' definition – as what is good for us to believe – so we don't need

> an account of a relation between beliefs and objects called 'correspondence', nor an account of human cognitive abilities which ensures that our species is capable of entering into that relation. . . . From a pragmatist point of view, to say that what is rational for us now to believe may not be *true*, is simply to say that somebody may come up with a better idea. It is to say that there is always room for improved belief, since new evidence, or new hypotheses, or a whole new vocabulary, may come along.[18]

That new vocabulary – like the ones previously in use and which were themselves once thought of as being true – will not in turn be true, but will simply be a vocabulary which works better relative to the things we want to do.[19] And if we recognise this, then we see that science and philosophy, say, are not privileged vocabularies accessing the world plain, but that their practitioners go about getting the ostensibly 'knowable' by using the same sorts of banal methods that all discursive practitioners tend to use. That is, they

> check off examples against criteria; they fudge the counter-examples enough to avoid the need for new models; they try out various guesses, formulated within the current jargon, in the hope of coming up with something which will cover the unfudgeable cases. We shall not think there is or could be an epistemologically pregnant answer to the question 'What did Galileo do right that Aristotle did wrong?', any more than we should expect such an answer to the question 'What did Plato do right that Xenephon did wrong?' . . . We shall just say that Galileo had a good idea, and Aristotle a less good idea. . . . Galileo's terminology was the *only* 'secret' he had – he didn't pick that terminology because it was 'clear' or 'natural', or 'simple', or in line with the categories of the pure understanding. He just lucked out.[20]

Consequently, Rorty thinks that what passes for epistemology and method is, in fact, just being 'pragmatically rational' in any given area.[21] And what he means by that phrase, is that we understand the conventions of a given discipline, that we don't fudge the data too much, that we don't rule out new roads of inquiry and so on, that in effect we have 'good epistemic manners'. In that sense, being 'pragmatically rational' means something like 'sane' or 'reasonable' rather than 'methodical':

> It names a set of moral virtues: tolerance, respect for the opinions of those around one, willingness to listen, reliance on persuasion rather than force. These are the virtues of which members of a civilised society must possess if the society is to endure.[22]

Accordingly, and pulling all this together, from this perspective Rorty thinks it was a mistake to have tried to turn the philosopher or the scientist into a new type of 'modernist' priest; a link between the human and the non-human who got the best (True) results when his human interests were denied in favour of nature's own interests. For, to shed our humanity is something we humans cannot, and should not want, to do. For there is no way that we can rise above all and every community in order to find some sort of transcendental or even divinised sky-hook to lift us beyond contingencies and mere human agreement to something like a human agreement with a known non-human reality; to something like correspondence with reality as it is in itself.[23] No, that just isn't possible, and a world where it was accepted that it wasn't possible would be nothing less than a 'paradise for pragmatists':

> Pragmatists interpret the goal of inquiry (in any sphere of culture) as the attainment of an appropriate mixture of unforced agreement with tolerant disagreement . . . Such a reinterpretation of our sense of responsibility would, if carried through, gradually make unintelligible the subject–object model of inquiry, the child–parent model of moral obligation, and the correspondence theory of truth. A world in which those models, and that theory, no longer had any intuitive appeal would be a pragmatist's paradise.[24]

In this political heyday of the pragmatist, then, there would be as little reason to be self-conscious about the nature and status of philosophy and science and the other disciplines, as, in the ideal democratic community, about the status of one's race or sex:

> For one's ultimate loyalty would be to the larger community which permitted . . . this kind of freedom and insouciance. This community would serve no higher end than its own preservation and self-improvement, the preservation and enhancement of civilization. It would identify rationality with that effort, rather than with the desire for objectivity. So it would feel no need for a foundation more solid than reciprocal loyalty.[25]

SECTION THREE: ON METAPHOR

In all of the areas which have just been discussed – Truth, Epistemology, Method, Science, Objectivity and so on – the point has been hinted at that Rorty has been using a concept of language which doesn't see it as a transparent and/or neutral medium for appropriating phenomena plainly (for putting us in some sort of correspondence with reality, for enabling us human beings to becoming better suited to the purpose for which God or Nature designed us) but simply as a tool; as something to help us get done the things we want to get done. Which means, in turn, that Rorty is not only able to envisage language in terms which are Darwinian (as enabling us to survive and adapt to situations) and Hegelian (as a thoroughly historical phenomenon) but also in terms that can allow him to privilege *metaphor* as the key way by which to think of meaning and meaning production as such. And it is Rorty's use of metaphor that I wish to discuss at this juncture, for with the idea of metaphor we have arrived at something of a turning point in my reading of Rorty. For henceforth Rorty's more negative comments as to what language *is not* (it's not a variously envisaged medium) will give way to what language *is* (it's a tool) in a more creative way. By the notion of metaphor, Rorty will stitch together his understanding of the best way to view language with the best way to view politics, in that the radical openness and potential of metaphor interpenetrates with the radical openness and potential for freedom of his sort of liberalism. So, how does this work, why and how is metaphor so crucial to Rorty?

At the beginning, of his essay,' Philosophy as science, as metaphor and as politics',[26] Rorty makes what he calls a dogmatic claim; namely, that there are 'three ways in which a new belief can be added to our previous beliefs, thereby forcing us to re-weave the fabric of our beliefs and desires – viz., perception, inference, and metaphor'.[27] Rorty goes on to say that the first two (perception and inference) are conservative notions of language, in that they both leave our language and thus our perceptions of our linguistically constituted world unchanged:

> They alter the truth-values of sentences, but not our repertoire of sentences. To assume that perceptions and inference are the *only* ways in which beliefs ought to be changed is to adopt what Heidegger identified as the 'mathematical' attitude. It is to assume that the language we presently speak is, as it were, all the language

there is, all the language we shall ever need. Such a conception of language accords with the idea that the point of philosophy is . . . to map out all possible logical space. . . . It supports the claim, common to Husserlian phenomenology and to analytic philosophy, that philosophising consists in clarification, in patiently making explicit what has remained implicit. [28]

By contrast, however, Rorty thinks of metaphor as a radical way of re-weaving our old beliefs and desires in that it enables us to think of language, logical space and the realm of possibility as open-ended. For metaphor, as Rorty puts it, is a voice from *outside* of logical space rather than an empirical filling up of that space or a logical–philosophical clarification of it; in fact, metaphor is something of a call

> to change one's language and one's life, rather than a proposal about how to systematize either. [29]

For what metaphors do is to precisely expand the boundaries and horizons of our 'present world' by taking the form of sentences which on the face of it seem obviously false or odd, but which eventually become (if they are successful) acceptable – and even acceptable 'truths'. Thus, by taking a trivial example before going on to more important ones, Rorty explains what he means by all this:

> 'Once upon a time . . . rivers and bottles did not, as they do now, literally have mouths.' To take more important cases, the first time someone said 'Love is the only law' or 'The earth moves around the sun' the general response would have been 'You must be speaking metaphorically'. But, a hundred or a thousand years later, these sentences become candidates for literal truth. Our beliefs were, in the interval, re-woven to make room for these truths – a process which was indistinguishable from the process of changing the meanings of the words used in these sentences in such a way as to make the sentences literally true.[30]

Consequently, Rorty's view of metaphorical sentences as forerunners of new language games by which old ones are eclipsed, enables him not only to envisage the possibility of fashioning new metaphors to erase the traces of the (in fact equally metaphorical) components of the 'longest lie', but at how such fashionings may occur, Rorty arguing that strange and crazy ways of looking at things might best be carried into social formations from outside the 'dominant discourses'; by outsiders and by strangers; by what Rorty sometimes refers to as the 'idiosyncratic genius'; by poets, visionaries and utopianists: by the likes of Nietzsche; . . . and indeed Rorty himself. For these are the kinds of people whose strange utterances make us think in auditory metaphors: of 'a voice from far off . . . a word spoken out of the darkness'.[31] These are people who spark off intellectual revolutions, who dabble in discomforting re-descriptions, who don't let the existing ways of looking at the world remain stable, who disrupt the surface calm of everyday common sense, apparently crazy people of the sort to whom Heidegger pinned the label 'Thinkers'.

For for Heidegger (and for Rorty who, at this point, begins to follow Heidegger) the proper role for such 'Thinkers' in any social formation is not to keep on replaying traditional philosophical tunes, but rather it is to 'free us from the language we presently use by reminding us that this language is not that of "human reason" but is the creation of the thinkers of our historic past', these thinkers being, in Heidegger's jargon, 'the poets of Being, the transcribers of "Being's poem – man"'. Consequently, for Heidegger and for Rorty too:

> To remind us of these thinkers, and to permit us to feel the force of their metaphors in the days before these had been leveled down into literal truths, before these novel uses of words were changed into familiar meanings . . . is the *only* aim which philosophy can have at the present time – not to facilitate but only to make more difficult, not to re-weave our fabric of belief and desires but only to remind us of its historical contingency.[32]

Accordingly, Rorty hopes his type of philosophy – his anti-essentialist, anti-foundational, ironic, historicist, nominalist, conversationalist philosophy, will help undercut 'the longest lie', and so 'free up' people to think new and daring thoughts and so 'blaze new trails', trails which in their blazing, will normalise those once 'crazy' suggestions that set them on their way until they become new norms; until such once new metaphors become 'dead metaphors', i.e. new truths, new truths which will then in turn become victims of further re-describing metaphors. Consequently the view that Rorty has of such 'Rorty-style' philosophers of the future goes as follows:

> He thinks of the thinker as serving the community, and of his thinking as futile unless it is followed up by a re-weaving of the

community's web of belief. That re-weaving will assimilate, by gradually literalizing, the new metaphors which the thinker has provided. The proper honour to pay to new, vibrantly alive metaphors, is to help them become dead metaphors as quickly as possible, to rapidly reduce them to the status of tools of social progress. The glory of the philosopher's thought is not that it initially makes everything more difficult (though that is, of course, true) but that in the end it makes things easier for everybody.[33]

Thus we arrive at Rorty's belief that his sort of philosopher should, as already suggested, serve a politics of an anti-foundational, anti-representational, anti-epistemological and anti-essentialist type, a polity inhabited by free-wheeling, freedom loving metaphoricians, Rorty at this point dropping the snobberies and élitism of Heidegger for the democratic Dewey. For,

> whereas Heidegger thinks of ... this liberating of culture from obsolete vocabularies ... as a process of banalisation, the pragmatist thinks of it as the only suitable tribute to render the great philosopher. Without this utilisation of his work, the great philosopher would have no social role to play, no political function. ... [Thus] whereas Heidegger thinks of the social world as existing for the sake of the poet and the thinker, the pragmatist thinks of it the other way round. For Dewey as for Hegel, the point of individual greatness is its contribution to social freedom, where this is conceived of in terms we inherit from the French Revolution.[34]

Dewey's pragmatism is thus seen by Rorty as a useful contribution to his own attempt to clear the ground for the realisation of the kind of social formation which the French Revolution had promised but failed to deliver; a sort of modernity 'Mark II' beyond the modern and the postmodern. A post postmodernity in which every human potential is given 'a fair chance':

> In the terms I have been using ... this aspiration amounts to the hope that every new metaphor will have its chance for self-sacrifice, a chance to become a dead metaphor by having been literalised into the language. More specifically, it is the hope that what Dewey calls 'the crust of convention' will be as superficial as possible, that the social glue which holds society together – the language in which we state our shared beliefs and hopes – will be as flexible as possible.[35]

Now, of course, as Roy Bhaskar has pointed out,[36] it may well take a lot more than a shift in language to begin to 'shift' capitalist social formations along the lines of Rorty's aspirations. But, that not inconsiderable point having been registered, for the moment we might note that Rorty does indeed think that we stand as good a chance as any of achieving this by all of us trying to become metaphorical/neo-pragmatic Rorties; by accepting this his philosophical position is, although not true, 'true enough' to act as a contingent 'basis' for a liberal utopia.

On this view, the most appropriate foundation for a liberal democracy is a conviction by its citizens that things will go better for everybody if every new metaphor is given a hearing, if no belief or desire is held so sacred that a metaphor which endangers it is automatically rejected. Such a conviction amounts to the rejection of the claim that we, the democratic societies of the West, know what we want in advance. . . . This amounts to suggesting that we try to eschew scientistic pronouncements which take for granted that we now have a secure grasp on the nature of society, or of the good. It means admitting that . . . we shall *always* need new metaphors, new logical spaces, new jargons, that there will never be a final resting-place for thought. [37]

Accordingly, if today we are to break free from the way we have been encultured into 'certaintist discourse', then we must work to create splits and fissures within our current social formations so that new ideas can work to subvert and remove any constraining edifices still wrought in the shadow of 'the longest lie'. Thus as Rorty puts it, we can only hope

to transcend our acculturation if our culture contains (or, thanks to disruptions from outside or internal revolt, comes to contain) splits which provide toeholds for new initiatives. Without such splits – without tensions which make people listen to unfamiliar ideas in the hope of . . . overcoming those tensions – there is no such hope. The systematic elimination of such tensions, or of awareness of them, is what is so frightening about *Brave New World* and *1984*. So our best chance for transcending our acculturation is to be brought up in a culture which prides itself on *not* being monolithic – on its tolerance for a plurality of sub-cultures and its willingness to listen to neighbouring cultures. This is the connection which Dewey saw between anti-representationalism and democracy. [38]

And so does Rorty. For whatever good in the past such ideas as Objectivity, Absolutes, Truth, and Transcendence may once have done for cultures, today better things can be obtained by the idea of a community which strives after novelty, agreement and solidarity; by a democratic and pluralist community of the sort of which Dewey dreamt:[39]

> If one reinterprets objectivity as intersubjectivity, or as solidarity ... then one will drop the question of how to get in touch with 'mind independent and language independent reality'. One will replace it with questions like 'What are the limits of our community? Are our encounters sufficiently free and open? Has what we have recently gained in solidarity cost us our ability to listen to outsiders who are suffering? To outsiders who have new ideas?' These are political questions.... Dewey seems to me to have given us the right lead when he viewed pragmastism not as grounding, but as clearing the ground for, democratic politics.[40]

If this is done, if the ground is well and truly cleared of the remaining accumulations of 'the longest lie', so we 'citizens of the future' can switch to new metaphors of a Rorty kind which will liberate us by making it clear

> that there are no objects of loyalty or sources of comfort other than actual and possible human communities: that there is nothing like Truth or Reason or The Scientifically-Knowable Nature of Reality towards which we need be humble, or on which we can rely for support. It tells us that we are as friendless, as much on our own, as the panda, the honeybee or the octopus – just one more species doing its best, with no hope of outside assistance, and consequently no use for humility. The best we can do is to take full advantage of our ability to use language by becoming ever more social animals, banding together in ever more complex ways for mutual support. Given this view, it is natural for philosophy to shelve epistemology and metaphysics and to concentrate on politics. [41]

And so we arrive at where I think Rorty's philosophy has been taking us all the time: at the political.

SECTION FOUR: A POLITY OF RORTIES

So, what would Rorty's polity be like? Who, ideally, would consistute its best citizens (for Rorty isn't sure that everyone could go much beyond a radical nominalism and historicism to fully embrace 'the best'); citizens who would simply have forgotten about the now itself crazy-looking longest lie and relax in their new freedoms? Rorty's answer is clear. They would be political liberals and philosophical ironists:

> I borrow my definition of 'liberal' from Judith Shklar, who says that liberals are the people who think that cruelty is the worst thing we do. I use 'ironist' to name the sort of person who faces up to the contingency of his or her own most central beliefs and desires – someone sufficiently historicist and nominalist to have abandoned the idea that those central beliefs and desires refer back to something beyond the reach of time and chance. Liberal ironists are people who include amongst these ungroundable desires their own hope that suffering will be diminished, that the humiliation of human beings by other human beings may cease.[42]

That is, says Rorty, fleshing out the ironic characteristics of his ironist a little, such a person might be more extensively described as someone who fulfills the following three conditions:

> (1) She has radical and continuing doubts about the final vocabulary she currently uses [the vocabulary in which she formulates her long-term projects, her deepest self-doubts and her highest hopes] because she has been impressed by other vocabularies, vocabularies taken as final by people or books she has encountered; (2) she realises that argument phrased in her present vocabulary can neither underwrite nor dissolve these doubts; (3) insofar as she philosophizes about her situation, she does not think that her vocabulary is closer to reality than others, that it is in touch with a power not herself. Ironists who are inclined to philosophize see the choice between vocabularies as made neither within a neutral and universal metavocabulary nor by an attempt to fight one's way past appearances to the real, but simply by playing the new off against the old. [43]

Rorty calls such people ironists because, additionally, they are people who realise as Rorty does himself (for of course the picture Rorty is drawing of the liberal ironists is a picture of himself) that anything can be made to look good or bad, useful or useless, by being redescribed, and that the renunciation by ironists of the attempt to formulate real criteria for choices between final vocabularies puts them in the position Sartre called meta-stable; that is, 'never quite able to take themselves seriously because always aware that the terms in which they describe themselves are subject to change, always aware of the contingency and fragility of their final vocabularies, and thus of theirselves'.[44] And not only that, for understandably given that the liberal ironist and Rorty are one and the same, she too adopts Rorty's mode of 'polemical' engagement:

> The ironist's preferred form of argument is dialectical in the sense that she takes the unit of persuasion to be a vocabulary rather than a proposition. Her method is redescription rather than inference. Ironists specialise in redescribing ranges of objects or events in partially neologistic jargon, in the hope of inciting people to adopt and extend that jargon. An ironist hopes that by the time she has finished using old words in new sentences, not to mention introducing brand-new words, people will no longer ask questions phrased in the old words. [45]

Ironists have the above characteristics then, but why should they be liberals? Why couldn't they be post-Marxist ironists, neo-socialist ironists, or indeed ironists of a type whose final political vocabulary has not yet been formulated? And I think that on my reading of Rorty, his preference for liberalism has all to do with the way in which he thinks that it will be able to further erase the shadow of the longest lie; that his sort of liberalism helps his anti-Platonic, anti-essentialist, anti-representational position. This, I think, is clear in many places in Rorty's works, but it is conveniently stated for my current purposes at the beginning of his *Contingency, Irony, and Solidarity*, wherein he puts his views as follows.

In the Introduction to the above work, Rorty gives two reasons why the ironic heroine of that book is a liberal. First because she accepts the (bourgeois) distinction between the private and the public spheres and the consequences of that distinction (a bifurcated person and a bifurcated polity which gets its solidarity through the adjacency of its differences), and second, because, as we have seen, she accepts Judith Shklar's definition of a liberal as someone who thinks that 'cruelty is the worst thing we do'. She is liberal in the first sense (which is the sense I want to develop here) because she rejects the attempt, dominant throughout the Western Tradition until today, to try and fuse the private and the public into one all-embracing philosophical position. This is the tradition – begun by Plato, continued by Christianity and still held by some classical liberals, some Marxists and others – that argues that, for example, one must find 'oneself' and become what one really/essentially is within an organic unity. Or which claims that self-realisation is to be found by working for the self-realisation of others. Or which postulates (in the case of classical liberalism) that there is something in the Enlightenment notion of a universal human nature, wherein things called 'rights' are embodied. In other words, that we ought to believe that what is 'most important to each of us is what we have in common with others – that the springs of private fulfillment and of human solidarity are the same'.[46]

However, comments Rorty, since Hegel, thinkers of an increasingly historicist and culturalist turn of mind have denied that there exists some demonstrable essentialist/naturalist 'upper case' human nature or some pristine unity such as 'the self', preferring to see as more plausible the idea that before culturalisation human beings are perfectly plastic and that a constitutive culturalisation therefore 'goes all the way down'. Such writers tell us, says Rorty, that we should replace questions such as 'What is it to be a human being?' with questions like, 'What is it to inhabit a rich twentieth-century democratic society?' or 'How can an inhabitant of such a society be more than an enactor of a role in a previously written script?' Yet, although questions of the latter type have, says Rorty, certainly helped us to escape from the constraints of metaphysics, theology and an essentialist humanism, the old tension between the public and the private – that old tension handed down to us as part of 'the longest lie' – still runs today, and not least across bourgeois social formations:

> Historicists in whom the desire for self-creation, for private autonomy, dominates (e.g. Heidegger and Foucault) still tend to see socialization as Nietzsche did – as antithetical to something deep within us. Historicists in whom the desire for a more just and free human community dominates (e.g. Dewey and Habermas) are still inclined to see the desire for private perfection as infected with 'irrationalism' and 'aestheticism'.[47]

So, how does Rorty go beyond this old public/private problematic; how does he square this particular circle? His answer is that one shouldn't try. To him it seems best to just leave the squares as squares and the circles as circles and not try to subsume or inter-penetrate the one with the other. Rather, what one should do is to give them equal weight relative to their different purposes:

Authors like Kierkegaard, Nietzsche, Baudelaire, Proust, Heidegger, and Nabokov are useful as exemplars, as illustrations of what private perfection – a self-created, autonomous, human life – can be like. Authors such as Marx, Mill, Dewey, Habermas, and Rawls are fellow citizens rather than exemplars. They are engaged in a shared, social effort – the effort to make our institutions and practices more just and less cruel. We shall only think of these two kinds of writers as *opposed* if we think that a more comprehensive philosophical outlook would let us hold self-creation and justice, private perfection and human solidarity, in a single vision.[48]

But given that, for Rorty, such a synthesis is impossible, then the only plausible answer to the public/private problem is just to keep the two spheres separate. Thus, in their private lives citizens can be as individualistic and crazy, as creative and as 'irrational' as they wish, the only proviso being – and Rorty sees there being practical (if actually pretty much unspecified) ways of ensuring this – that they cause no harm to others and use no resources needed by those less advantaged. Here, in private, people can weave their own fantasies; here they can be Bloom's 'strong poet', recoiling with horror from the thought that they may be only a copy or a replica or a role in someone else's story: 'The hope of such a poet is that what the past tried to do to her she will succeed in doing to the past: to make the past itself, including those very causal processes which blindly impressed all her own behavings, bear *her* impress.' But such a strong poet is not for the public sphere, and Rorty recoils with some distaste from thinking of the consequences of what happened when a Hitler or a Stalin had the power to impress their own private fantasies on others. No, what is needed in the public sphere is a pragmatic, conversational, democratic, workaday liberal philosophy to ensure that, as it were, the trains run on time, electricity is subject to a switch, and water is on tap:

> The vocabulary of self-creation is necessarily private, unshared, unsuited to argument. The vocabulary of justice is necessarily public and shared, a medium for argumentative exchange.[49]

For Rorty, then, the different philosophies informing the public and private spheres are just two different sorts of tools – 'as little in need of synthesis as are paintbrushes and crowbars' – each relevant to its own job but hopeless for doing the other, each getting us what we publicly and privately want but each, in its own way, irrelevant to the other. Here both public and private moralities are, within their separate spheres, *right*, and there is no need to speak just one, single language.

Such, in general terms, are the ideas which seem to lie behind Rorty's liberal utopia, a liberal utopia wherein ironism in the relevant sense is universal. So, how might this liberal utopia be realised? Well, Rorty has little by way of a concrete answer to this, little by way of socio-economic, political or cultural analyses to suggest how some kind of transformation from the present into the desired future could take place. And perhaps one shouldn't expect such details, not least because Rorty is only sketching in what he rather guardedly calls a utopia – and utopias don't have, as Marx correctly pointed out, the details of 'the transition'. Nevertheless, Rorty hasn't been entirely silent on at least two aspects of 'how to get into the future'. One of these sees the goal as being achieved by way of 'imaginative projection', the other sees the desired future as one stretching forwards from the actuality of America and the North Atlantic Democracies.

Thus, attending to the first, Rorty thinks that human solidarity will not be seen by clearing away prejudice or burrowing down to previously hidden depths, but by the 'ethnographic' ability to see strange people as fellow sufferers:

> Solidarity is not discovered by reflection but created. It is created by increasing our sensitivity to the particular details of the pain and humiliation of other, unfamiliar sorts of people. Such increased sensitivity makes it more difficult to marginalise people different from ourselves by thinking, 'They do not feel it as *we* would,' or, 'There must always be suffering, so why not let *them* suffer?' This process of coming to see other human beings as 'one of us' rather than as 'them' is a matter of detailed description of what unfamiliar people are like. . . . This is a task not for theory but for genres such as ethnography, the journalist's report, the comic book, the docudrama, and, especially, the novel.[50]

For Rorty it is the above genres (and not at all philosophy, which Rorty has by now unprivileged by seeing it as just another form of discourse) and especially fiction, that gives us the details which we need to know 'about kinds of suffering being endured by people to whom we had previously not attended' (such fiction as that of Dickens, Henry James, Orwell and Nabokov) which is why in Rorty's utopia such genres as the novel would replace the sermon and the treatise as the principal vehicles of moral change and progress. And history too would have a place here. This history would not resemble that academic/bourgeois way of considering it as a study of the past for its own sake après, say, Elton, but more in keeping with Carr's explicitly practical usage (though shed of any notion that history's narratives are discovered and not created), history would take the form of edifying narratives which would pragmatically connect the hoped-for liberal utopia of the future with the past in order to make that future relatively attractive:

> A historicist and nominalist culture of the sort I envisage would settle . . . for narratives which connect the present with the past, on the one hand, and with utopian futures, on the other. More important, it would regard the realisation of utopias, and the envisaging of still further utopias, as an endless process – an endless, proliferating realisation of Freedom, rather than a convergence toward an already existing Truth.[51]

And so to Rorty's second and much criticised move – his decision to choose America and the North Atlantic Democracies as the best place from which to create his desired utopia. For it is this attachment to bourgeois, liberal, democratic America as the best pragmatic place to start, that has made Rorty a particular target for the left. In the end, the charge goes, Rorty's philosophy is really little more than an apology for and rationalisation of America at home and America in the world; the legitimation of what is but a new type of *Pax Americana*.[52]

Now, these critiques are useful to me here. For they allow me to reflect upon Rorty's position as described hitherto before going on to say how the sorts of debates Rorty *et al.* are engaged in constitute much of today's intellectuality, an intellectual world of which Hayden White is a part.

SECTION FIVE: DEBATING RORTY

In the Introduction to volume one of his *Philosophical Papers*, Rorty claims that whilst many of his critics on the left are 'fairly well disposed toward the anti-representationalism I advocate', nevertheless, they see themselves as standing outside of the sociopolitical culture of liberalism with which he identifies. So, he adds, when

> I say ethnocentric things like 'our culture' or 'we liberals', their

reaction is 'who, we? ...' [For whereas] I see the culture of the
liberal democracies as still providing a lot of opportunities for self-
criticism and reform ... they ... seem to see themselves as
inhabiting a prison-house, one from which they must escape
before starting to tear it down.[53]

However, whilst it is correct to see many of Rorty's left wing
critics as indeed suspicious of his championing of liberal, bourgeois
democracies, not all are quite as sanguine about his anti-representationalism as he may suppose. For some left critics it is not only his
politics which are problematic, but also his apparently cavalier
attitude towards Truth, Reason, Science, Epistemology, Method,
Plato, Kant, the 'values of the Enlightenment' and so on. Thus, taking
Bhaskar and Norris as two representative examples, Section One of
Bhaskar's *Philosophy and the Idea of Freedom* (entitled 'Anti-
Rorty') is a 130-page critical dissection of Rorty's position on
science, ontology, epistemology, politics and so forth, whilst Norris
has repeatedly returned to take on Rorty's apparent jettisoning of
rationality and truth in favour of forms of what he calls Rorty's 'ultra-
relativism'.[54]

How far are these criticisms valid? My own position on this area
is as follows. I think that some of the detailed and often technical
arguments levelled at Rorty by, say, Bhaskar, are not always
adequately addressed by Rorty *at that level*. That much can be
conceded. But such details notwithstanding, it is not obvious that
these critiques take away the interest of Rorty's overall position so
that, at the general level, Rorty's basic anti-representationalism/anti-
foundationalism/anti-essentialism may well be able to stand. If this
is the case, if Rorty can be defended in general terms, then the
question I want to consider is: what sort of typical arguments has he
got to be defended against? And to deal with this, I want to turn to
the general criticisms that have been levelled against Rorty by
Christopher Norris, a Norris who has returned so often to criticise
Rorty that one is almost spoilt for choice as to which of his texts to
go to. However, in a few pages of his *Uncritical Theory: Postmodernism, Intellectuals and the Gulf War*,[55] Norris runs a convenient critique of both Rorty's philosophical *and* political position
such that I think Norris can legitimately be made to stand in here as
a representative voice of 'the left'.

We are living today, says Norris, in a period of widespread drift
towards varieties of ultra-relativist thinking in matters of historical,

political and ethical judgement, of which postmodernism is merely the most extreme 'desire to have done with all truth-claims beyond what is presently and contingently "good in the way of belief"', postmodernism going along with the current neo-pragmatist line as argued by Rorty *et al.*, 'that the only kind of truth that counts is the power to persuade members of one's own interest-group, "interpretive community", or professional guild'. In which case, adds Norris, the issues raised by the Gulf War (the Gulf War standing in here as an object upon which to exercise this general approach) must resolve into a matter of consensus opinion amongst those – chiefly the US and 'Allied' communities – whose understandings of events will (as the dominant discourse) dominate discussion and determine how the story gets told. That is to say, it is Norris' point that if postmodernists like Rorty are right, then such a discourse could not be challenged in the name of 'the truth' or 'the facts', because if

> all truth-claims eventually come down to a question of suasive appeal within this or that cultural context, then it follows that any appeal to 'the facts', to valid arguments, 'just war' principles and so forth could never do more than provide extra rhetorical or psychological back-up for beliefs that already commanded some measure of communal agreement. Thus rhetoric ... goes 'all the way down', and theory-talk is redundant.[56]

Here, Norris says that it is worth noting that the first generation of pragmatists would have found it difficult to go along with Rorty's interpretation of pragmatism as these pioneers apparently understood it. Norris argues that Dewey was actually a 'stickler for factual truth', that Pierce hung on to a regulative notion of 'truth at the end of inquiry', and that William James heavily criticised America's involvement in the Philippines campaign of 1910–11.[57] In short, says Norris, there is an enormous difference between the critical stance adopted by such early pragmatists and 'the current (postmodern) use of their ideas as a knock-down argument against all forms of dissident or critical–interventionist thought'. Norris argues that this difference has much to do with that turn towards post-structuralist ideas of language, discourse and representation which deny 'any access to reality or truth except by way of signifying systems which would render such access strictly impossible'. For, if one accepts this turn, then

of course the way is open for neo-pragmatists to draw the familiar conclusion: that truth is *always and only* what counts as such within a given 'interpretive community' ... or at a given stage in the ongoing cultural 'conversation of mankind'. ... And it will then appear flatly impossible that any counter-argument on factual, historical, or ethically principled grounds could ever carry weight or even make sense to members of the relevant community. ... [thus] What has occurred across a range of disciplines – and often in the most 'advanced' sectors of speculative thought – is a full-scale reversal of the commonsense view that holds language to be normally and properly accountable to standards of truth-telling probity.[58]

In other words, Norris has detected that there is a path that leads very directly from the neo-pragmatist/textual suspension of determinate truth-claims to the attitude of a

supine moral and political acquiescence that equates truth with some existing state of received consensus belief. For on this view there could be no warrant ... for any argument that went clean against the prevailing socio-cultural drift.[59]

How convenient that is for Rorty, says Norris, for this enables him to sustain a conversation laid down by membership of a community whose parameters are those of 'North Atlantic Post-modern Bourgeois Democracy', for such is the best hope for intellectuals like himself who are, after all,

well placed to enjoy the benefits on offer, and who can have no sensible reason for wanting to disrupt the conversation on behalf of other, less privileged mortals. That those others might feel themselves excluded – if not forcibly dragooned or bombed into compliance – in the name of a New World Order conceived on the US model is, of course, a possibility that Rorty can scarcely entertain, concerned as he is to relegate such conflicts to the margins of civilised debate.[60]

For Norris then, postmodern/neo-pragmatist thought, Rorty-style, is nothing other than yet another version of the 'end of ideology' thesis devised in the 1950s by Daniel Bell and other apologists for a previous phase of US expansionism; I mean, says Norris, how lucky that just at this moment

the high ground of cultural debate should be captured by a group of theorists ... who proclaim the obsolescence of enlightened critique, the ubiquity of consensus values, and the advantages to be had by going along with this emergent sense of a New World Order equated – so it happens – with the interests and priorities of current US strategic policy.[61]

Consequently – and pulling all this together – Norris concludes with the following points:

> There are few things more depressing ... than this collapse of moral and political nerve brought about – or ... influenced – by various forms of postmodern–pragmatist thought. For the result of such ideas is firstly to undermine ... the epistemological distinction between truth and falsehood, and secondly to place *ethical* issues beyond reach of argued, responsible debate ... what emerges at the end of this revisionist line is an outlook of deep-laid scepticism ... not only to the truth-telling claims of Enlightenment *Ideologiekritik* but also ... that it is our duty as responsible citizens to *think for ourselves* on matters of significant moral and political choice, and to base such commitments on the *best available knowledge* of their real-world conditions and consequences.[62]

Now there are, of course, things which one recognises in these charges against Rorty *et al.* Yet, whilst it is certainly the case that postmodern-pragmatism can very easily be put to the service of the status-quo by undercutting the grounds for the truth-claims of any opposition, it is another to demonstrate that this is actually Rorty's intention or affect. Of course, Rorty does align himself with the sociopolitical culture of the liberalism of the North Atlantic democracies, but it is another thing to show Rorty is supportive of current US strategic policy, or that his idea of a liberal–ironist culture is what those who control the current US status quo would recognise themselves as articulating or wanting. Again, against the charge that Rorty's style of philosophy is one unable to challenge a dominant discourse, given that Rorty *et al.* have deconstructed the whole of the foundational Western Tradition from Plato on down – and it's not easy to think of a discourse more dominant than that – this success (which is, of course, precisely what Norris is worried about) is scarcely conceivable unless, intellectually, Rorty *et al.* possessed precisely that critical reason and independence of thought Norris denies them. But these are debating points and might be left at that at this point. For Norris may also have made a series of more substantial misreadings when he accuses Rorty of being one of postmodernism's 'ultra relativists', that Rorty's definition of truth is the impotent 'what is good by way of belief', and that Rorty's acceptance of 'America' is an acceptance – for it is admittedly *an* acceptance – easily given. So I turn, briefly, to these possible 'misreadings' now.

Thus, against Norris' charge that Rorty's neo-pragmatism is just one more postmodern version of that 'ultra-relativism' that stalks the land, it is directly to the point that Rorty explains very clearly that relativism is precisely not something which his form of pragmatism, nor pragmatism as such, actually holds:

> 'Relativism' is the view that every belief on a certain topic, or perhaps about *any* topic, is as good as every other. No one holds this view. Except for the occasional cooperative freshman, one cannot find anybody who says that two incompatible opinions on an important topic are equally good. The philosophers who get *called* 'relativists' are those who say that the grounds for choosing between such opinions are less algorithmic than had been thought. . . . So the real issue is not between people who think one view as good as another and people who do not. It is between those who think our culture, or purpose, or intuitions cannot be supported except conversationally, and people who still hope for other sorts of support.[63]

This seems clear. So, why is Rorty's pragmatism still confused with relativism? Rorty's answer is because critics don't see the difference between (upper case) *philosophical theories* on the one hand and (lower case) *real theories* on the other. To explain.

In a certain *limited* sense, says Rorty, pragmatists are philosophical relativists at the level of the upper case; at the level when one has to choose between one *whole* vocabulary and another, say between theories of a typical foundational type (for example, between Kantianism and Marxism). For:

> Such theories are attempts to ground some element of our practices on something external to these practices. Pragmatists think that any such philosophical grounding is . . . as a wheel that plays no part in the mechanism. In this, I think, they are quite right. No sooner does one discard the categories of the pure understanding for a Newtonian age than somebody draws up another that would do nicely for . . . an Einsteinian one. No sooner does one draw a

categorical imperative for Christians than somebody draws up one which works for cannibals. . . . The reason this game is so easy to play is that none of these philosophical [upper case] theories have to do much hard work. The real work has been done by the scientist . . . or the societies which developed the moralities and institutions in struggle and pain. All the Platonic or Kantian philosopher does is to take the finished first-level product, jack it up a few levels of abstraction, invent a metaphysical or epistemological or semantical vocabulary . . . and announce that he has *grounded* it.[64]

But of course he hasn't. And, because such groundings are impossible (you can always get another equally axiomatic ground), then Rorty argues that the only thing that matters are *real theories*:

Nobody really cares if there are incompatible alternative formulations of a categorical imperative. . . . We do care about alternative, concrete . . . detailed proposals for political change. When such an alternative is proposed, we debate it, not in terms of categories or principles but in terms of the various concrete advantages and disadvantages it has.[65]

Consequently, Rorty thinks that the reason relativism is talked of as a problem is because people (like Norris) seem to think that being relativistic about the possibility of *grounding* upper case philosophy leads pragmatists to being relativistic about lower case *real* theories. Accordingly, since

the time of Kant, it has become more and more apparent to non-philosophers that a really professional philosopher can supply a philosophical foundation for just about anything [i.e. nothing]. This is one reason why philosophers . . . have come to strike our fellow-intellectuals as merely comic.[66]

There is another comment to make here too. Because relativism only makes sense if opposed to absolutes, then because there are no (upper case) absolutes (grounds) in that sense, then there is nothing to be sceptical/relativistic about. Given that there are no 'truths' in that sense, all such truths are therefore 'positions'. For pragmatists, then, Norris' accusation of relativism (in the way he has construed it) seems to aim at a target that does not exist; for all we have (and all we have ever had) are our own positions which we can try and defend using the best means – the best *reasons* – we can think of. And

Rorty does this too of course, which suggests that Norris' claim that Rorty's definition of truth does not provide him with the possibility of having any 'reasons' for any truths, may be also wide of the mark. To be sure, Rorty has no ultimate reasons for his overall vocabulary, but at the *real theory* level – and this is the level at which Rorty always operates – he does. And so we might look at this now.

The point here is simply this: that Norris is criticising a definition and a use of a definition of truth (without 'reasons') that Rorty does not hold. That is, when criticising Rorty, Norris invariably says that Rorty works with a definition of truth as 'that which is good by way of belief'. But in fact he doesn't; for the definition which Rorty actually uses (although he does not always give the full rendition) is the rendition that has been used throughout this discussion of him; namely, that truth is – and here some emphasis might be added – 'the name of whatever proves itself to be good in the way of belief, *and good, too, for definite, assignable reasons*'. Rorty is therefore well able to *support* his position with the usual sorts of definite, assignable reasons generally available, and these are not of course restricted to the notions of his 'community', if by community one restricts the 'community of ideas' to the geo-political region of the North Atlantic democracies. For Rorty, like Norris, roams all over the world of ideas; his intellectual community stretches back thousands of years and its parameters are global, so that the fact that Rorty is within his actual community no more stops him from criticising it than the fact that Norris is within his community stops him from criticising his – for he does so all the time. And not only that. The suggestion that Rorty gives no 'reasons' to back up his ideas is not the case. For, at a very obvious level, Rorty has written thousands of words explaining precisely *why* he is an anti-foundationalist, explaining *why* his heroine is a radical, anti-dogmatic ironist, explaining *why* he is not a relativist, and explaining why he sees, and *how* he sees, the North Atlantic democracies as the best place from which to *start* towards his utopia. Moreover, whilst Rorty is indeed committed to free and open conversation he nevertheless believes – for reasons to do with his substantive liberal idea that hurting other people is the worst thing we do – that there are some people one should not converse with:

> In finding a . . . stance to adopt toward Nietzsche or Loyola [or a Hitler or a Stalin] we liberal democrats are faced with a dilemma. To refuse to argue about what human beings should be like seems

to show a contempt for the spirit of accommodation and tolerance, which is essential to democracy. But it is not clear how to argue for the claim that human beings ought to be liberals rather than fanatics without being driven back on a theory of human nature. ... I think we must grasp the first horn. We have to insist that not every argument needs to be met in the terms in which it is presented. Accommodation and tolerance must stop short of a willingness to work within any vocabulary that one's interlocutor wishes to use, to take seriously any topic that he puts forward for discussion.[67]

This presumably means, *pace* Norris, that one doesn't need to take seriously *any* current discourse one doesn't want to take seriously, including that of US strategic planners. And, from these positions on relativism, truth and 'reasons for positions', Rorty thinks that he is justified in being indignant about the way he is 'mis-read' by people like Norris; accusations that try to make out that his sort of 'fuzzy pragmatists' have no weapons to use against their enemies:

When Dewey urged that we try to create such a [pragmatist's] paradise, he was said to be irresponsible. For, it was said, he left us bereft of weapons to use against our enemies; he gave us nothing with which to 'answer the Nazis'. When we new fuzzies try to revive Dewey's repudiation of criteriology, we are said to be 'relativistic'. We must, people say, believe that every coherent view is as good as every other, since we have no 'outside' touchstone for choice among such views. We are said to leave the general public defenseless against the witch doctor, the defender of creationism, or anyone else.

Nobody is [therefore] convinced when we fuzzies say that we can be just as morally indignant as the next philosopher. ... Even when we actually display appropriate emotions we get nowhere. ... When we suggest that one of the few things we know ... about truth is that it is what wins in a free and open encounter, we are told that we have defined 'true' as 'satisfies the standards of our community'. But we pragmatists do not [*pace* Norris] hold this relativist view. We do not infer from 'there is no way to step outside communities to a neutral standpoint' that 'there is no rational way to justify liberal communities over totalitarian communities' .... What we in fact infer is that there is no way to beat totalitarians in argument by appealing to shared common premises, and no point in pretending that a common human nature makes the totalitarians unconsciously hold such premises. . . . Anti-pragmatists fool themselves when they think that by insisting . . . that moral truths are 'objective' . . . they have provided us with weapons against the bad guys. For the fascists can, and often do, reply that they entirely agree that moral truth is objective, eternal and universal [and fascist]. . . . Dewey made much of the fact that traditional notions of 'objectivity' and 'universality' were useful to the bad guys, and he had a point.[68]

So to America. And here, whilst it is true that this is Rorty's starting point for his political utopia, it is both *the* starting point and *a* starting point not uncritically accepted. One sometimes thinks when reading Norris that because he cannot himself see many/any desirable features issuing from America, that only dupes or doltish time-servers could. But it is doubtful if Rorty is either of these things. No, Rorty's optimism and normally laidback style seems to be sorely tried by the condition of America. And nowhere is this more clearly expressed (though it is expressed in many other places so it is surprising it has been so much overlooked) than in his essay, *Unger, Castoriadis, and the Romance of a National Future*.

For, what Rorty likes about the Brazilian philosopher, Roberto Unger, is that he is something of a poet and romantic; is someone who has precisely what Rorty wants; namely, visions of new communities beyond foundationalism. For Rorty, Unger still retains the sort of optimism and large-scale 'future thought' that America may now have lost, Rorty quoting with approval Unger's view that

> At this time in world history, an attitude once confined to great visionaries had become common among decent men and women. They could no longer participate in political struggle out of . . . personal ambition. . . . They also had to feel that they were sharing in an exemplary experiment in the remaking of society. . . . He wished . . . [Brazil] to become a testing ground for . . . the options available to mankind.[69]

To which Rorty's immediate comment is wistful; nostalgic even. For, to get in the mood to read this sort of thing he remarks, 'we rich, fat, tired North Americans must hark back to the time when our own democracy was newer and leaner', at a time when a new future lay excitingly ahead. Irving Howe, says Rorty, described the 'American newness' of 150 years ago as a time when people began to feel invigorated by the idea that they could determine their own fate: 'He continues bleakly: "What is it like to live at such a time? The opposite of what it is like to live today".'

So why is Rorty so downcast and on his way in this essay to characterise himself not so much in terms of 'we liberal democrats' or 'we liberal utopians', but as a member of a new group – 'we *tragic liberals?*' Well, the problem is, *pace* Norris (and incidentally Michael Billig who, in a critical run-through of the first person plurals used by Rorty in his various writings, omits this one)[70] America, an America that Rorty feels is just not up to the task embraced by Unger's Brazil:

> Unger has us dead to rights when he speaks of 'the rich, polished, critical and self-critical but also downbeat and Alexandrian culture of social and historical thought that now flourishes in the North American democracies'. . . . In *Politics*, Unger is reacting against this bleak defensiveness and resignation.[71]

So, can America become revitalised and upbeat? Rorty is wary. He has little faith in the American working classes, and whilst there are pockets of radical optimism (in the women's movement, for example), and some radicals around who can 'single-handedly deconstruct a large social theory faster than a Third World village can construct a small elementary school', they do not take kindly to optimism and romance:

> Most radical critics of American institutions (for example, the admirers of Althusserian, Heideggerian, or Foucauldian social thought – the people for whom Harold Bloom has invented the sobriquet 'The School of Resentment') would not be caught dead with an expression of hopefulness on their faces. Their reaction to American inertia and impotence is rage, contempt, and the use of . . . 'subversive, oppositional discourse,' rather than suggestions about how we might do things differently.[72]

Is there, therefore, hope in those places where modernist experiments have not yet been tried? Might it be possible to create new utopias in Brazilias? Well, being a political romantic is not easy these days, muses Rorty, nevertheless,

> Realising that Unger is a *Brazilian* philosopher lets us Alexandrians convert our initial reaction to his book to something more like, 'We hope to Heaven these [new] imaginary institutions do sell in Brazil; if they should actually *work* there, maybe then we could sell them here'.[73]

But, if this is a possibility, if there is hope in underdeveloped social formations and in the Third World, the main vehicle for that change will not come, says Rorty, from 'the workers of the Third World', but rather from something he calls the *national imaginary*. For today political imagination is, he opines, almost always a national imagination. He thinks this not only because he considers it as Unger's view, but because he agrees with Cornelius Castoriadis that we are still locked into the national and hence, because nations are always *imagined communities*, into the possibility of imagining different ones:

> Political imagination is, almost always, national imagination. To imagine great things is to imagine a great future *for a particular community*. . . . Political romance is, therefore, for the foreseeable future, going to consist of psalms of *national* futures rather than of the future of 'mankind'.[74]

To break free from history, to do at the national level what Rorty sees the liberal ironist doing at the personal level, endlessly redescribing herself, is thus at least a possibility:

> 'The *only* thing that is not defined by the imaginary in human needs', Castoriadis says, 'is an approximate number of calories per day'. Every other 'constraint' is the fossilized product of some past act of imagination.[75]

And so Rorty returns yet again to America. Can America will a new political romance, or is it too fossilised? Rorty, the tragic liberal, is still not sure:

> we tragic liberals fear . . . in the contemporary United States – and, more generally, in the rich North Atlantic democracies . . . [that] Certain constraints may come to seem so firm . . . that their sense of themselves as a community will not outlast [their] . . . elimination. . . . The institutions that empowered our past . . . may strangle our future – with the poor and weak getting strangled first, as usual. The institutions that are our only protection against quasi-fascist demagogues may also be the constraints which prevent us from renouncing our insolent greed. . . . Maybe North Atlantic politics have frozen over to such a degree that the result of breaking the ice would be something even worse than what we have now. . . . A century after Whitman's death it may seem that, as Orwell said, 'the "democratic vistas" have ended in barbed

wire'. . . . Maybe the Brazilians (or the Tanzanians, or *somebody*) will be able to dodge around that barbed wire – despite all that the superpowers can do to prevent them.[76]

Despite his pessimism about America then, in the end Rorty forces himself to be generally more optimistic; maybe there will be new romantic metaphors of freedom, and maybe new experiments from the Third World. Here is his optimism in a nutshell, an optimism that isn't in any way uncritical of America:

> To say, as I have been saying here, that if there is hope it lies in the imagination of the Third World, is to say that the best any of us here in Alexandria can hope for is that somebody out there will do something to tear up the present system of imaginary significations within which politics in (and between) the First and Second Worlds is conducted. . . . Only some actual event, the actual success of some political move made in some actual country, is likely to help. No hopeful book by Unger or Habermas, any more than one more hopeless 'oppositional', unmasking book by the latest Resenter, is going to do the trick. Unger, however, has an advantage over the rest of us . . . he is aware of 'the exemplary instability of the Third World'. . . . His theoretical writing is shot through with a romanticism for which we Alexandrians no longer have the strength. His book has a better chance than most to be linked, in the history books, with some such world-transforming event.[77]

Now, this may not exactly be revolutionary, but is this nuanced and tragic/optimistic Rorty one that we can glean from the pages of a Norris? I think not.

SECTION SIX: ON HISTORY – FROM RORTY TO WHITE

In his book, *Doing What Comes Naturally*,[78] Stanley Fish argues that whilst there are many ways of reading the history of Western thought, one of the most interesting and illuminating is to identify as the motif which runs through it from the Greeks to the present day, a prolonged and fiercely engaged antagonism between foundationalist (of, say, a Platonic type) and rhetorical (of, say, a Sophist type) philosophical positions. Of course there have been important differences in the way this antagonism has been conducted and articulated and the relative weight its component parts have, on occasion, exercised. Nevertheless, in Fish's view, that quarrel between foundationalism and rhetoricism

> survives every sea-change in the history of Western thought, continually presenting us with the (skewed) choice between the plain, unvarnished truth straightforwardly presented and the powerful but insiduous appeal of 'fine language', language that has transgressed the limits of representation and substituted its own forms for the forms of reality.[79]

Whilst, in that long history, rhetoric has (apparently) come out almost entirely on the losing side, today that is no longer the case. For today, in one discursive practice after another, rhetoric trips across the field, such that it now saturates Western intellectual and cultural expressions. Accordingly, Fish thinks that there is now abundant evidence to suggest that our world is clearly in 'the grip of the rhetorical', and that what this has made us realise – retrospectively as it were – is that although in its long engagement with foundationalism, rhetoricism has not been overtly successful (that *Rhetorical Man* has not been much triumphant over foundational, *Serious Man*), in fact, that struggle has never actually been one fought *between* two separate positions at all, but by two positions both of which have developed *within* rhetoricism. That is, says Fish, that today we realise that the seriousness of the ostensibly *Serious Man* is itself just a rhetorical construction; that seriousness is nothing more than another rhetorical trope; just one more affectation to try and help this man get what he wanted to get. In other words, what is now clear is that *Serious Man* is himself a rhetorical man and that, if only we had known it, rhetoric has always been 'the only game in town'.[80]

Now I mention this to help bring my discussion of Rorty to a close. Because, although Rorty might be wrong about liberalism (that as I have said already, maybe we could have, say, a post-Marxist ironist instead of a liberal ironist as our *focus imaginerius*), and whilst he may still be too American despite his reflexive, tragic outlook, it seems unlikely that we are wrong to see intellectual constructions as being rhetorical and, in their rhetoricism, ironic. Today it really does seem implausible to think that we can go much beyond Rorty and think seriously about foundations as though the very notion of foundation was not a metaphor, a useful fiction, a rhetorical device, a long, long lie. It may be, of course, that in this area Rorty gets some of the details wrong; that careful dissection (as in Bhaskar) can unthread some of the weft and weave of Rorty's position and so create holes. But is it now possible to think that today there really are non-rhetorical/non-ironic grounds for Foundationalism? For Essentialism? For a Correspondence Theory of Truth? For Objectivity? For Epistemology? For Method? For Theory? For Ontology? For an upper case History or a lower case 'history', both of which claim that they are identical to its ostensible genus? Well, I think this is unlikely.

So, we return from Rorty to history after what, for some, may have seemed like a long detour. But it has been made – to recall – not so that we can understand by just a very brief – and no doubt partial and 'slanted' reading of Rorty – the very specific question of what is history today, but rather that such a reading might help us to understand the sort of answer which may be plausible in that postmodern condition inscribed, as it were, in Rorty's general position; a condition which makes – does it not – the 'certaintist' answers that Carr and Elton give to 'the history question' appear *passé*. Rorty has been examined here because in his writings – whether one agrees with all or every aspect of them or not – there is so much that is of the 'post'; so much that exemplifies the general anti-essentialist, anti-representationalist, anti-foundationalist thrust of the postmodern condition as it redescribes old canons and shibboleths and overtly politicises discursive practices *per se*. In this sense Rorty helps us to begin to see – almost before we have looked – a lot of the general things which Hayden White will be saying.

For, although White has his own spin on things, much of the position he holds has similarities to Rorty's. White too is critical of any correspondence theory of Truth; of any incorrigible or entailed reading between the past and historiography. White is also anti-essentialist, anti-teleological, anti-foundational and utopian. Like Rorty, White has no time for the idea that we know what history really is, therefore freeing it up to be whatever we want it to be, a history that, for White, is useful for his own notion of utopia. This is not to say – yet again – that the actuality of the past did not exist exactly as it did, but it does mean that White thinks it can be (as it always has been) used as people desire. And White makes all this very clear.

But, in addition to considering the question of history in these sorts of ways, White does something else which Rorty does not do and which no historian has done to anything like the same extent: he offers a *formal* analysis of the dominant mode of historical representation, the narrative. White is therefore not only an extremely stimulating theorist of history in that 'post' condition which Rorty in so many ways embodies and expresses, but he also gives us a way of thinking about what a historical interpretation is arguably like in its formal ('universalistic like') 'form' – whether the historians doing that 'forming' know it or not. This is not to say that White's structuralist approach is therefore 'correct' so that, after all these years, we have finally got it plain and true. Of course not. For in this respect White is again similar to Rorty. No, it is, to repeat, rather that White is to be looked at as an illuminating example of the currently plausible; an example that Carr and Elton's renditions don't suggest. Indeed, White has views on history which, in their 'inventions', are not even 'imagined' by them.

Chapter 5

On Hayden White

With regard to the two questions which are now to be posed to Hayden White, namely, what does he think history is and what use is his answer to those studying the question of what is history today, I think that, in a way, we know something about these areas already. That is, we know that White's most succinct response to the question of what is history, is that it is a narrative discourse, the content of which is as much imagined/invented as found. We also know some of the reasons why White thinks this: because in the construction of their historical narratives historians inevitably combine known or found parts (facts) with ultimately unknown and thus imagined/invented wholes; because the attempt to make truth claims about the past beyond the level of the statement and/or the chronicle based upon some sort of correspondence between the stories they tell and the stories lived in the past, breaks down when it is realised that there are no stories in the past to correspond to – that past 'events' just don't have in them the shapes of stories. Additionally, we know how White's definition of history when combined with his general textualism problematicises any kind of realist empiricism and/or mimeticism, points to the inescapable present-centredness and positional nature of all historical interpretations/readings, queries old distinctions between 'proper' history and historicism by virtue of, for example, their common metahistorical status, and generally ideologises all history in whatever case. And so on and so forth: these are already significant indications as to the possible 'uses' of White's views on history.

But there is more to it than that. For, whilst we 'know' the above mentioned things, we know them only through the occasional reference to, or use of, White to illustrate points relating to, say, general remarks on 'history today' or in connection with Elton's position on 'writing', rather than by a study of White in his own right. But now that White is being looked at 'in and for himself', then it is obvious that the two questions can be considered in a fuller way. So, how will White be tackled?

My consideration of White will be in four sections. In section one ('The Politics of Historical Interpretation') the argument will be put that White's views on history are as they are because of his political (utopian) position. This is a point that has been mentioned before, but now it will be 'fleshed out' to form the basis of the reading given here. This fleshing-out is important. For whilst we know already how White defines history; whilst we know that he thinks the past in all its sublimity can never be grasped fully in narrative form; and indeed, whilst we have already suggested that this way of looking at history is connected to his utopianism, we haven't yet seen exactly how White's political hopes *arguably determine* his view of the past, and how this leads him to not only recognise narrative forms of historical representation as epistemologically problematic, but also why he criticises narrative discourses as such insofar as they conceal the 'reality' of the past which is precisely that it is 'non-narratable'. Of course, White recognises very well indeed that epistemologically the conviction that one can make no sense of past (his view) stands at exactly the same level of plausibility as the conviction that one can, but it is White's point that the kind of politics that can be justified by an appeal to history differs according to whether one proceeds on the basis of the former or the latter belief. And White is convinced that his sort of 'visionary politics' can proceed only on the former – which is why he holds it. By examining the details of all this, then, we should be able to see how White's epistemological arguments with regard to the impossibility of imposing narrative closures on the past (in either upper or lower case varients) derives from his political view that such closures – such 'disciplinary orderings' of the past – are undesirable, this approach enabling us to gain an understanding of precisely what White thinks history is and why he holds such views. This, at any rate, will constitute the content of the first section on White.

The second section (entitled 'On Narrative') relates to the further crucial aspect of White's usefulness. For, whilst the area covered in the first section is itself useful for making us aware of, for example, the ideological nature of history as White construes it, he is useful again for another reason which we have already mentioned. Because, as we know, White also offers in his work a structural analysis of the *form* in which he thinks all histories beyond the level of the statement and/or the chronicle are articulated whether he likes that form or not; namely the narrative form, it being White's argument that all such histories are *metahistories*. Accordingly, section two of this discussion of White will be an analysis of what he means by metahistory and its implications for thinking about the way historical knowledge is produced. And it is hoped that when this section is added to the first then it might be possible to reflect back over not only the 'nature of history debates' as found in Carr and Elton, but also over much of the discursive field of contemporary historiography. To help with this more general 'reflecting', two short sections will bring my reading of White to a close. First, there will be a consideration of the issues raised throughout the entire discussion of this book but now seen from the vantage point of having 'read' White, and finally, I have drawn up a summary definition of what I think history is, both as a résumé of all the arguments I have been running including those on White, and as a possible basis for further work.

SECTION ONE: THE POLITICS OF HISTORICAL INTERPRETATION

Because White feels that on occasion he has been accused of encouraging in some of his writings the kind of nihilism that invites radical, or even revolutionary, activism of an irresponsible kind, he has deemed it necessary to register as an 'item of personal belief' that he is, in fact, no revolutionary: 'I am against revolutions, whether launched from "above" or "below" in the social hierarchy and whether directed by leaders who profess to possess a science of society and history or be celebrators of political "spontaneity".'[1] Besides, White adds, in today's advanced industrial states at least, political revolution (which he anyway thinks 'always misfires') is likely 'to result in the further consolidation of oppressive powers rather than the dissolution thereof. After all, those who control the military–industrial–economic complex hold all the cards.'[2] Admittedly, says White, he is – if not a nihilist – certainly a historical relativist, but even then he somewhat underplays this, arguing that so far as he is concerned such relativism is to be seen as a basis for social toleration and not as a licence to 'do as you please'.[3]

Yet, these disclaimers taken into account, White still has a series of radical answers to the question of 'why study the past?' which seem to have stayed with him pretty much since his 1966 essay, *The*

Burden of History. The gist of that work was that historical study should show people how the past can be used to effect an ethically responsible transition from the present to the future in ways which prioritise the responsibilities of the individual by inducing in them an awareness that any given 'present' condition is always, in part, a product of specifically human choices which can therefore be changed by further human action 'in precisely that degree'. Consequently, White thinks that we need a way of thinking about the past which will 'educate us to discontinuity ... for discontinuity, disruption and chaos are our lot'. For life is lived all the better if history is read as having no single meaning (succumbs to no single narrative) but many different ones, a history that keeps on the agenda a future-directed utopianism that will help people be released from 'the burden of history' as construed as a single 'closure'.[4] And for the reading of White that I will be offering, the preliminary point that I want to develop is his view that disruption and chaos are our lot.

The idea that the past has neither rhyme nor reason to it; that it is grotesque, or absurd, or sublime, is a lesson that White seems to have learned from his 'existential' readings of Burckhardt, Schopenhauer, Nietzsche, Camus and Sartre *et al.*, and never forgot, White seemingly going along with, for example, Burckhardt's perspectival cutting-up of the past to suit his own purposes, Burckhardt having abandoned the 'dream of telling the truth about the past' by means of a coherent story because he had long since abandoned the belief that history had any inherent meaning or significance. The only 'truth' that Burckhardt recognised, says White, was that which he had learned from Schopenhauer, namely, that 'every attempt to give form to the world, every human affirmation, was tragically doomed in the end, but that individual affirmation attained to a worth of its own insofar as it succeeded in imposing upon the chaos of the world a momentary form'.[5]

The reason why I think that White hasn't forgotten this way of reading the past is simply because it consistently appears within his texts, the idea that most historiography is the attempted imposition of meaningful form onto a meaningless past seeming to lie behind and/or within the bulk of the essays in *Tropics of Discourse*, in *The Content of the Form*, and in his book *Metahistory*. The importance of this relatively constant perspective – which I think to all intents and purposes constitutes the motif which runs throughout White's work – is that it is the embodiment of his political views as articulated in historiography. I believe that nowhere is this seen better than in White's 1982 essay *The Politics of Historical Interpretation: Discipline and De-Sublimation*.[6] For there White argues that narrative histories of both the upper and lower case need to be critiqued (out of existence) insofar as their various 'disciplinings' of the past have erased the one thing that it is essential never to erase – the sublime nature of the past – if one is to keep on the agenda the politically utopian:

> Let me try to put this somewhat more clearly. It seems to me that the kind of politics that is based on a vision of a perfected society can compel devotion to it only by virtue of the contrast it offers to a past that is understood in the way that Schiller conceived it, that is, as a 'spectacle' of 'confusion', 'uncertainty', and 'moral anarchy'. Surely this is the appeal of those eschatological religions that envision a 'rule of the saints' that is the very antithesis of the spectacle of sin and corruption that the history of a fallen humanity displays to the eye of the faithful. . . . But modern ideologies seem to me to differ crucially from eschatological religious myths in that they impute a meaning to history that renders its manifest confusion comprehensible to either reason, understanding, or aesthetic sensibility. [consequently] To the extent that they succeed in doing so, these ideologies [therefore] deprive history of the kind of meaninglessness that alone can goad living human beings to make their lives different for themselves and their children, which is to say, to endow their lives with a meaning for which they alone are fully responsible. [7]

White concludes these thoughts by adding that, from this perspective, however radical Marxism may once have been – and indeed may still be – as a social philosophy and as a critique of capitalism, as a philosophy of history it is no more visionary than its bourgeois counterparts. [8]

Here, then, we can surely see the political basis for what White thinks narrative history is in both its upper and lower case forms – an overwhelmingly political mode of disciplining the past – as well as what it ought to be; namely, a study of the past that fully recognises the openness and uncontrollable nature of it in order to encourage an open and different emancipatory future. As White goes on to say, in his opinion one can never move with any political confidence from an apprehension of the way things actually are, or have been, to the moral insistence that they should be otherwise without passing through a feeling of repugnance for, and negative judgement on, the conditions to be superseded,[9] so that insofar as history is disciplined in such a way that that repugnance is controlled or negated or made palatable (which is what we have just seen White thinks most histories do) then history is removed from any connection with the visionary politics of the kind White likes and is instead consigned to a service that will always be anti-utopian in nature, a view that is again as true of a Marxist reading of the past as it is of the bourgeois historians' concern with a study of the past 'for itself alone'. [10]

Now, there is a sense in which all this seems very clear; this is White's general position on history. So, do we need to add to it? I believe we do. For it might be useful not to leave White's *The Politics of Historical Interpretation* at this point but to dwell on some (if not all) of its arguments for a little longer. For, as well as simply making the points just discussed, White also fits them into a (self-conscious) narrative of his own which leads him (in 1982) to be relatively optimistic about the possibility of a utopian historico-politics. That is to say, that in this essay White seems to put the following four arguments: (1) that prior to the end of the eighteenth century, the past as history was relatively undisciplined; that it admitted to the 'sublime'; (2) that during the nineteenth and into the twentieth century radical (i.e. Marxist) and liberal and conservative ideologies, all variously disciplined the past into the forms that suited them; (3) that these disciplinisations were basically aestheticisations (sometimes expressed in the ordered/aestheticised discourse of science) of the past that snuffed-out the sublime; but that (4) today, in our postmodern condition, various theories of discourse have now opened up the possibility (or threat) of criticising out of existence such aestheticised closures, this 'condition' explaining that sense of crisis which postmodernism signifies in contemporary social formations for their exponents and beneficiaries, as the narrative myths and certaintist disciplinary procedures which have helped form the narrative glue that holds such social formations together (and which indentures the bulk of its citizens to impoverished lives) have become unstuck, thereby offering at least the possibility of histories of discontinuity and difference based on the rearticulation of the past as sublime. Let me now unpack just a little of White's interesting argument: it goes as follows.

If, begins White, one wanted to know what consistituted the historian's field of phenomena in the eighteenth century, then the answer to that query would be simply 'the past', a past conceived as the source and repository of tradition, moral exemplars and admonitory lessons to be investigated by one of the modes of interpretation into which Aristotle divided various kinds of rhetorical discourse: ceremonial, forensic and political, with the preliminary ordering of this field of phenomena being consigned to the disciplines of chronology and the ordering of documents into the form of annals. As for the uses to which historical reflection was to be put, well, says White, these were as wide as rhetorical practice, political partisanship and confessional variation allowed, whilst as for what history could tell people about human society, this either fell under the charge of Christian myth or its secular, Enlightenment counterpart (the myth of Progress), or, it displayed a panorama 'of failure, duplicity, fraud, deceit, and stupidity'.[11] Consequently, when at the end of the eighteenth century Kant asked what a study of history could teach mankind, he came to three conclusions: (1) that the human race was progressing continually; (2) that the human race was degenerating continually; and (3) that the human race remained at the same general level of development continually, calling these three notions of historical development eudaemonism, terrorism, and farce.[12]

Now, the crucial point to note about these 'lessons from history', is that they do, of course, leave the past entirely open to any sort of equally plausible interpretation, and that it is accordingly this interpretive danger which White sees post-eighteenth-century historical narratives as attempting to close down. White puts his argument to this effect as follows:

> The important point [here] is that the variety of uses to which written history's subordination to rhetoric permitted it to be put exposed historical thinking to the threat of being conceived solely in terms of Kant's third type, the farce; as long as history was subordinated to rhetoric, the historical field itself (that is, the past or the historical process) had to be viewed as a chaos that made no sense at all or one that could be made to bear as many senses as wit and rhetorical talent could impose upon it. Accordingly, the disciplining of historical thinking that had to be undertaken if history considered as a kind of knowledge was to be established as arbitrator of the realism of contending political programmes, each attended by its own philosophy of history, had first of all to consist of a rigorous de-rhetoricisation.[13]

White says that this is precisely what happened. In effect history was to become a discipline in a quite literal way. He argues that this was

done by distinguishing the narratives of history from those of fiction
via the rigorous application of the 'rules of evidence' to the 'historical
record' as facticity, so eventually pushing out the rhetorical, the
speculative, the incomprehensible and the sublime, so gradually
affirming that the stories historians told were 'found' in the cor-
roborated 'evidence' rather than being 'imagined'. Accordingly, in
this way historians of all ideological persuasions soon came to argue
that the order, coherence, structures and developments embodied in
the historical narratives that they produced, actually corresponded
to the order, coherence, structures and developments that 'the past'
really did 'objectively' possess.[14]

Consequently, White argues that through these developments
narrative history took on the form of the ordered, the measured
and the beautiful, as opposed to a view of a past that lacked these
aesthetic proportions, so that the aesthetic tamed the irregularities
and grotesqueness of the sublime. And here, at this point in his own
narrative, White lines himself up alongside the German philosopher
who didn't succumb to the blandishments of the aesthetic as purged
of the sublime: Schiller.

For White's Schiller, that 'bizarre savagery' which he found in
physical nature equated to the delight which he considered one might
feel in contemplating 'the uncertain anarchy of the moral world',[15]
Schiller going on to add that meditation on the confusion that the
'spectacle' of history displayed could produce a sense of a specific
type of human freedom which, insofar as it did so, made 'world
history' appear to him as a 'sublime object', transforming the '"pure
daemon" in human kind into grounds for belief in a "dignity" unique
to man'. Here, says White, the sublime was seen as a necessary
complement to the beautiful if an 'aesthetic education' was to be
made into a complete whole.[16]

This would have been, as it were, the best of all possible outcomes
so far as White is concerned. But, unfortunately, Schiller's vision was
not to become a dominant one. Instead, as the nineteenth century
unfurled, so the aesthetic relentlessly displaced the sublime right
across the political spectrum so that, by its end, a generally accredited
aesthetic theory was as uncritically accepted by once radical Marxists
as much as by their conservative and liberal opponents. As White
puts it:

> What must be recognised . . . is that for both the Left and the Right,
> this same aesthetics of the beautiful presides over the process in

which historical studies are constituted as an autonomous scholarly discipline. It takes little reflection to perceive that aestheticism is endemic to what is regarded as a proper attitude towards objects of historical study in a certain tradition, deriving from Leopold von Ranke and his epigones, which represents the nearest thing to an orthodoxy that the profession possesses. For this tradition, whatever 'confusion' is displayed by the historical record is only a surface phenomenon: a product of lacunae in the documentary sources, of mistakes in ordering the archives, or of previous inattention or scholarly errors.... Historical facts are [thus] politically domesticated precisely insofar as they are effectively removed from displaying any aspect of the sublime that Schiller attributed to them.... By this I mean ... the following: insofar as historical events and processes become understandable, as conservatives maintain, or explainable, as radicals believe them to be, they can never serve as a basis for a visionary politics more concerned to endow social life with meaning than with beauty. In my view, the theorists of the sublime had correctly divined that whatever dignity and freedom human beings could lay claim to could come only by way of what Freud called a "reaction-formation" to an apperception of history's meaninglessness.[17]

Hence White's arguments – which we are already familiar with from our earlier remarks and which in this narrative we have been in a sense 'contextualising' – that insofar as any history renders the 'manifest confusion' of the past comprehensible to either reason or aesthetic sensibility, then such ideological closures deprive history of that openness and meaninglessness that can 'alone goad living human beings to make their lives different for themselves and their children'.[18] Insofar as history is disciplined to understand the past in such a way 'that it can forgive everything or at best to practice a kind of "disinterested interest" of the sort that Kant imagined to inform every properly aesthetic perception, it is removed from any connection with a visionary politics' whatever its radical rhetoric may, as in the case of Marxism, suggest.[19] As White somewhat reluctantly puts it,

Marxism is anti-utopian insofar as it shares with its bourgeois counterpart the conviction that history is not a sublime spectacle but a comprehensible process the various parts, stages, epochs, and even individual events of which are transparent to a consciousness endowed with the means to make sense of it in one way or another.[20]

And so we return directly to historical narrative and the politics of history today. For, isn't it obvious from this account, asks White rhetorically, that historical narrative is a general ideological instrument of anti-utopian closure? And if it is – and clearly for White it is – then is it not imperative in these postmodern days to imagine a 'deconstructive' history that would signal (and here White begins to critique academic history especially, his utopianism, as it were, now standing in for a moribund Marxism) its 'resistance to bourgeois ideology' by refusing to attempt a narrativist mode for the representation of its 'truth'? And if this is a possibility – if histories of rupture and discontinuity and of difference and 'the other' are at least now on the agenda – then couldn't this refusal to effect narrative closures signal a recovery of the historical sublime that bourgeois historiography repressed in the process of its disciplinisation? And more than that, goes on White, if this is the case, then cannot the possible recovery of the historical sublime act as a necessary precondition for the production of a historiography 'charged with avenging the people'? Well, concludes White, 'This seems plausible to me.'[21]

Accordingly, White in his more radical mood refuses to accept a politics of interpretation in historical studies that instructs us that 'the war is over' and that we should 'forgo the attractions of a desire for revenge'. For, it seems obvious to White that such instruction always emanates from centres of established power and that 'this kind of tolerance is a luxury only devotees of dominant groups can afford'. For

> subordinate, emergent, or resisting social groups, this recommendation – that they view history with the kind of 'objectivity', 'modesty', 'realism', and 'social responsibility' that has characterised historical studies since their establishment as a professional discipline – can only appear as another aspect of the ideology they are indentured to oppose.[22]

Nor, adds White, will such groups gain any help from other ideologies – Marxism included – which offer only their own version of this 'objectivity'. No, such opposition can be carried forward only on the basis of the historical record, as being not a window through which the past 'as it really was' can be apprehended but rather a wall that must be broken through if the 'terror of history' [après Kant] ... is to be directly confronted and the fear it induces dispelled.[23]

For in the end, says White, if one wants to liberate oneself from narrative closures of the past, then everything depends on how one studies it and to what end. And for White, nothing 'is better suited' to an undesirable end as a study of the past that is either 'reverential' or 'convincingly objective' in the way that conventional historical studies across the board now tend to be. No, for White, one of the things which one can learn from historiography, is that no study of the past is innocent, ideologically or otherwise, whether launched from the political perspective of the left, the right or the centre. And this is because the

> very notion of the possibility of discriminating between the Left, the Right and Centre is in part a function of the disciplinization of historical studies which ruled out the possibility – a possibility that should never be ruled out of any area of inquiry – that history may be as meaningless 'in itself' as the theorists of the historical sublime thought it to be.[24]

This, then, concludes my reading of further aspects of White's essay, and I think that after the explicitness of the last few remarks we should now be able to see very clearly why White regards those narrative histories which emerged in the nineteenth century as forms of narrative closure vis-à-vis the sublime as being 'ripe for critique'. And I also think that we should now have a further reason to add to our previous understanding of why White defines history as 'a narrative discourse the contents of which are as much imagined/ invented as found', and why, in the name of individual freedom, emancipation and empowerment via an acknowledgement of the sublime, he can offer a critique of such narration in favour of history as 'rupture', 'discontinuity' and 'dislocation'. For,

> Since the second half of the nineteenth century, history has become increasingly the refuge of all those 'sane' men who excel at finding the simple in the complex and the familiar in the strange. This was all very well for an earlier age, but if the present generation needs anything at all it is a willingness to confront heroically the dynamic and disruptive forces in contemporary life. The historian serves no one well by constructing a specious continuity between the

present world and that which preceded it. On the contrary, we require a history that will educate us to discontinuity more than ever before; for discontinuity, disruption and chaos is our lot.[25]

Yet, having said all this, it still has to be noted – and this point seems to be as true now as it was in the late 1970s and early 1980s – that unfortunately White has not gone on to explain how either his politics or his history of discontinuity would actually work in much detail. There are intimations in parts of his work, but if it's practical examples of historical 'discontinuity' and 'rupture' allied to politics that we are after, then perhaps Michel Foucault is a better theorist for us to go to, as White himself does on occasion.[26] For, in Foucault, 'rupture', 'discontinuity' and the examination of the violent appropriation of the past by power-based historical perspectives runs throughout and indeed constitutes his work, his notion of *effective history*, for example, working within traditional historiography (in both upper and lower cases) to show the caprice and contingency of all 'interpretations' including those dominant renditions so 'objectively' in place, Foucault deliberately skewing his past against the grain so as to bring out the slanted 'nature' of all history. Accordingly, Foucault's language and perspective are much more radical than those of White but, unfortunately, an analysis of this lies beyond the scope of this present study.[27] At the moment White is at the centre of our concerns and must remain so. So I now want to bring this discussion of White to a close whilst at the same time beginning to move on to Section Two of this chapter, something I think I can do by saying that with regard to White's final answer to the question of what is history I can conclude by making the two following points.

First, White thinks that what history *is* is predominantly a form of narrative discourse, the content of which is as much invented/imagined as found and which on the whole is not expressive of discontinuity and the positive acceptance of the sublime. Second, he thinks that what history/historiography *ought* to be, is a series of discontinuous histories the content of which is as much imagined/invented as found, but which acknowledges the presence of the sublime as a 'useful fiction' on which to 'base' movements towards a more generous emancipation and empowerment than is currently in place in order to realise a radical, liberal – but not much detailed – utopia. This seems to me to embrace much if not all of White's answer to the question of 'What is History?' and the reasons he has for thinking in the ways he arguably does.[28] And so to Section Two of this examination of aspects of White. For, as already indicated, irrespective of what White thinks history is or ought to be, in *Metahistory* in particular (though in other essays too) he also offers a view of how all narrative histories are formally constructed, over the years White being concerned to try and identify what the 'ideal–typical structure of the historical work in narrative form might consist of', a formal approach that he sees as being an attempt to construct a general theory of historical narrative. What is therefore of great interest in White so far as this reading is concerned, is how, in his attempts to show how the 'formless' past is made into historiography, he goes far beyond the old shibboleths of Carr and Elton into a richness of analysis not even hinted at in their texts. For this is a way of thinking about historical construction which if we don't go to White we will not be able to get from anyone else.

Consequently, White's views on how the past becomes narrative historiography deserve careful consideration.

SECTION TWO: ON NARRATIVE

In the preliminary 'methodological' remarks at the start of *Metahistory*, White puts before his readers three points: (1) a (partial) definition of what he thinks historiography most manifestly is; (2) some of the conclusions about the nature of historiography so defined that he has arrived at as a result of his studies, and (3) an outline of the 'methodological categories' he has used in order to dissect historiography into its constitutive elements, these constitutive elements being, at one and the same time, identical to his methodological categories; that is (as we shall see) White will use, for example, the category of emplotment to explain precisely how emplotment – as a constitutive element of history – works. Accordingly, I think that it might be best to begin my exposition of White's work by following him through these 'preliminaries' so that we can see the general shape of White's approach via an overview before going on to examine his arguments in more detail.

Thus, with regard to (1) White says that in his theory of historiography as metahistory he will treat the 'historical work as what it most manifestly is: a verbal structure in the form of a narrative prose discourse' (to which we might add the by now familiar 'content' clause, 'the content of which is as much imagined/invented as found'). And he goes on almost immediately to explain that, as a result of both his methodological investigations and his study of aspects of 'historical consciousness', he is able to draw (and this is point (2) seven 'conclusions' about the nature of historiography so defined which he thinks might be offered at this early stage of the proceedings so that they can be kept in mind as outcomes towards which his analysis will be heading in general terms:

(1) There can be no 'proper history' which is not at the same time 'philosophy of history'; (2) the possible modes of historiography are the same as the possible modes of speculative philosophy of history; (3) these modes, in turn, are in reality *formalizations* of poetic insights that analytically precede them and that sanction the particular theories used to give historical accounts the aspect of an 'explanation'; (4) there are no apodictically certain theoretical grounds on which one can legitimately claim an authority for any one of the modes over the others as being more 'realistic'; (5) as a consequence of this, we are indentured to a *choice* among contending interpretative strategies in any effort to reflect on history-in-general; (6) as a corollary of this, the best grounds for choosing one perspective on history rather than another are ultimately aesthetic or moral rather than epistemological; and, finally, (7) the demand for the scientization of history represents only the statement of a preference for a specific modality of historical conceptualization, the grounds of which are either moral or aesthetic, but the epistemological justification of which still remains to be established.[29]

So to White's third point, the methodological categories which will enable him to both dissect the component parts of historiography whilst seeing them as constitutive of it. And because this area will include in it the elements which I will be most concerned with in the exposition which follows – and because there are so many of them – then this third point will need to be more extensively examined at this early juncture than the previous two.

White begins by saying, then, that in order to carry out his analysis of what he thinks historiography is, he finds it useful to distinguish initially between what he calls the 'primitive' and effectively the 'non-primitive' elements of the historical account. What does this distinction mean? Well, White means by the primitive elements of the historical account those ways whereby the 'traces of the past' are prepared for the 'non-primitive' part of the historians' task, namely, the construction of history into a narrative form. That is, like Tony Bennett, White assumes that the formless (and for him) the sublime past, cannot ever be appropriated directly, can never be re-presented plainly, but can only be interpreted textually through its 'always already' historicised traces (the 'textual' records, archives, relics, etc.) in the ways in which they are currently constituted. White calls these textual traces the 'relatively unprocessed historical record'. And he says that what historians first have to do to begin to turn this record into history, is to organise the 'data' it contains into a chronicle and thence into a story on the basis of which they will then be able to transform these 'primitive elements' (the unprocessed historical record, the chronicle and the story) into a narrative. And to do this, to transform these elements into a narrative (i.e. to get from the primitive to the non-primitive) White thinks that historians have to use three types of explanation and one type of 'configuring conceptual strategy'. By which he means that all historians working in whatever case must, in order to be able to explain the past in ways which enable them to be understood by others, use three types of explanation; namely, explanation by argument, explanation by emplotment, and explanation by ideology. And within each of these White then identifies what he refers to as four possible modes of articulation by which the historian can gain an explanatory affect of a specific kind. For explanation by argument these are the modes of formism, organicism, mechanism and contextualism; for explanation by emplotment these are the archetypes of romance, comedy, tragedy and satire, whilst for explanation by ideology, these are the tactics of anarchism, conservatism, radicalism and liberalism. And White argues that the specific selections and combinations (permutations) of these modes comprise what he calls the historiographical 'style' of a particular historian or philosopher of history. But it is not only that. For White then argues that to relate these modes to one another, historians also have a set of 'conceptual strategies' by which to explain or represent their 'data'. On this level, White believes that the historian performs a poetic act in which he/she prefigures the historical field and constitutes it as a domain upon which to bring to bear the specific theories he/she will use to explain 'what was really happening' in it. This act of prefiguration, White adds, may take a number of forms, forms which White, borrowing from a 'tradition of interpretation as old as Aristotle but more recently developed by Vico, modern linguists, and literary theorists' calls by the four tropes of poetic language: metaphor, metonymy, synecdoche and irony. It is White's theory that this 'dominant tropological mode and its attendant linguistic protocol comprise the irreducibly "metahistorical" basis of every historical work'.

White effectively summarises much of this as follows.

I begin by distinguishing among the following levels of conceptualization in the historical work: (1) chronicle; (2) story; (3) mode of emplotment (4) mode of argument; and (5) mode of ideological implication. I take 'chronicle' and 'story' to refer to 'primitive elements' in the *historical account*, but both represent processes of selection and arrangement of data from the *unprocessed historical record* in the interests of rendering that record more comprehensible to an *audience* of a particular kind. As thus conceived, the historical work represents an attempt to mediate among what I will call the *historical field*, the unprocessed *historical record*, other *historical accounts*, and an *audience*.[30]

Now, at this point it might look as though what White will be saying about how histories are 'made up' (or 'written up' as historians like to say) is extremely complicated. And this is not least because he has enumerated so many variables to arrive at his 'conclusions'; I mean, White is arguing that historical accounts are constructed through working an interpenetration of (always-to-be-interpreted) categories and sub-categories of which at least nineteen are available.

Thus, initially we have the primitive elements:

(1) Traces
(2) Chronicle
(3) Story

and then the non-primitive 'narrative' elements of argument, which include the modes of:

(4) Formism
(5) Organicism
(6) Mechanism
(7) Contextualism

emplotment, which include the modes of:

(8)   Romance
(9)   Comedy
(10) Tragedy
(11) Satire

ideology, which include the modes of:

(12) Anarchism
(13) Conservatism

(14) Radicalism
(15) Liberalism

and tropes, which include the modes of:

(16) Metaphor
(17) Metonymy
(18) Synecdoche
(19) Irony

However, whilst this is indeed a far cry from, say, the relative simplicities of Carr and Elton with regard to how histories are made, and whilst it is admittedly somewhat complicated, it is not 'that complicated'. For, whilst White doesn't make many allowances for his readers, with some slight rearrangements and perhaps elements of simplification, his ideas are accessible and clear. Accordingly, it is this slightly rearranged and more 'popular' White that I now want to explain in detail. I start at that point where White sees the historian beginning to shape the shapeless traces of the past (the unprocessed historical record) by way of transforming them into a chronicle.

What, then, does White mean by a chronicle? His answer is this. A chronicle is the arrangement of the events and people to be dealt with – as derived from the historicised traces – 'in the temporal order of their occurrence'. In principle, says White, chronicles are 'open ended'. Having no logical *inaugurations* or *endings*, they simply begin when the historian-as-chronicler begins, and end when he/she ends. Stories, however, are different, in that White thinks that the chronicle is organised into a story form by the 'further arrangement of the events into the components of a "spectacle" or process of happening, which is thought to possess a beginning, middle, and end'. And this transformation of the chronicle into a story is accomplished by characterising some of the 'events' in the chronicle as having a certain location and a certain importance relative to other events so that, as White puts it, a 'hierarchy of significance' is established, summarising these points as follows: 'Historical *stories* trace the sequence of events that lead from inaugurations to (provisional) terminations of social and cultural processes in a way that *chronicles* are not required to do. . . . Stories . . . have a discernable form (even when that form is an image of a state of chaos) which marks off the events contained in them from other events that may appear in a comprehensive chronicle of the years covered in their unfoldings.'[31]

Now, in order to stress the extent to which the interventions, and indeed the *inventions*, made by the historian to give the chronicle a story form play a part at even this early stage of the proceedings (for to recall, White defines history as a narrative discourse the content of which is as much *invented* as found), White reflects upon the assertion often made by traditional historians that the aim of the historian is to explain the past by simply 'uncovering' or 'finding' the stories that already lie buried in the 'factual' chronicle – in the 'events of the past' – and that the difference between historical accounts and fictional stories resides in the fact that the historian 'finds' his or her facts/stories, whereas the writer of fiction 'invents' his or hers. But to White the first idea – that events already have in them the shapes of stories – just makes no sense, whilst with regard to the second, White argues that this 'traditional' understanding of the historian's task 'obscures the extent to which "invention" also plays a part in the historian's operations'.[32] For we can see already the way in which the historian has to invent a story form to accomplish the transformation of the events/facts of the chronicle into a story that in themselves the event/facts could *never* produce. In other words, to transform the events/facts of the chronicle into what they *become* in a story (i.e. a series of events/facts arranged in 'a hierarchy of significance' relative to a beginning, a middle and an end) is a form of fiction-making. This is not to say, to repeat the now obvious point, that the events/facts did not truly happen in exactly *the way they did*, but that in the story (and the finished narrative) they happen in exactly *the way they do*: historians deal with 'truth' alright, but that truth has about it 'the truth of fiction'.

Now, in *Metahistory*, White's discussion of the way the 'primitive elements' are turned into stories is fairly short, for he almost immediately goes on to distinguish between his conception of the chronicle and the story *and* the completed narrative (of which the story is but an early stage). But before following White here, it might be useful to further clarify what he means more precisely by a *hierarchy of significance* and the relationship, at this stage, of 'fact and fiction'. And to do this it is necessary to look for just a short time at White's essay, *The Historical Text as Literary Artifact*.

White points out in this essay that whilst most historians may not like to think of their work as translations of fact *into* fiction, by endowing sets of past events with meanings over and above what might be suggested by a chronicle so as to make a comprehensible (if primitive) story of them, then this is effectively what they do. Of course some historians may well grant at least something of this point, but then go on to insist that 'beneath' all the stories 'the facts remain'. And in a sense so they do. But to recall an earlier phrase from White, such facts relate only to that aspect of the historian's work called the chronicle, and not to the historical story which, by precisely *not* being a chronicle already has an element of interpretation in it. And to illustrate how the facts cannot pin down the significance the story form gives them, White gives an example of how a series of facts – let us call them a, b, c, d, e ... n – can be endowed with different meanings and significance without violating their integrity as facts or the imperatives of sequence/chronology in any way.

Thus the series of facts may be arranged as follows:

1 A b c d e . . . n
2 a B c d e . . . n
3 a b C d e . . . n
4 a b c D e . . . n
5 a b c d E . . . n

whereof the capitalised letters indicate the privileged status of certain events/facts which are endowed with an explanatory force either as causes explaining the structure of the whole series 'or as symbols of the plot structure of the series considered as a story of a specific kind'.[33] Thus, for example, in series 1, by making 'A' the decisive factor, then we might say that it *determines* what follows; hence it is prioritised as *the* explanatory factor. It has more significance than b, c, d, e, ... n. On the other hand, giving 'E' priority would suggest that all the previous events/facts of the sequence were leading up to 'E' so that, although 'E' comes last in the story it has, by being its climax, determined both the story form and, by assigning itself and the other elements in the series their relative positions, so their relative significance within 'the hierarchy of significance'. In other words, what White is doing here (as well as, as it were, rearticulating Hirst's point about the unity of significance) is making a distinction between what one might call the *syntax* and the *semantics* of history in that, whilst one can accept that historians pretty much 'constitute/find' the *syntax* of the past (the facts/the statements/the chronicle) they *never* find its *semantics* (its story/narrative forms) that is to say, its meaning; its 'true' significance.

From which illustration and 'conclusion' White draws three (further) points. *First*, that if the historian simply recorded the events/facts then he/she would not be a historian at all but merely a chronicler. *Second*, to turn a chronicle into history thus requires what is effectively an act of translation, and to speak of translation is to always speak of the incomplete. For as Iain Chambers puts it: 'to translate is always to transform'; it always 'involves a necessary travesty of any metaphysics of authenticity or origins'.[34] Thus, with regard to White's series, for example, it is easy to see that one doesn't even have to violate the syntax in any way at all to yield alternative yet equally plausible interpretations/translations of 'the same things'. Thus, *third*, histories, as White puts it, are never just about the events/facts of the past *per se* but also 'about the possible sets of relationships that those events [facts] can be demonstrated to figure'.[35] And here it is the word 'figure' that is important. For given, says White, that history has no generally accepted *technical language*; given that there is no general agreement as to what history 'really' is; given that history has no single *method* which historians *qua* historians subscribe to to get from syntax to semantics, and given that historians' characteristic mode of meaning-making is just 'ordinary educated speech', so all this implies,

> that the only instruments that he has for endowing his data with meaning, of rendering the strange familiar, and of rendering the mysterious past comprehensible, are the techniques of *figurative* language. [consequently] All historical narratives presuppose figurative characterisations of the events they purport to represent and explain. And this means that historical narratives, considered purely as verbal artifacts, can be characterised by the mode of figurative discourse in which they are cast [by the rhetorical tropes of metaphor, metonymy, synecdoche and irony]. . . . In point of fact [therefore] history . . . is made sense of in the same way that the poet or novelist tries to make sense of it, i.e. by endowing what originally appears to be problematical and mysterious with the aspect of a recognisable . . . form. It does not matter whether the world is conceived to be real or only imagined; the manner of making sense of it is the same.[36]

Accordingly, the conclusion White draws from these three thoughts is to suggest a richness of historical explanation which is wholly to the good. As he puts it:

> If we recognize that there is a fictive element in all historical narrative, we would find in the theory of language and narrative

itself the basis for a more subtle presentation of what historiography consists of than that which simply tells the student to go and 'find out the facts' and write them up in such a way as to tell 'what really happened'.[37]

This is the small digression I have made from White's arguments in *Metahistory* and so, having made it, I turn again to White's major text, picking up the point – to recall – that there is a difference between what White has been talking about so far (the primitive elements of traces, chronicles and stories) and a narrative. And this difference is one which White now begins to explain by saying that whereas the 'figuring out' of the chronicle into a story raises such questions as, 'what happened next?' and 'how did it all come out in the end?', these questions about the connections between events which make up a *followable* story have to be distinguished from questions of a different kind, namely: 'what does it all add up to?'; 'what does it all mean?'; 'what is the point of it all?' For these questions, says White,

> have to do with the structure of the *entire set of events* considered as a *completed* story and call for a synoptic judgement of the relationship between a given story and other stories that might be 'found', 'identified', or 'uncovered' in the chronicle. They can be answered in a number of ways. I call these ways (1) explanation by emplotment, (2) explanation by argument, and (3) explanation by ideological implication.[38]

Consequently it is to these three areas – the areas which White thinks transform stories into narratives – that I now turn, beginning by considering White's 'explanation by argument'.

Within that part of his analysis which he calls 'explanation by formal argument', White argues that it is possible to distinguish between its four types (the modes of formism, organicism, mechanism and contextualism) in two ways. First, on the basis of the direction that the argument is presumed to take (along a spectrum towards either *dispersion* or *integration*) and, second, on the basis of the *paradigm* of 'the general aspect that the explicated set of phenomena will assume at the end of this operation'. What do these two things mean?

Well, by the *direction* the explanation will take, White means that historical explanations can be located along a spectrum which runs, as just noted, from dispersion to integration. Thus, some historians will favour a historical explanation constituted by a set of dispersed entities each of which is clearly discernable as a unique and discrete thing and which, when put together, have nothing in common except 'their inhabitance of a single neighbourhood of occurrences'. That is to say, that at this end of the spectrum the explanation is *analytical* in that it leaves the various elements which make up the explanation *un-reduced* either to the status of, say, general causal laws, or to general classificatory categories. As White puts it:

> For historians governed by this conception of what an explanation should consist of, a field which *appears* at first glance to be a vague congeries of events is revealed at the end of the analysis to consist of a set of essentially autonomous particulars subsumable under no general rule, either of causation or of classifcatory entailment.[39]

Alternatively, at the other end of the spectrum, a fully explicated analysis will appear in an *integrated* way in that, although the elements which comprise it may appear at first glance to be unrelated to each other, by the end of the historians' analysis such individual elements are 'seen' to be connected either in some sort of *cause–effect* way (in which case White will consider this relationship to be a *mechanistic* paradigm) or in that of a *whole–part* relationship (in which case White will consider this to be or an *organicist* paradigm). Either way, for the integrative type of historian, his/her 'explanation by argument' will strive not for dispersion and analysis but precisely for integration and synthesis. And it is along this dispersive/analytical–integrative/synthetic spectrum that White (and this forms the second phase of his 'explanation by argument' approach) will locate (in ways which should seem rather obvious by now) his four paradigms: the formist (which incidentally in some writings White calls the 'idiographic'), the contextual, the mechanistic and the organic. What do these paradigms mean more exactly?

By a formist paradigm, White means that some historians see the argumentative part of their work as simply 'sorting out' the various entities which 'fall into' the area they are studying so that 'their outlines appear more precise'. Such historians see their function as being a kind of magnifying glass for their readers so that 'when they have finished with their work, the particulars in the field appear clearer to the (mind's) eye'.[40] That is to say, the formist-type historian will consider the explanation to be complete when a given set of objects has been properly identified, its class, generic, and specific attributes assigned, and labels attesting to its particularity attached to it.[41] In this way White compares such an explanation to the notes collected by a naturalist or anthropologist in the field but with one difference; namely, 'whereas both the naturalist and the anthropologist regard their observations of data to be worked up subsequently into generalizations about the structure of the field as a whole, the [formist] . . . historian conceives of his work as finished when the phenomena he has observed have adequately been represented in precise descriptive prose'.[42] Accordingly, the formist mode of explanation is to be found in any historiography in which the depiction of the variety, uniqueness, colour and vividness of the field is taken to be the aim of historical representation. Of course White is aware that such historians (he lists a number from Herder to Trevelyan) may be inclined towards *some* generalisations, but he argues that in formist modes of argumentative explanation, these tend to stress the uniqueness of the different agents, agencies and acts which make up the events to be explained simply because these are held to be what is central to one's inquiries, as distinct from the 'ground' or 'scene' against which these entities arise.[43] Consequently, those historians who go in for the setting of such 'contexts' are simply called *contextualists*.

The informing presupposition of contextualism is that past events can be best explained by being set much more deliberately in their contexts, this procedure then yielding, says White, such 'historiographical favourites' as periods, trends, eras, movements and so on, which enables us to see the whole historical process as a succession of relatively discrete 'movements' each with its own unique, governing features. And White argues that it is when 'events' have been set within such contexts ('against their backgrounds') by the method which W. H. Walsh called *colligation*, that the historian's task is said to be complete. Thus, in the contextual mode of argumentation, the entities in the field still remain dispersed, but they are now modestly and 'provisionally integrated' with one another as occupants of a shared context or, as it is sometimes said, are objects bathed in a common atmosphere.

Consequently, although contextualism is 'modestly integrative' in its general aim it does not, says White, encourage either an organicist synthesis of the whole field (in the manner of Hegel) or a mechanistic reduction of the field in terms of universal causal laws (as in the manner of Marx). From which it follows that for historians with a mechanistic or organic conception of the form that the explicated historical area must take, the attempts by both formists and contextualists to explain what happened in the past are 'radically un-satisfactory'.

Because organicist arguments are much more integrative, White argues that they are necessarily *reductive*, in that an organicist historian insists on considering the various contexts as mere parts of a greater whole which is almost always 'history-in-general' (i.e. some form of upper case history). Consequently, an organicist argument must take the form of a synthesis in which the historian strives to identify the principles by which the different aspects of history can be integrated into a single macrocosmic process of, say, *development*. And this means that explanation must take the form of a synthesis in which each of the parts of the whole must be shown either to mirror the structure of the totality, or to prefigure the form of either the end of the whole process, or at least the latest phase of the process. In this way the specific events of the past are thus effectively taken to be *expressive* of some sort of underlying *essence*, it being in this tendency to posit a permanent (if often latent) essence which gives to arguments cast in this form their often abstract or overtly 'philosophical' character. And it is because the organicist is inclined to posit and talk about 'ideas' or 'principles' or 'the spirit' of history, rather than *laws*, which, for White, distinguishes organicist arguments from mechanical ones. Thus, says White:

> it is the search for such laws, by which the events in the historical field can be reduced to the status of manifestations of impersonal causal agencies, that characterises the analytical strategy of the mechanistic theory of historical explanation in general. The mechanist, in short, does not see the elements of the historical field as being related in terms of part–whole relationships, but rather in terms of part–part relationships and in the modality of causality.[44]

Consequently, the mechanistic historian will carefully distinguish between those things that are causes from those which are effects, the historical field being explained when he/she has satisfactorily distinguished between causal agencies and the effects of these agencies' operations, and thus provide the necessary and sufficient conditions for their specific configurations at specific times and places within the whole process.

These, then, are the four types of 'explanation by formal argument' identified by White, and clearly there is a lot of difference between them (I mean, one can easily see the 'argumentative' and dispersed/integrative 'differences' between say Trevelyan and Marx). Moreover, because such differences are not differences that lie in the past itself (i.e. these are methodological procedures brought *into* the field from outside to do the job it precisely cannot do – organise itself) then the explanatory 'unities' which run across the dispersed–integrated spectrum are clearly 'imagined'. But White also adds three comments of his own on this state of affairs, comments which are useful to note briefly.

First, whilst White thinks he has identified the four basic types of explanatory argument (and whilst he thinks that in any given historical work the mode favoured is identifiable) and whilst there will often be (as will be seen shortly) an 'elective affinity' between any given explanatory argument and the mode of emplotment used, this is not the case in any absolutely necessary way; thus, 'these designations of modes of explanation ... are not exhaustive of the specific tactics used by ... historians'.[45] *Second*, White stresses that in the whole of this discussion he is of course speaking about the level on which the historian is trying to grasp the nature of the *whole field of phenomena* that is being presented in the narrative, not the level on which the historian 'searches for the necessary conditions of a given event's occurrence within the field'. Thus,

> A historian may decide that a decision to go to war was a result of policy choices of a given individual or group; and he can be said to have explained thereby why the war broke out at one time rather than another. But such [actually always problematical] 'explanations' as these have to do with the constitution of the chronicle of events that still require 'interpretation' in order to be transformed into a comprehensive [narrative] ... by its emplotment [and troping] as a particular story form. And such explanations are to be distinguished from the general theory of significant relationships by which a field thus emplotted is provided with an 'explanation' of why it has the form that it has in the narrative.[46]

Third (and this is the crucial ideological point), whilst any of the four argumentative modes might be used in a historical work to provide something like a formal argument of the 'true' meanings of the events depicted, these different modes have not enjoyed 'equal authority among the recognized professional [academic] practitioners of the discipline since its academicization in the early Nineteenth Century'. Indeed, says White, amongst academic (bourgeois/lower case) historians, formist and contextual modes have been the orthodox stock in trade, organicist and mechanistic arguments being regarded as unfortunate lapses from 'proper' history into the 'philosophy of history'. And, as White notes, the reason for this is not epistemological (i.e. it's not that formist and contextual arguments can be shown to give you a *better* explanation of what happened in the past and why), nor methodological (because, given that there is no such thing as the definitive method, all methods are instrumental 'tools' for getting what is required – and what is required is not defined by the tools that try and get it for you) but ideological. That is:

> Commitment to the dispersive techniques of Formism and Contextualism reflects only a *decision* on the part of historians not to attempt the kind of integrations of data that Organicism and Mechanism sanction as a matter of course. This decision . . . rest[s] on precritically held opinions about the *form* that a science of man and society *has to take*. And these opinions, in turn, would seem to be generally ethical, and specifically ideological, in nature.[47]

This third and final point thus brings us directly to the ideological. But because White generally considers the mode of emplotment before the ideological mode, in order to keep my explanation close to White's at this stage I will do the same. (Although, in fact, this point about the way in which White generally sequences his 'modes' – in *Metahistory* and elsewhere – raises some questions about the impression readers may get from White by virtue of this sequencing, however, I feel such critical reservations might best be considered after White's whole theory of historical narrative has been outlined, and so I now turn, as he does, to *emplotment*.)

Explaining the meaning of a story by identifying the kind of story that is basically being told, is thus called 'explanation by emplotment', emplotment being the way a sequence of events is fashioned into a narrative that is gradually seen to be of a particular kind. White identifies (after Northrop Frye) four modes of emplotment: romance, tragedy, comedy and satire. So, we might ask, why emplotment, why these four modes, and how do they work?

The reason which White gives for emplotment is simply that for a history to be what it is – a narrative in which the content is as much invented as found – it cannot remain in its chronicle or even in its story form; to change a sequential story into a meaningful narrative it must be emplotted; it must be *encoded*. And because (to recall) the past itself doesn't have a plot written into its events to be discovered and told, then the *production* of a plot is, in the final analysis, an arbitrary production: any given set of real events/facts can be emplotted over and above the story and the chronicle in any number of different narrative ways (as Rorty has put it, anything can be re-described):

> Since no given set or sequence of real events is intrinsically tragic, comic, farcical, and so on, but can be constructed as such only by the imposition of the structure of a given story type on the events, it is the choice of the story type and its imposition upon the events that endow them with meaning. . . . There is no way that one could conclude on logical grounds that any set of 'real' events *is* a farce. This is a judgement [a value which cannot be entailed from the 'facts'] . . . and it is a judgement that can be justified only on the basis of a poetic troping [and emplotting] of the 'facts' so as to give them . . . the elements of the [desired] story form.[48]

If this is indicative of the reason for emplotment (and as we shall see for tropes) then why just the four modes of romance, tragedy, comedy and satire? If the past can be emplotted in any number of ways, why not another number? And White's answer is that these four modes are the main modes of emplotment which the 'myths of the Western literary tradition sanction as appropriate ways of endowing human processes with meaning'. Of course there may be others, such as epic, whilst White allows that any given historical account may mix modes at specific points. Nevertheless, for White, a given history tends to emplot the whole set of stories making up its total narrative in one comprehensive or archetypal form so that it can be understood by its readers: historians, thinks White, if they are to get their stories across, must be 'culturally resonant' story-tellers.

Now, all this might seem a little complicated, and so it might be useful to just spend a paragraph or so explaining further what White means by the 'myths' of the Western literary tradition and why such myths 'have to be used' by historians to gain 'culturally resonant' meanings that can be communicated to an audience. White's 'reasons' are something like the following.

Drawing on the work of Northrop Frye, White says that a historical interpretation, like a poetic fiction, can be 'said to appeal to its readers as a plausible representation of the world by virtue of its implicit appeal to those "pre-generic plot-structures" or arche-typal story forms that define the modalities of a given culture's literary endowment'. That is to say, historians, like poets and novelists, gain their 'explanatory affect' – over and above whatever formal arguments they offer – by building into their narratives 'patterns of meaning similar to those more explicitly provided by the literary art of the cultures to which they belong'. In other words, to be understood, historians must draw upon the 'fund of culturally provided *mythoi*' from within their social formation in order to constitute 'the facts' as figuring a story of a particular kind so that their readers can recognise it, appealing to their encapsulation within that same 'fund of *mythoi*' so that they can understand the historian's account of the past and its significance/meaning. In that sense, it is White's argument that the historical narrative is understood when and insofar as the events that make up the chronicle and story are recognised in the narrative form they are emplotted in. White pulls this all together thus:

> When the reader recognizes the story being told in a historical narrative as a specific kind of story – for example as . . . romance, tragedy, comedy. . . . [then] On this level of encodation, the historical discourse directs the reader's attention to a secondary referent, different in kind from the events that make up the primary referent; namely, the plot structures of the various story types cultivated in a given culture [this enabling the reader to comprehend] . . . the meaning produced by the discourse. This comprehension is nothing other than the recognition of the form of the narrative.[49]

For these reasons then – for the story the historian is telling to be understood by the culture in which he/she lives – such stories have to be encoded in recognisable, cultural forms. And there is a political point to all this as well. For (to again recall an earlier point) it is when all this is seen and understood; that is, when it is recognised (as the literary, the rhetorical, the deconstructive and other 'turns' of post-modernism make us recognise) that the stories that a given culture tells about itself and its past are seen precisely as *mythical* and thus arbitrarily constructed (that is, when histories are recognised as being metaphorical and allegorical) that ushers in that 'crisis' (if one has and/or does benefit from such myths) or that 'opportunity' (if one has not and/or does not benefit from them) signified by 'post-modernism', White seeing this as an opportunity of course (as we have already seen in Section One), the chance for the development of his own non-narrative histories of 'discontinuity'.

These explanations – on why emplotment, on why four modes and on how they work having been given – there now remains only the task of describing how White more specifically characterises romance, tragedy, comedy and satire *vis-à-vis* his general understanding of the formal way in which they combine to help transform/translate the past and its 'primitive' elements into narrative.

With regard to romance, White sees this form as effectively that of a heroic type of release from, or transcendence of, the situations in which individuals or groups or nations, etc., have found themselves. These will be emplotments which stress the triumph of, say, good over evil, of virtue over vice, of the struggle and (maybe) victory of the oppressed over their oppressor(s). For example, the defeat of slavery by abolitionists, the sometime resistance of the working classes to various forms of exploitation, the 'individual' rags-to-riches 'life story', the victory of democracy over fascism and totalitarianism(s), and so on. And the archetypal theme of satire is the precise opposite of the romantic, 'a drama dominated by the apprehension that man is ultimately a captive of the world rather than its master'; that in the end decay and death visit all and everything.[50] Consequently, histories emplotted in this mode are histories of suffering without any obvious redemption: the genocide afflicted on the indigenous American Indians; the Holocaust; the 'slave camps under the flag of freedom'.

Comedy and tragedy fall between romance and satire. In emplotments of a comedy type, hope is held out for at least the temporary triumph of man over his situation, and these are celebrated. But knowingly, and half expectedly, things can and do go wrong. And in tragic emplotment they invariably do, but not often enough or thoroughly enough to cast the tragic into the category of the satirical:

> The reconciliations which occur at the end of Comedy are reconciliations of men with men, of men with their world and their society; the condition of society is represented as being purer, saner, and healthier as a result of the conflict among seemingly inalterably opposed elements in the world; these elements are revealed to be, in the long run, harmonizable with one another. . . . The reconciliations that occur at the end of Tragedy are much more sombre; they are more in the nature of resignations of men to the conditions under which they must labour in the world [e.g. 'You'll never get rid of envy and greed and thus, say, social classes . . .']. . . . They set the limits on what may be aspired to and what may be legitimately aimed at for security and sanity in the world.[51]

These four archetypal emplotments, then, says White, provide us with a means of characterising the different kinds of explanatory effects a historian can use at the level of narrative emplotment. And of course the point of all this is simply the very obvious one by now – a point I noted briefly in Chapter 1 – that a narrative account is always a figurative account; is always an allegory.[52]

Turning now from emplotment to ideology, White argues that, whether historians know it or not, there is an irreducible ideological component in every historical account of the past, in that the claim to have discerned some form of coherence in a past which actually does not have any, 'brings with it theories of the nature of the historical world and of historical knowledge itself which have ideological implications for attempts to understand "the present", however this "present" is defined'. That is to say:

> Commitment to a particular *form* of knowledge predetermines the *kinds* of generalizations one can make about the present world, the kinds of knowledge one can have of it, and hence the kinds of projects one can legitimately conceive for changing that present or for maintaining it . . . indefinitely.[53]

And it is this last point – that all historians whether working in the upper or lower case are necessarily 'present-centred' – which draws White to the writings of Karl Mannheim to explain how this seems to work. (That is, that the argument that White will be running is that it just is the case that all of us invariably carry with us *into the past and back out again* a view of it which is not radically at odds with the way we read the present and the future; I mean could you see Geoffrey Elton ever writing an E. H. Carr history or thinking E. H. Carr's thoughts on history *per se*? And if you cannot – and you cannot – then might it not be plausible to suggest that this has something to do with how they read the present and the future in terms of ideological differences that transcend arguments about evidence not least because, as already noted, it is precisely the evidence that they are arguing about?) Anyway, in this context, how does White use Mannheim?

What White finds to the point in Mannheim is his view that the different positions on the ideological spectrum of class-divided (capitalist) societies – liberal, conservative, radical and anarchist – each have their own forms of 'social time-consciousness' and a notion of the extent to which historical processes can be 'rationally' understood. And also, White appreciates Mannheim's view (as expressed *inter alia* in his *Ideology and Utopia* and his essay,

Conservative Thought) that it is possible to demonstrate the ideo-logical bases and implications of 'the Rankean ideal of an objective historiography' as established as the academic *doxa* during the second half of the nineteenth century.[54]

Thus, says White, according to Mannheim, ideologies can be classified according to whether they are 'situationally congruent' (i.e. generally satisfied with the *status quo*) or 'situationally transcendent' (i.e. critical of it). Consequently, even those historians who profess that their works carry within them no particular ideological commit-ment are still ideological in that their very rejection is itself ideo-logical (for example – and to recall – to cultivate a study of the past 'for its own sake' is, at a time when such a view suggests that a study of the past for, say, 'women's sake', is illegitimate, is precisely as 'ideologically positioned' as the illegitimacy they seek to criticise). As White sums all this up:

> even those historians who professed no particular ideological commitment and who suppressed the impulse to draw explicit ideological implications from their analysis of past societies could be said to be writing from within a specifiable ideological frame-work, by virtue of their adoption of a position *vis-à-vis* the form that a historical representation ought to take . . . a 'contemplative' historiography is [thus] at least consonant with, when it is not a projection of, the ideological positions of the liberal and con-servative, whether its practitioners are aware of this or not.[55]

Consequently, it just being a fact that for White 'every history is attended by specifically determinable ideological implications', then he thinks that the four ideological positions that concern him each have their own specific views on (a) social change (b) the pace of change (c) different time orientations and (d) the temporal location of the utopian ideal. What do these things signify?

With respect to (a) social change, White argues that whilst all four ideological positions recognise its inevitability, they have different views as to both its desirability and the 'best' rate of change: conservatives are the most suspicious of changes to the *status quo*, whilst liberals, radicals and anarchists are less so, being corre-spondingly less or more optimistic about the prospects of *rapid* transformations of the social order. As to (b) the pace of change, White sees conservatives well-versed in the notion of a natural/ organic rhythm, liberals as holding, say, the 'social rhythm of the parliamentary debate' and evolutionary/piecemeal change, whilst

radicals and anarchists envisage the possibility of 'cataclysmic transformations' with the former more sensitive to the 'inertial pull of
inherited institutions' and therefore more concerned with the pro-
vision of the organisational means of effecting such changes than the
latter. With regard to (c) different time orientations, conservatives
tend to see historical evolution as the progressive elaboration of the
structure that currently prevails, and that this is just about the best
one can hope for for the time being. Liberals, on the other hand,
imagine a reformed *status quo*, whilst radicals and anarchists hope
for a significantly different future, the latter seeing the possibilities
of transformation more 'spontaneously' than the former. Finally
with regard to (d) the temporal location of any utopian ideal, White
follows Mannheim in suggesting that conservatives are the most
'socially congruent', anarchists the most 'socially transcendent', with
liberals and radicals in between. But for White the point to all this is
that all four take the prospect of change seriously, it being this which
accounts 'for their shared interests in history and their concern to
provide a historical justification for their programs': all four ideologies need to 'go to history'.

Consequently, all history is ideologically affected. And, this being
the case, White sees no possibility of there being some extra-
ideological grounds on which to arbitrate between these different
understandings of the historical process and their construction of
what counts as historical knowledge. Accordingly, White is interested in ideology not so that he can 'judge' the extent and degree of
conflicting ideological views on history, but merely to indicate 'how
ideological considerations enter into the historian's attempt to
explain the historical field and to construct a verbal model of its
processes in a narrative'.

Leaving ideology at this point and summing up so far, we can thus
say that for White, interpretation enters into historiography in at
least the three ways mentioned so far – in terms of argument,
emplotment and ideology. So, does this mean, asks White rhetorically, that the various combinations of these three modes is just a
matter of personal whim which may suggest that there are as many
interpretations in history as there are historians? White's answer is
no. For two reasons. First, White argues that an interesting pattern
has emerged with regard to how interpretation enters at the different
levels identified *vis-à-vis* the construction of a given historical
narrative:

The analysis of plot structures yields four types: Romance,

Comedy, Tragedy and Satire. That of explanatory strategies has produced four paradigms: [formist] . . . organicist, mechanistic, and contextualist. And the theory of ideology has produced four possibilities: anarchism, conservatism, radicalism, and liberalism. And although I have denied the possibility of assigning priority to one or another of the levels of interpretation . . . I believe that the types of interpretive strategies identified are structurally homologous. . . . Their homology can be graphically represented in the following table of correlations.

Mode of Emplotment	Mode of Explanation	Mode of Ideology
Romance	Formist	Anarchist
Comedy	Organicist	Conservative
Tragedy	Mechanistic	Radical
Satire	Contextualist	Liberal[56]

Now, of course, White is not suggesting that such correlations appear in the work of every historian – and in *Metahistory* itself White takes some four hundred pages to work out the correlations present in a group of nineteenth-century historians. Nevertheless, on the basis of this analysis, White is able to make a second point which leads him toward his theory of tropes. And it is this.

White argues that the recurrence of patterns in the various levels on which interpretation takes place suggests to him that such an arrangement might be held together by something operating at a more basic level which, as it were, metaphorically 'underpins' them. And for White if there is such an underpinning, then in history's case (as in other discourses as yet unreduced to the relative certainties of a science) it is a linguistic one: the theory of tropes. He puts it this way:

This [underpinning] ground is that of language itself, which, in areas of study such as history, can be said to operate *tropologically* in order to prefigure a field of perception in a particular modality of relationships. If we distinguish between those areas of study in which specific terminological systems . . . have been constituted as orthodoxy – as in physics . . . and those areas of study in which the problem is still to produce such a system of stipulated meanings and syntactical rules, we can see that history certainly falls into the latter field. This means that historiographical disputes will tend to turn, not only upon the matter of what are the facts, but also upon that of their meaning. But meaning, in turn, will be construed in terms of the possible modalities of natural language itself, and specifically in terms of the dominant tropological strategies by which unknown or unfamiliar phenomena are provided with meanings by ... [metaphors]. If we take the dominant tropes as four – metaphor, metonymy, synecdoche, and irony – it is obvious that in language itself, in its generative or prepoetic aspect, we might possibly have the basis for the generation of those types of explanation that inevitably arise in any field of study not yet disciplined.[57]

So we arrive at White's theory of tropes.

Now, there is no doubt that historians (let alone history students) find White's 'explanation by tropes' the most difficult area of his work to grasp. Consequently, so that we are not in that position, a few preliminary remarks may be in order rather than plunging straight away into a description of how tropes work, building, to begin with, on some of the points White has himself made in the quotation given immediately above: that is, we can say that White comes to his theory of tropes for (at least) the following sorts of argument.

History is not a science. It does not have a technical language. It does not have a language with specific terminological systems, with stipulated meanings for lexicographical elements and with the sort of explicit syntactical rules and grammar which, say, physics or chemistry has. Therefore, without such a generally agreed technical language and indeed, no agreement, actually, on what kinds of events make up their specific subject matter and how to categorise them, the historian has therefore no alternative but to make the unfamiliar (and ultimately unfathomable) past familiar through the use of figurative language: 'the historian's characteristic instrument of encodation, communication, and exchange is ordinary educated speech'.[58] And because this is the case – because for White ordinary language works metaphorically (and White is similar to Rorty at this point) to make the unfamiliar familiar through its 'figures of speech' – then such figurative 'tropes' are, as it were, 'literally' the only ways we have to 'figure things out'. Rhetorical tropes are therefore not some sort of optional extra to give an account a few flourishes and stylistic embellishments; rather, rhetorical tropes constitute one of the main ways in which ordinary language works in order to make meanings. And if all this is the case, then White seems correct to point out that all historical narratives (of whatever case, for we must recall that this is a formal theory of historical representation *per se*) presuppose figurative characterisations of the events/facts they purport to be representations of. This means at least two things. First, that 'historical narratives, considered purely as verbal artifacts, can be characterised by the mode of figurative discourse in which they are cast', and second, that it may well be that the kind of emplotment that the historian decides to use to give meaning to a set of events is 'dictated by the dominant figurative mode [tropes] of the language he has used to *describe* the elements of his account *prior* to his composition of a narrative', that tropes come 'before' the narrative and *pre-figure* (set up) the field.[59]

Within this preliminary context what, more specifically, is White driving at, and how, in a more detailed way, do tropes work? Well, in his *The Historical Text As Literary Artifact* (which, incidentally, contains material extremely useful for understanding some of the more cryptic remarks in *Metahistory*) White tells us that at a conference 'many years ago', he heard the literary theorist Geoffrey Hartman remark that to write a history meant that the historian had to place an event within a context by relating it as a part to some sort of conceivable (imagined) whole. And White says Hartman went on to say that, so far as he was aware, there were only two ways to relate parts to wholes: by the metaphors of metonymy and synecdoche. And White tells how, having been working on the thought of Vico and Hegel as well as Kenneth Burke, Hartman's remark confirmed his growing understanding that all historical knowledge seemed to have to be articulated through the four principle modes of figurative, linguistic representation: metaphor, metonymy, synecdoche and irony:

> My own hunch – and it is a hunch which I find confirmed in Hegel's reflections on the nature of nonscientific discourse – is that in any field of study which, like history, has not yet become disciplinized to the point of constructing a formal terminological system for describing its objects ... it is the types of figurative discourse that dictate the fundamental forms of the data to be studied.[60]

Which means, as White goes on to explain, that the figure – the shape – of the relationships which, in the finished account, will appear to be inherent (intrinsic in) the events of the area under study, will actually have been externally imposed on the field of study by the historian. In other words, because the events of the past cannot describe themselves and their 'relationships' (that they cannot 'figure themselves out') then it is the historian who, 'in the very act of *identifying* and *describing* the objects that he finds [in the past] . . . constitute[s] their subjects as possible objects of narrative representation by the very [tropological] language they use to *describe* them'.[61]

In other words – and to pull this together here – the four rhetorical tropes which ordinary language historians have to employ so that they can make meaningful/significant relationships amongst the events/facts they are discussing, pre-figure and thus underwrite and shape the way 'the past' will then be 'figured out' via the various modes of explanation by argument, emplotment and ideology; that is, that it is the linguistic tropes which shape and ultimately define the type of narrative account which then passes for an account of 'what the past as described (configured) was really like'. For White then, language – no matter how clear and common-sensical – or rather precisely because it is so common-sensical and 'ordinary' – is not some sort of Elton-like innocent medium for representing the past in the forms (relationships) in which they really were; rather, the events of the past are related to each other by virtue of the way language works, because of the way rhetorical tropes make relationships meaningful: by relating parts to wholes, wholes to parts, and so on. White goes on to explain and apply all this in detail. That is to say, he goes on to argue that whilst metonymy, synecdoche and irony are types of metaphor, they differ from each other and from the notion of metaphor itself in the kinds of reductions or integrations they 'cause' in the types of historical interpretations constructed. Thus, 'Metaphor is essentially *representational*, Metonymy is *reductionist*, Synecdoche is *integrative*, and Irony is *negational*'.[62] What does this mean 'historically'?

Taking metaphor itself in the first instance, White argues that an historian using metaphor as the governing trope will be giving a formist historiographical representation. Thus, for example, the metaphorical expression, 'the saviours of humanity – the working classes', affirms the adequacy of the working classes to the task of saving humanity in a figurative sense; that is, as an indication of the qualities of human decency and so on, possessed by the working classes. But in this metaphorical construction the saviours of humanity are not reduced to the working classes (as they would be if the phrase was read metonymically) nor is the essence of humanity taken to be identical to the working classes (as it would be in a synecdoche). Nor is the expression an implicit negation of what is explicitly affirmed, as it would be in the case of irony.

Following on from this, White comments that metonymy and synecdoche are secondary forms of metaphor. Metonymy is basically reductive, and thus provides the model for the form of explanation White has termed mechanistic. In metonymy, the reduction of the whole to the part is done in such a way as to assign priority to the parts for the ascription of meaning to any putative whole. So, for example, a form of explanation that is metonymic might see individual acts of resistance to colonialism as giving meaning to (as constituting) third-world nationalism, such individual acts 'standing in for' the general phenomena. Again, individual resistance to capitalist forms of factory discipline might be seen as giving meaning to the notion of working-class consciousness. In these ways two different objects are being compared as explicitly bearing a part–whole relationship.

Alternatively, a synecdochical trope would sanction a 'figuring out' movement in the opposite direction (from whole to parts); towards the integration of all apparently particular phenomena into a whole so that the particulars are understood in terms of that whole, as expressive of some sort of totality. And White thinks synecdoche is the basis for all organicist type explanations. So if, for example, one starts with the idea that all history is the history of class struggle (Marx) or all history is the deathbed of aristocracies (Pareto) so all and every act of class struggle or aristocratic decline can be treated as particular expressions of the general no matter how tenuous that whole–part relationship might 'appear'; in the end that relationship will always be 'found', that is, 'imposed'. Finally, White sees irony as a negational relationship constitutive of scepticism and cynicism; of comical or tragic modes of explanation. Thus, if one asserts that the working classes can be seen as if they are the saviours of mankind, then one can either mean it or, if it is written or delivered in a certain way, mean its opposite: that is, it would be ironic to think that the herd-like working classes are the saviours of humanity.

In other words, what all this amounts to is that if an historian has an attitude towards 'history' that leads him/her to favour, say, a synecdochical trope, then the way he/she will represent the past, the way he/she will 'figure it out' and shape it, will be to everywhere find particular signs of some type of overarching purpose or trajectory. Such an overarching totality/purpose is not actually to be 'found' in the past, of course, but adherence to this linguistic trope will suggest that it is. On the other hand, a series of negative ironies will cause the past to be 'read' as having no essence to be expressed in particularities, but will everywhere find the unexpected, the accidental, the comic, the tragic. Not that the comic or the tragic are actually inherent in the events/facts of the past – not least because an historian working in the synecdochical can 'explain' the same events/facts as non-tragic and non-comic. Indeed, as expressions of a whole trajectory – it being simply that if the historian has a disposition (an ideological predisposition) to trope the past, say, ironically, then ironic that past will definitely be seen (be made) to be.

To pull this together further and to start to sum up White on tropes. White thinks that *before* the historian brings to bear upon the historicised traces/data/chronicle under analysis the conceptual apparatus that he/she will use to explain it, he or she will have prefigured the field tropologically in order to prepare it for an overarching act of interpretation of a particular tropological kind. In this way the narrative account that the historian will eventually give – although it purports to be a verbal representation or picture (icon) of this or that aspect of the past – will always be a 'problematic' established tropologically and then solved by the various arguments of explanation simply because no problematic is inherent in the past itself. For the past itself does not have 'problems', only historians have those: 'historical problems' are the problems which historians themselves both 'create' and 'solve'. As White comments on all of this:

> Historical accounts purport to be verbal models, or icons, of specific segments of the historical process. But such models are needed because the documentary record does not figure forth an unambiguous image of [itself]. . . . In order to figure [out] 'what *really* happened' in the past, therefore, the historian must first *prefigure* as a possible object of knowledge the whole set of events reported in the documents. This prefigurative act is *poetic* . . . insofar as it is constitutive of the structure that will subsequently be imaged in the verbal model offered by the historian as a representation and explanation of 'what *really* happened'. . . . It is also constitutive of the *concepts* he will use to *identify the objects* that inhabit that domain and to *characterise the kinds of relationships* they can sustain with one another. In the poetic act which precedes the formal analysis of the field, the historian [therefore] both creates his object of analysis and predetermines the modality

of the conceptual strategies he will use to explain it. . . . In short, the theory of tropes provides us with a basis for classifying the deep structural forms of the historical imagination in a given period of its evolution.[63]

And to help make all this abundantly clear, let me end with an example which I hope makes White's point. It employs a rather vulgar Marxism.

Thus, let us imagine that in this Marxist account, all history is seen as a history of class struggle. Simply seeing history in this way (as a synecdoche) will thus pose for the historian the problem to be tackled (i.e. of explaining how certain events are examples of class struggle) and the way to tackle them (as relating such events to the overall notion of class struggle). Thus, this will be an example of a history written in the upper case. Once prefigured in this way, the relationship of whole to parts will be seen organically in terms of argumentation, with mechanistic elements to explain cause–effect details within the overarching framework. The mode of emplotment will be heroic and triumphalist and 'serious' – not tragic or comic or satirical – whilst the ideological input will be radical. In this reading of the past – prefigured by synecdoche and propelled by radicalism – the historical past just cannot possibly be seen as something to be explained by the argumentative mode of, say, formism, or emplotted satirically, even though exactly the same detailed events could be so construed by somebody else. Alternatively, it is barely conceivable that (say) Elton should trope his past as a synecdoche, in ideologically radical ways and use a romantic emplotment. And so on and so forth.

Accordingly, it would appear at least plausible to think that tropes work in the way White suggests and that all histories are metahistories. In which case metahistory – as a formal theory of historical representation in narrative form which points to 'the fact' that, precisely because of the arguments that are constitutive of the term metahistory historical 'content' is as much invented as found – seems to be a theory that all historians should at the very least consider. And they should of course consider it very critically – more critically than has been done in the description/exposition offered here. But for now, and in keeping with the positive reading given to White, he can be given the last word; a word from his own 'Conclusion' to *Metahistory*:

> In my view, no given *theory* of history is convincing . . . to a given public solely on the basis of its adequacy as an 'explanation' of the

'data' contained in its narrative, because, in history ... there is no way of pre-establishing what will count as a 'datum' and what will count as a 'theory' by which to 'explain' what the 'data' mean. In turn, there is no agreement over what will count as a specifically 'historical' datum. The resolution of this problem requires a metatheory. ... In history, I have argued, the historical field is [therefore] constituted as a possible domain of analysis in a linguistic act which is tropological in nature. The dominant trope in which this constitutive act is carried out will determine both the kinds of objects which are permitted to appear in that field as data and the possible relationships that are conceived to obtain among them. ... These precritical commitments to different modes of discourse and their constitutive tropological strategies account for ... different interpretations of history.[64]

SECTION THREE: ON THE USE OF WHITE

So, what might be the use of White today for history students coming to the question of what is history (my comments in this section concentrate on White's *Metahistory* having looked already at some of the consequences of White's views of 'what is history' in Section One)? My answer is twofold.

First, in these postmodern days, in these days of narrative, linguistic, discursive 'turns', students arguably ought to include an examination of White's ideas as the minimum starting point in terms of their thinking about how histories are made and what history might conceivably be. White's is not the final word, not least because White himself has moved on from his metahistory days, and beyond this injunction to take White seriously as a starting point for their own analyses, attention again needs to be brought to those critical of White. But although White may himself have moved on, I think that most of us have a lot of catching up to do, especially if we have lived our historical/intellectual lives in the relatively cramped intellectual habitat of the old Carr–Elton debate and formulations not dissimilar to it. For the point is that White himself inhabits a more interesting and arguably a far richer, more generous, more suggestive and open-ended world than Carr and Elton, and that, as I have said, White's world cannot be reached – indeed cannot even be imagined – from their vantage points. To illustrate how useful White's general ideas might arguably be for students, I want to draw up a list of the processes by which I think all histories are put through, then going

on to pose the question of how many variables seem to be unnecessary for any understanding of how histories might be made. At
the same time, the list I want to give is one which will not actually
be in the same order as White's categories as expounded in, say,
Metahistory, so that in this way the order of my list is something of
a criticism of White's ordering and perhaps the impression created
thereby. For, although White's categories are probably 'essential', I
think his order of presentation may be 'wrong' and that, more
particularly, he rather unexpectedly down-plays the ideological.
Thus, for example, White says that historians *initially* trope the
field and that tropes therefore *prefigure* and *precede* the modes of
argument, emplotment and ideology; that tropes come *first*. But, in
his presentations White – as we have seen and noted – invariably
discusses tropes *last*, hence giving the sometime impression that
tropes are something of an 'extra' and that they somehow 'come last'
not just in terms of presentation but in terms of analytical importance
too. And the particular point to add to this general one is that White
may also be wrong in again giving the impression that although
tropes are a manifestation of our attitudes (our ideological positions)
tropes come before ideology, whereas on my reading it is precisely
because one is of, say, a certain type of lower case historian (say
Elton) or a certain type of upper case historian (say Carr) that one
will be drawn to a particular way of 'figuring things out' in the first
place, and that it is therefore the ideological mode which *pre-
determines* which trope will be used to metaphorically do so.
However, be that as it may, the following list, which outlines how
the past is mediated and transformed into historiography, uses
White's categories but not his order. The question to be kept in mind
is this: how many of the categories are inessential to an understanding
of how histories are made today?

1 The actual past has gone. It has in it arguably neither rhyme nor
reason: it is sublime. The presence of the past is manifested only
in its historicised traces accessible now; such traces signify an
'absent presence'.

2 From work on that historicised archive, historians and those acting
as historians in the 'historical public sphere' (as historians in
universities and other places) informed by the extant historiography relevant to the area in question and their general notion
of what doing historical work might be like in the context of their
lives, extract from the traces of the historicised archive various

'data'/facts and so forth. Here ideology is at work. Consequently, at this point:

3 White's ideological modes of conservatism, liberalism, radicalism and anarchism become determinate;

4 these, in interpenetrative ways, then attract to them tropological modes of configuration: the tropes of metaphor, metonymy, synecdoche and irony. Subsequently,

5 these themselves interpenetrate with the modes of emplotment – romance, tragedy, comedy and satire – to then interpenetrate with the

6 modes of formist, contextual, mechanical and organic argumentation. Then,

7 the historian goes to work. The traces of the past are worked up into a chronicle and then

8 into a story form, a story form which answers such questions as, what comes next? What happened then? Here, already at all these stages, the modes of ideology, argument, emplotment and the tropes will already have been active (I mean: it's not as though the historian does all these things without a trope in his/her head) such modes, however, coming into their own as

9 the story is transformed into the narrative structure; such a structure being part trace and part imaginative configuration *vis-à-vis* the types of narrative forms existing in the culture in general (and the 'history culture' in particular) so as to re-order the resultant historiographical construct understandable, consumable, and thus, as an artifact – as a commodity like any other commodity – to exercise its various effects *vis-à-vis* the forces at work within any given social formation.

Now, the question to be put to those who might see White as being too complicated or too 'theoretical' (or even irrelevant) is simply this: in the construction of what now passes for historical knowledge, which of White's categories do historians, and which of White's categories could historians, do without? I mean, do they and could they do without the notion of the past as an 'absent presence'? Could they access 'it' in ways not archival, i.e. textual? Is there not a difference between trace, source, data, evidence, chronicle, story – and narrative? Is it not the case that narratives – narratives ideologicised, troped, emplotted, argued for – are not in those forms in 'the past'; in the 'past itself'? And if they are not, if the past is never history but just 'material', contingently waiting to be appropriated with reference to the social formation wherein the appropriations are being variously legitimated (or not), then, if ordinary language/ textuality is the basis for such histories as narrative, how can such constructions be made if not through language of a certain non-technical and thus metaphorical kind? And how can such metaphor-ical/rhetorical modes work if not metaphorically and rhetorically? And so on and so forth. In other words, just how many categories which White has identified are not very obviously in all histories of whatever case? And if it looks as if they are all necessary, then isn't it therefore plausible to suggest that White's is an 'essential' way of thinking, in preliminary ways, about how all this works both in White himself and how it might be extended, reorganised and possibly gone well beyond? Might it not be a good idea that historians, when constructing their histories, make quite explicit in their introductions and throughout their texts whenever appropriate, the ideological positions they are writing from, the dominant trope they are using, the type of argumentative mode and emplotment they favour, and that they make – to recall Barthes' point made in the Introduction – explicit the way they have consitituted their referent. And if this could be done – as it arguably should be done in order to make the histories that one is getting clean and 'upfront' – is it likely that, having gone on this journey of clarification, one would ever return to Carr and Elton except for the occasional nostalgic visit; a remembrance of things past? Well, these matters must be for the reader to decide.[65] But for me, I don't mind lining up with the sentiments White expresses for the sorts of advantages which might accrue if students start to think critically along these lines. This constitutes my second and last point on White. It runs as follows.

At the end of *The Historical Text as Literary Artifact*, White tries to justify both his own way of understanding history and the way in which that way of understanding might be useful to history students. These sentiments (from 1974) are now almost as old as Elton's *The Practice of History*, but they speak from another intellectual place, in a different register, and in an alternative way of thinking about and doing history. And they still have a resonance; a pertinence. Of course – and as has already been noted – in the years since then White has himself moved on, but not least because of the relative theoretical backwardness of history as a discourse *vis-à-vis* other discourses, White's comments might be reiterated in a concluding fashion now: they're still to the point. So what does White say?

He begins by saying that, of course, his insistence on the imaginative/fictive element in all historical narratives is certain to arouse the ire of historians who think they are doing something entirely different from the novelist in that they deal with the 'real' whilst novelists deal only with 'imagined' events. But they ought to think again. For 'history' is arguably made sense of in the same way that novelists and poets make sense, by endowing what originally appears problematical by a recognisable, familiar, disciplining form. In which case the different referents, real and imagined, are not to the point, for the way of making sense of them is the same. This – and this is a point not to be overlooked – in no way detracts from the status of the knowledge which is ascribed to historiography. For in a way nothing has changed. For if historiography has, as it were, always been metahistorical then, as in the same way that it has always been textual, different historians can, and will, go on filling such formalities by their own substantive narratives, save only for the fact that they now have a reflexive understanding of how the discourse they are involved in perhaps works. Maybe in the end that is the point of the whole exercise – for people to be in control of their own discourse; not to be fumbling in the half-light and not to claim that their view of the past is effectively the past's own. But maybe it is not only that either. For, conscious of the ideological component in all historiography, White argues that if historians were to recognise the fictive element in their history, then they would be aware of any and every history that bore down on them wearing the emblem of 'Truth'. For, by drawing history nearer to its literary sensibility, argues White, we should be able to easily identify the ideological and certaintist element both in other people's histories and our own. And if, he says, we thus recognise and make explicit the fictive element in our histories, then our understanding of historiography could move to a higher level of self-consciousness than most of us currently occupy. And White sees this raising of the consciousness of his students to be part of his task as a teacher. For,

> What teacher has not lamented his inability to give instructions to apprentices in the *writing* of history? What graduate student has not despaired at trying to comprehend and imitate the model which his instructors *appear* to honour but the principles of which remain uncharted? If we recognize that there is a fictive element in all historical narrative, we would find in the theory of language and narrative itself the basis for a more subtle presentation of what historiography consists of than that which simply tells the student

to go and 'find the facts' and write them up in such a way as to tell 'what really happened'.

In my view, history . . . is in a bad shape today because it has lost sight of its origins in the literary imagination. In the interests of *appearing* scientific and objective, it has repressed and denied to itself its own greatest source of strength and renewal. By drawing historiography back once more to an intimate connection with its literary basis, we should not only be putting ourselves on guard against *merely* ideological distortions; we should be by way of arriving at that 'theory' of history without which it cannot pass for a 'discipline' at all.[66]

SECTION FOUR: LOOSE ENDS

There are no further conclusions I wish to draw in this text: Carr, Elton, Rorty and White can be left at this point. Yet at the same time it might be useful for me to pull together, in the form of a 'definition', some of the strands of thought I have tried to present in an introductory way. This definition, like all definitions of this type, is obviously not definitive. In fact it is not really a definition at all, being more like a summary of some of the 'key' areas discussed. And I am aware that in these 'postmodern days' even 'definitions' of this kind are – what else? – the stuff of cliché. Nevertheless, with all its faults and limitations and provisionality, it is sometimes useful to have this kind of summary/definition available for discussion and perhaps for future work. And so I end with what, for me, history might – in the context of this text only – be read as today:

> History is arguably a verbal artifact, a narrative prose discourse of which, après White, the content is as much invented as found, and which is constructed by present-minded, ideologically positioned workers (historians and those acting as if they were historians) operating at various levels of reflexivity, such a discourse, to appear relatively plausible, looking simultaneously towards the once real events and situations of the past and towards the narrative type 'mythoi' common – albeit it on a dominant-marginal spectrum – in any given social formation. That past, appropriated by historians, is never the past itself, but a past evidenced by its remaining and accessible traces and transformed into historiography through a series of theoretically and method-ologically disparate procedures (ideological positionings, tropes,

emplotments, argumentative modes), such historiography – as articulated in both upper and lower cases – then being subject to a series of uses which are logically infinite but which, in practice, correspond to the range of power bases that exist at any given juncture and which distribute/circulate the meanings drawn from such histories along a dominant–marginal spectrum. Understood in this way, as a rhetorical, metaphorical, textual practice governed by distinctive but never homogeneous procedures through which the maintenance/transformation of the past is regulated (après Bennett) by the public historical sphere, historical construction can be seen as taking place entirely in the present, historians *et al.* organizing and figuring this textual referent not as it was but as it is, such that the cogency of historical work can be admitted without the past *per se* ever entering into it – except rhetorically. In this way histories are fabricated without 'real' foundations beyond the textual, and in this way one learns to always ask of such discursive and ideological regimes that hold in their orderings suasive intentions – *cui bono* – in whose interests?

Notes

INTRODUCTION: HISTORY, THEORY, IDEOLOGY

1 K. Jenkins, *Re-Thinking History*, London, Routledge, 1991. Like *Re-Thinking History*, this text is not meant to be scholarly; it is no monograph. Rather it is written in a popular, 'teacherly' but hopefully challenging way with the aim of encouraging students to develop an interest in the areas it touches upon such that they might go on to the more scholarly debates, some of which I cite in my footnotes.

2 Books of an introductory nature which do look at 'movements', general approaches and so on include: A. Marwick, *The Nature of History*, London, Macmillan, 3rd ed. 1989; J. Tosh, *The Pursuit of History*, London, Longman, 2nd ed. 1991; G. McLennan, *Marxism and the Methodologies of History*, London, Verso, 1981; A. Callinicos, *Making History*, New York, Cornell University Press, 1988.

3 The works I mainly draw on are, for Hayden White: *Tropics of Discourse* (1978), *Metahistory* (1973), *The Content of the Form* (1987), all Baltimore, Johns Hopkins University Press. For Richard Rorty: *Philosophy and the Mirror of Nature*, Princeton, Princeton University Press, 1979; *Consequences of Pragmatism*, Minneapolis, Minnesota University Press, 1982; *Contingency, Irony, and Solidarity*, Cambridge, Cambridge University Press, 1989; *Objectivity, Relativism and Truth* and *Essays on Heidegger and Others, Philosophical Papers*, vols 1 and 2, both Cambridge, Cambridge University Press, 1991.

Of course Rorty and White have written articles and reviews which have appeared in other places, but because of the introductory nature of this book I have used primarily those works which students coming to Rorty and White for the first time might find most accessible and most available. In passing, I shall myself have occasion to refer to some of Rorty and White's other pieces, but my treatment of both of them is quite consciously based on the works (for these are their major works) cited above.

4 E. H. Carr, *What is History?* London, Macmillan, 1961, and London, Pelican, 1964; 2nd ed. 1987, reprinted in Penguin Books, 1990.

5 G. Elton, *The Practice of History* (1967), the edition used, London,

Fontana, 1969; *Political History: Principles and Practice*, London, Penguin, 1970; *Return to Essentials*, Cambridge, Cambridge University Press, 1991. R. W. Fogel and G. Elton, *Which Road To The Past?* London, Yale University Press, 1983. I completed the final draft of this book on 23 November 1994 and I learnt of the sad death of Sir Geoffrey Elton (on 4 December 1994) shortly afterwards. Because this text has much to say which is critical of Elton, and because it will be published so soon after his death, I would point out that my views on Elton are not, of course, views on the man himself, but only on his ideas on the nature of history and the way these are articulated. I say this not least because I am very much aware of Elton's enormously sustained, rich, suggestive and provocotive scholarship in his own chosen historical field, and that this side of Elton's work – its main side – must be evaluated by those who also work in this area. My comments on Elton are restricted, then, to his views on the nature and practice of history; it is no part of the remit I have set myself to be concerned with issues other than those.

6   D. LaCapra, *History and Criticism*, London, Cornell University Press, 1985, p. 137.

7   For a bibliography of Rorty's works from 1959 to 1989, see, A. Malachowski (ed.) *Reading Rorty*, Oxford, Blackwell, 1990, pp. 371–8.

8   H. A. Veeser (ed.) *The New Historicism*, London, Routledge, 1989. Since the publication of *The Content of the Form* in 1987, White has written several pieces which have appeared either in journals or as chapter contributions to books. For an analysis of some of these pieces and their critical reception see Wulf Kansteiner's article, 'Hayden White's Critique of the Writing of History', in *History and Theory*, 32, 3 (1993), pp. 273–95. Kansteiner's excellent footnotes will lead those interested not only to White's recent writings but also to most of the critical discussion of White which has appeared recently.

9   See T. Bennett on this, *Outside Literature*, London, Routledge, 1990, ch. 3 *passim*.

10 Another way of putting the argument I am running is to see it as an 'end of history' argument; that is, that given our histories in both upper and lower cases are modernist, then with the end of modernity, so we reach the end of modernity's versions of the past. An interesting approach to this problem and its implications for social history not only epistemologically and methodologically but ideologically, is in a forthcoming article by Patrick Joyce, 'The End of Social History', in *Social History*, 20, 1, Jan. 1995. I am grateful to Patrick Joyce for early sight of this paper.

The kind of postmodernism I have depicted is articulated somewhat differently by Hans Bertens in his *The Idea of the Postmodern*, London, Routledge, 1995. Nevertheless Bertens' Introduction and especially his Conclusion seem to me to substantiate the general drift of my argument.

11 See, for example: R. J. Bernstein, *The New Constellation*, Oxford, Polity Press, 1991; A. Malachowski (ed.) *op. cit.*; R. Bhaskar, *Philosophy and the Idea of Freedom*, Oxford, Blackwell, 1991; C. Norris, *Uncritical Theory*, London, Lawrence and Wishart, 1992; C. Norris, *The Truth about Postmodernism*, Oxford, Blackwell, 1993.

On 'Rorty bashing', Bernstein comments that 'Rorty has offended and antagonised just about everyone – the political left and right, traditional liberals, feminists, and both analytic and Continental philosophers. His "strong" readings of key figures strike many as idiosynscratic creations of his own fantasies. He has been accused of being "smug", "shallow", "elitist", "priggish", "voyeuristic", "insensitive", and "irresponsible". "Rorty-bashing" is rapidly becoming a new culture industry' (p. 260). Yet, although Bernstein's own critique is extremely perceptive, he argues that even if Rorty doesn't always answer the questions he raises, his importance is that he raises them, concluding that 'Rorty helps to accomplish for our time what that other great ironist, Socrates, did in his historical context' (p. 291). This may be a little over the top, but the Rorty that is presented in this text is, in a way, that sort of Rorty.

12 See, for example, the collection of essays in *History And Theory*, Beiheft, 19 (1980); *Metahistory: Six Critiques*, and the debates over epistemology and narrativity which run throughout *Knowing and Telling History: The Anglo-Saxon Debate*, in *History and Theory*, Beiheft 25 (1986); P. Zagorin, 'Historiography and Postmodernism: Reconsiderations', in *History and Theory*, 29 (1990), pp. 263–74. See also one of the most insightful essays on White; namely, H. Kellner, 'Narrativity in History; Post-Structuralism and Since', in *History and Theory*, Beiheft 26 (1987), pp. 1–29.

I have already (note 8 above) cited Kansteiner's article, which, because it is the last critical essay to appear directly on White which I have seen, very usefully brings criticism of White pretty much up to date. An exchange (which I suspect will be of a popular type) between Arthur Marwick and Hayden White on 'the nature of history' is due to appear in the January and April 1995 issues respectively of the *Journal of Contemporary History*. A preview of this exchange appeared in the *Times Higher Education Supplement*, November 25th 1994, pp. 17–18. White's presence also lies behind much of Chris Lorenz's article, 'Historical Knowledge and Historical Reality: A Plea for "Internal Realism"', *History and Theory*, 33, 3 (1994). Again, Lorenz's footnotes will lead readers to many of the critics and critiques of White's work.

13 LaCapra, *op. cit.*, pp. 135–6.

14 D. MacCannell, *Empty Meeting Grounds*, London, Routledge, 1992, pp. 9–10.

CHAPTER 1: HISTORY TODAY

1 T. Bennett, *Outside Literature*, London, Routledge, 1991; see also, K. Jenkins, 'Marxism and Historical Knowledge: Tony Bennett and the Discursive Turn', *Literature and History*, Third Series 3/1, 1994, pp. 16–30.

2 Bennett, *op. cit.*, p. 50.

3 ibid., p. 49.

4 ibid., p. 50.

5 ibid., pp. 50–1.

6 An interesting discussion of Derrida's expression there is 'nothing outside the text' has been analysed and related to its Nietzschean 'origins' in *Nietzsche's Case* by B. Magnus, P. Stewart and J. P. Mileur, London, Routledge, 1993, p. 14 *et passim*.

7 H. White, *Tropics of Discourse*, Baltimore, Johns Hopkins University Press, 1978, p. 82; *Metahistory*, Baltimore, Johns Hopkins University Press, 1973, p. 2.

8 H. White, *The Content of the Form*, Baltimore, Johns Hopkins University Press, 1987, pp. ix–xi.

9 F. R. Ankersmit, 'Reply to Professor Zagorin', *History and Theory*, 29 (1990), pp. 275–96. Ankersmit's argument is basically derived from White – whom he champions – and has a complexity and richness only hinted at here. See also H. Kellner, 'Narrativity in History; Post-Structuralism and Since', *History and Theory*, 26 (1987), pp. 1–29, for comments on both Ankersmit and White.

10 ibid., p. 278. White and Ankersmit have been challenged by many historians and philosophers of history for their relativism. The article by C. Lorenz, 'Historical Knowledge and Historical Reality: A Plea for "Internal Realism"', in *History and Theory*, 33, 3 (1994), is one of the latest attempts to refute the sort of position White and Ankersmit allegedly occupy. My own view is that Lorenz's position does not lead to a convincing critique of White and Ankersmit but this sort of detailed critique cannot be conducted in this particular text. More specific than Lorenz is David Carr's rejection of 'impositional narratives' in *Time, Narrative, and History*, Indianapolis, Indiana University Press, 1986.

11 H. White, *The Content of the Form*, p. 57.

12 ibid., p. 48.

13 H. White, *Tropics of Discourse*, p. 3.

14 L. Stone, 'History and Post-Modernism', in *Past and Present*, 131 (1991), pp. 217–8; L. Stone, 'History and Post-Modernism', in *Past and Present*, 135 (1992), pp. 189–94; G. M. Spiegel, 'History and Post-Modernism', in *Past and Present*, 135 (1992), pp. 194–208. See also, G. M. Spiegel, 'History, Historicism, and the Social Logic of the Text in the Middle Ages', in *Speculum*, lxv (1990), pp. 59–86. See also, the article in favour of postmodernism by Patrick Joyce and Catriona Kelly, 'History and Postmodernism', in *Past and Present*, 133 (1991), pp 204–13.

15 L. Stone, *Past and Present*, 135, p. 190. Lawrence Stone has discussed White's relativism in the following terms: 'I agree in denouncing the appalling corruption of style in the writing of history by social science jargon and linguistic and grammatical obfuscation. I also agree that we should fight to preserve from the attacks by extreme relativists, from Hayden White to Derrida, the hard-won professional expertise in the study of evidence that was worked out in the late-nineteenth century.' L. Stone, 'Dry Heat, Cool Reason: Historians under Siege in England and France', in *TLS*, 31 January, 1992.

In this respect Stone is close to Elton as well as other advocates of 'hard professionalism' such as Arthur Marwick (see for example Marwick's article, '"A Fetishism of Documents"?: The Salience of Source-Based History', in H. Kozicki (ed.), *Developments in Modern Historiography*, New York, St Martin's Press, 1993, pp. 107–38.). Accordingly, as Kansteiner points out, in the minds of such historians as Stone, 'the source material contains the narrative rationalisation of past agents which represents one relevant version of the past and which through the hindsight and the questions of the historian can be rendered into a historically relevant and truthful account.' Kansteiner also makes the point, which I think supports my own argument with regard to my critique of 'revisionists', that the 'relativism' of White brings together in a common defence of 'proper history' not only professional historians such as Stone *et al.* but also philosophers of history (such as Dray and Mandelbaum) and some Marxists (such as Eagleton who accuses White of idealism) concluding: 'This reaction shows that White has struck a widely held, sensitive consensus about the political and social functions of historical writing: the task to render justice and to provide political orientation on the grounds of facticity. The charge of relativism has [thus] limited his practical influence among historians, and at times unified a fragmented discipline against White's critique.' W. Kansteiner, 'Hayden White's Critique of the Writing of History', in *History and Theory*, 32, 3 (1993), pp. 273–95, pp. 287–8.

16 G. M. Spiegel, *Past and Present*, 135, pp. 195–7.

17 G. Elton, *Return to Essentials*, Cambridge, Cambridge University Press, 1991, p. 54.

18 See, for example, C. Norris, *The Truth About Postmodernism*, Oxford, Blackwell, 1993; T. Eagleton, *Literary Theory: An Introduction*, Oxford, Blackwell, 1983; A. Callinicos, *Against Postmodernism*, Oxford, Polity Press, 1989; F. Jameson, *Postmodernism, or, the Cultural Logic of Late Capitalism*, London, Verso, 1991; R. Samuel, 'Reading the Signs I', *History Workshop Journal*, 32 (1991), pp. 88–109, and, 'Reading the Signs II', *History Workshop Journal*, 33 (1992), pp. 220–51.

19 E. Fox-Genovese, 'Literary Criticism and the Politics of the New Historicism', in H. A. Veeser (ed) *The New Historicism*, London, Routledge, 1989, pp. 213–24.

20 See, for example, Bennett, *op. cit.*, ch. 3.

21 G. McLennan, *Marxism and the Methodologies of History*, London, Verso, 1981, p. 234.

22 H. White, 'New Historicism: A Comment', in Veeser, *op. cit.*, pp. 293–302, p. 297.

23 S. Fish, 'Commentary: The Young and the Restless', in Veeser, ibid., pp. 303–16, p. 305.

24 H. White, 'New Historicism: A Comment', in Veeser, ibid., p. 296.

25 S. Fish, 'Commentary: The Young and the Restless', in Veeser, ibid., p. 305.

26 H. White, in Veeser, ibid., p. 295.

27 S. Fish, *Doing What Comes Naturally*, Oxford, Oxford University Press, 1989, *passim*.

28 B. McHale, *Constructing Postmodernism*, London, Routledge, 1992, pp. 4–5.

29 R. Samuel, 'Reading the Signs II', pp. 220–1.

30 Bennett, *op. cit.*; C. Mouffe and E. Laclau, *Hegemony and Socialist Strategy*, London, Verso, 1985; E. Laclau, *New Reflections on the Revolution of Our Time*, London, Verso, 1990; D. Hebdige, *Hiding In The Light*, London, Routledge, 1988.

31 B. K. Marshall, *Teaching the Postmodern*, London, Routledge, 1992, p. 4.
32 G. Elton, *The Practice of History*, London, Fontana, 1969, p. 11.
33 R. Rorty, *Contingency, Irony and Solidarity*, Cambridge, Cambridge University Press, 1989, p. 61 and p. xv.
34 ibid., p. 86.
35 H. White, *op.cit.*, p. 434.
36 H. White, *The Content of the Form*, p. 164.

CHAPTER 2: ON E. H. CARR

1 J. Tosh, *The Pursuit of History*, London, Longman, 1991, pp. 236, 29, 148.
2 G. McLennan, *Marxism and the Methodologies of History*, London, Verso, 1981, p. 103; D. LaCapra, *History and Criticism*, London, Cornell University Press, 1985, p. 137.
3 The continuing popularity and status of Carr's *What is History?* is difficult to explain. Thus, in *Myths of the English*, Roy Porter, in his introduction, writes that 'the questions of historical objectivity and historical method . . . have never been better discussed than in E. H. Carr's *What is History?*' Yet, this remark, in footnote 6 of Porter's Notes, is followed, in footnotes 7 and 8, by references to some of the most sophisticated contemporary discussions of these areas by, for example, Culler, Barthes, Baudrillard, Greenblatt, *et al.* Against such theorists Carr is banal. Thus, one can only conclude that Carr is just so established in 'our' historical consciousness that naming him in these sorts of contexts is a knee-jerk reaction; for certainly Porter's comment cannot be sustained. Perhaps Carr's 'deserved prominence' is one of our English myths! R. Porter (ed.), *Myths of the English*, Oxford, Polity Press, 1992, p. 7.
4 E. H. Carr, *What is History?* London, Penguin, 1987, p. 16.
5 ibid., pp. 9–10.
6 ibid., pp. 10–11.
7 ibid., pp. 11–12.
8 ibid., pp. 12–13.
9 ibid., pp. 19–20.
10 ibid., p. 3.
11 ibid., p. 4.
12 ibid., p. 5.
13 ibid., p. 6.
14 ibid., p. 6.
15 ibid., p. 20.
16 ibid., p. 21.
17 ibid., p. 22.
18 ibid., p. 22.
19 ibid., p. 22.
20 ibid., p. 26.
21 For a different reading of Collingwood which takes into account Carr, see P. Q. Hirst, *Marxism and Historical Writing*, London, Routledge & Kegan Paul, 1985, ch. 3, pp. 43–56.

22 Carr, *op. cit.*, p. 26.
23 ibid., p. 27.
24 ibid., p. 30.
25 ibid., p. 125.
26 ibid., p. 130.
27 ibid., p. 131.
28 ibid., p. 132.
29 ibid., p. 132.
30 ibid., pp. 123–4.
31 ibid., p. 123.
32 ibid., p. 123.
33 ibid., p. 121 and p. 132.
34 ibid., p. 162.
35 Tosh, *op. cit.*, p. 148.

CHAPTER 3: ON GEOFFREY ELTON

1 G. Elton, *Return to Essentials*, Cambridge, Cambridge University Press, 1991, p. 3.
2 G. Elton, *The Practice of History*, 1967; London, Fontana, 1969, pp. vii–viii.
3 ibid., p. vii.
4 ibid., p. viii.
5 G. McLennan, *Marxism and the Methodologies of History*, London, Verso, 1981, p. 102. The remark, 'We even get paid – isn't that marvellous' is taken from a BBC2 Programme, 'Thinking Aloud'.
6 Elton, *Return to Essentials*, p. 3.
7 McLennan, *op. cit.*, p. 102.
8 I have not referred in this text to Elton's *Political History: Principles and Practice*, London, Penguin, 1970, because it is hardly ever referred to by anybody else and my concern here is with the 'popular' Elton, especially the Elton of *The Practice of History* and *Return to Essentials*. In some ways certain chapters in *Political History* are more theoretical (ch. 4 'Explanation and Cause' for example). His final chapter, 'The End Product', is also interesting for his views on history having to be a story: 'in the end there will be a story to tell', especially in the light of White's critique of narrative. At the same time, much of Elton's 'position' is 'transferred' from *The Practice of History* and there is little or no 'new' insight on his view of history in his later text.
9 Elton, *The Practice of History*, p. 31.
10 ibid., p. 33.
11 ibid., p. 40.
12 ibid., p. 42.
13 Thus, on the theoretical nature of empiricism and lower case history, McLennan writes: 'In Britain, disagreement over the fundamentals of methodology has only quite recently become a notable feature of historians' discourse. Previous quietude, however, was not so much a rejection of philosophical underpinning as a consensus around [an ostensibly a-theoretical set of] *empiricist*, or at any rate particularistic,

norms. Of course, it is characteristic of empiricism that theoretical reflection is systematically discouraged in the promotion of the primacy of observational facts or data. This philosophical statement of priorities emerges in the guise of a common-sense embargo on "useless" speculation as a diversion from everyday practical consciousness (including that of the practical historian)' *op. cit.*, p. 97.

14 Elton, *Return to Essentials*, p. 26.
15 ibid., pp. 41–3.
16 ibid., p. 43.
17 Elton, *The Practice of History*, p. 19.
18 Elton, *Return to Essentials*, p. 8.
19 ibid., p. 9.
20 ibid., p. 49.
21 ibid., pp. 52–3.
22 ibid., p. 66.
23 ibid., pp. 66–9 *passim.*
24 ibid., pp. 72–3.
25 M. Stanford, 'History: Reflection on Principles and Practice', in *History Review*, 17 (1993), pp. 22–7, p. 23.
26 McLennan, *op. cit.*, p. 99.
27 ibid., p. 98.
28 Elton, *The Practice of History*, p. 177.
29 ibid., p. 77.
30 ibid., p. 71.
31 ibid., p. 71.
32 ibid., p. 73.
33 ibid., p. 73.
34 ibid., p. 74.
35 ibid., p. 74.
36 ibid., p. 74.
37 P.Q. Hirst, *Marxism and Historical Writing*, London, Routledge & Kegan Paul, 1985; R. Johnson (*et al.*) 'Popular Memory: theory, politics, method', in *Making Histories* (Centre For Contemporary Cultural Studies) London, Hutchinson, 1982, pp. 205–52; R. Barthes, 'The Discourse of History', in E. S. Shaffer, *Comparative Criticism: A Yearbook 3*, Cambridge, Cambridge University Press, 1981, pp. 7–20. See also D. Attridge, G. Bennington and R. Young (eds) *Post-Structuralism and the Question of History*, Cambridge, Cambridge University Press, 1987, *passim.*
38 Hirst, *op. cit.*, p. 78.
39 ibid., p. 78.
40 ibid., p. 78.
41 ibid., p. 78.
42 ibid., p. 79.
43 ibid., p. 79.
44 ibid., p. 81.
45 See D. Attridge *et al.* (eds), *Post Structuralism and the Question of History*, p. 3.
46 ibid., p. 3.

47 ibid., p. 3.
48 Johnson, *op. cit.*, p. 225.
49 ibid., p. 225.
50 H. White, *The Content of the Form*, Baltimore, Johns Hopkins University Press, 1987, p. 26.
51 ibid., p. 1.
52 Elton, *The Practice of History*, p. 124.
53 ibid., pp. 128–9.
54 ibid., p. 148.
55 ibid., p. 176.
56 ibid., p. 177.
57 White, *op. cit.*, pp. 26–57.
58 ibid., p. 27.
59 ibid., p. 30.
60 ibid., p. 31.
61 ibid., p. 31.
62 For some further 'introductory' approaches to reading texts, see R. Selden and P. Widdowson, *A Reader's Guide to Contemporary Literary Theory*, London, Harvester, 1993.
63 White, *op. cit.*, p. 31.
64 ibid., p. 31.
65 Elton, *Return to Essentials*, p. 3.
66 ibid., p. 3.
67 E. P. Thompson, *The Poverty of Theory*, London, Merlin, 1978.
68 ibid., p. 197.
69 R. F. Atkinson, *Knowledge and Explanation in History*, London, Macmillan, 1978, p. 7. As Atkinson goes on to add, 'Philosophers interest themselves in history for their own purposes: the instrumental value, or disvalue, of their investigations to history is wholly accidental', p. 8.
70 Elton, *Return to Essentials*, p. 28.
71 ibid., p. 36.
72 Deconstructionism as a concept has been variously interpreted. In his *Deconstruction: Theory and Practice* (Routledge, 1991) Christopher Norris offers the following definition of the verb to deconstruct: 'an ambivalent or middle voice verb [which includes reading] texts with an eye sharply trained for contradictions, blindspots, or moments of hitherto unlooked for complication' (p. 137). I think my own little piece of deconstruction comes close to this definition, but there are others, as Norris goes on to point out. For example, Norris talks of deconstruction as 'thinking that systematically challenges consensus values from a sceptical, dissenting or oppositional standpoint' (p.136); as taking things apart 'in a spirit of game-playing nihilist abandon and without the least concern for constructing some better alternative' (p.137) in the very Derridean sense of arguing that texts deconstruct themselves. That is, by careful readings texts themselves have unbearable tensions that destroy any univocal, unambiguous reading or essential meaning. Norris, now much less a fan of deconstructionism than he perhaps was, sees all these as just variants of the current postmodern turn across various areas of thought. I return again to some of Norris' increasingly anti-postmodern arguments in my chapter on Rorty.

CHAPTER 4: ON RICHARD RORTY

1 R. Rorty, *Consequences of Pragmatism*, Minneapolis, University of Minnesota Press, 1982, p. 208. Rorty's almost life-long engagement with (and renunciation of) the Platonic 'Western Tradition' is, for me, best described in his autobiographical essay, 'Trotsky and the Wild Orchids', *Common Knowledge*, Winter, 1992, pp. 140–53. I have found this essay not only informative but, in its recollections, strangely moving. For students coming to Rorty for the first time this essay (also published in the USA in M. Edmundson (ed.) *Wild Orchids and Trotsky*, New York, Penguin, 1993) could be read initially as an invaluable introduction to Rorty's general 'position'.
2 ibid., p. xxv.
3 R. Rorty, *Contingency, Irony, and Solidarity*, Cambridge, Cambridge University Press, 1989.
4 ibid., p. 5.
5 ibid., p. 5.
6 ibid., p. 5.
7 ibid., p. 6.
8 ibid., p. 6.
9 ibid., p. 7.
10 ibid., pp. 8–9.
11 ibid., p. 9.
12 Rorty, *Consequences of Pragmatism*, p. xiv.
13 See below, pp. 119–30.
14 R. Rorty, 'Solidarity or Objectivity', in *Objectivity, Relativism and Truth*, Cambridge, Cambridge University Press, 1991, pp. 21–34.
15 ibid., p. 21.
16 ibid., p. 21.
17 Rorty, *Consequences of Pragmatism*, ch. 11, 'Method, Social Science', and 'Social Hope', pp. 191–210 *passim*.
18 Rorty, *Objectivity, Relativism and Truth*, pp. 22–3.
19 Rorty, *Consequences of Pragmatism*, p. 193.
20 ibid., p. 193.
21 Rorty, *Objectivity, Relativism and Truth*, pp. 41–2.
22 ibid., p. 37.
23 ibid., p. 37 et *passim*.
24 ibid., pp. 41–2.
25 ibid., p. 45.
26 R. Rorty, *Essays on Heidegger and Others*, Cambridge, Cambridge University Press, 1991, pp. 8–26.
27 ibid., p. 12.
28 ibid., p. 12.
29 ibid., p. 13.
30 ibid., p. 13.
31 ibid., p. 14.
32 ibid., p. 16.
33 ibid., p. 17.
34 ibid., p. 18.

35 ibid., p. 18.
36 R. Bhaskar, *Philosophy and the Idea of Freedom*, Oxford, Blackwell, 1991; see especially pp. 70–8, et *passim*.
37 Rorty, *Essays on Heidegger and Others*, p. 19.
38 Rorty, *Objectivity, Relativism, and Truth*, pp. 13–14.
39 ibid., p. 13.
40 ibid., p. 13.
41 R. Rorty, 'Just One More Species Doing Its Best', in *London Review of Books*, vol. 13, no. 14, 25 July 1991, pp. 3–7, p. 6.
42 Rorty, *Contingency, Irony, and Solidarity*, p. xv.
43 ibid., p. 73.
44 ibid., pp. 73–4.
45 ibid., p. 78.
46 ibid., pp. xiii.
47 ibid., p. xiii–xiv.
48 ibid., p. 29. For a critique of Rorty's bifurcated polity, see, for example, Nancy Fraser, 'Solidarity or Singularity? Richard Rorty between Romanticism and Technocracy', in A. Malachowski (ed.), *Reading Rorty*, Oxford, Blackwell, 1990, pp. 303–21.
49 ibid., p. xiv.
50 ibid., p. xvi.
51 ibid., p. xvi.
52 M. Billig, 'Nationalism and Richard Rorty; The Text as a Flag for *Pax Americana*', in *New Left Review*, 202, 1993, pp. 69–84. For Rorty's own view of the various criticisms levelled at him from the political left and right, see his 'Trotsky and the Wild Orchids', *op. cit.*
53 Rorty, *Objectivity, Relativism, and Truth*, p. 15.
54 C. Norris, *Uncritical Theory: Postmodernism, Intellectuals and the Gulf War*, London, Lawrence & Wishart, 1992.
55 ibid., see especially chapters 3 and 6, pp. 52–158, et *passim*.
56 ibid., p. 64.
57 ibid., p. 64.
58 ibid., pp. 64–5.
59 ibid., p. 65.
60 ibid., p. 66.
61 ibid., p. 67.
62 ibid., p. 68.
63 Rorty, *Consequences of Pragmatism*, pp. 166–7.
64 ibid., pp. 167–78.
65 ibid., p. 168.
66 ibid., p. 169.
67 Rorty, *Objectivity, Relativism and Truth*, p. 190.
68 ibid, p. 42, and, 'Just One More Species Doing Its Best', p. 6.
69 Rorty, *Essays on Heidegger and Others*, *op. cit.*, pp. 177–92, p. 178.
70 Billig, *op. cit.*, *passim*.
71 Rorty, *Essays on Heidegger and Others*, p. 179.
72 ibid., p. 179.
73 ibid., p. 181.
74 ibid., p. 184.

75 ibid., p. 186.
76 ibid., p. 187.
77 ibid., p. 192.
78 S. Fish, *Doing What Comes Naturally*, Oxford, Oxford University Press, 1989.
79 ibid., p. 478.
80 ibid., p. 484.

CHAPTER 5: ON HAYDEN WHITE

1 H. White, *The Content of the Form*, Baltimore, Johns Hopkins University Press, 1987, p. 63.
2 ibid., p. 227. f.n. 12.
3 ibid., p. 227.
4 H. White, 'The Burden of History', in *Tropics of Discourse*, Baltimore, Johns Hopkins University Press, 1978, pp. 27–50. pp. 48–50. This point, that White would like his history to be directed towards a 'freedom' that would release us from the 'burden of history', is discussed by Hans Kellner in his essay 'White's Linguistic Humanism', in *History And Theory*, Beiheft 19, 1980, pp. 1–29. Here Kellner makes the point that White's 'existentialism' connects up to his reading of Nietzsche: 'Language, for Nietzsche, is the basic creative expression of a world of chaos; but when language congeals into a "legislation" that obscures its *made* nature, the way is clear for a tyranny of logic, "illusions about which one has forgotten that this is what they are". And history, as White makes plain, is equally a *made* object, which becomes a "burden" when it claims a privileged weight of truth' (p 7). Kellner also points out that White's criterion for what counts as a 'good history' is 'clear and simple'; namely, that historical writing should reinforce the sense of human mastery. 'His emphasis on *choice* (presented as both an aesthetic and a moral act) is repeated unmistakably; despite his full awareness of the claims of Marx and Freud, White persistently asserts human freedom' (p 17). I have found Kellner's essay, which 'places' *Metahistory* within the 'context' of White's 'career' up until the point of its writing, especially useful. See also, John Nelson's 'Tropal History And The Social Sciences: Reflections on Struever's Remarks', in the same volume, pp. 80–101, and Kellner's later essay, 'Narrativity in History: Post-Structuralism and Since', in *History and Theory*, Beiheft 26, 1987, pp. 1–29.
5 White *Tropics of Discourse*, p. 44.
6 White, 'The Politics of Historical Interpretation: Discipline and De-Sublimation', in *The Content of the Form*, pp. 58–82.
   Kansteiner argues in his 'Hayden White's Critique of the Writing of History', in *History and Theory*, 32, 3 (1993), pp. 273–95 that since the publication of *The Content of the Form* in 1987, White has tried, in several essays, to meet some of the criticisms he has been subjected to both before and since that date, criticisms which, coming from historians, philosophers of history and literary critics, divide their attention between White's 'relativism' and his 'structuralism/formalism'. As Kansteiner puts it: 'The two most frequent criticisms of White's work –

its relativism and formalism – mark the respective borders and illustrate White's peculiar [and little imitated] position within American academe' (p.294). However, Kansteiner then goes on to say that the revisions which White has made to meet various critiques have been unconvincing, stating that 'neither White nor his critics have been able convincingly to refute the argument that White developed most succinctly in his essay "The Politics of Historical Interpretation: Discipline and De-Sublimation". The narrative strategies which we employ to make sense of our past evolve independently of the established protocols for gaining and asserting historical facts. This [relativising] circumstance applies to all historical representations but is most disturbing when considered in the context of the representation of Nazism' (p.295).

I would make two points about Kansteiner's comments. First, Kansteiner is correct to think that White hasn't been successful in solving the problem of relativism, which allows us, I think, to still use White's essay 'The Politics of Historical Interpretation . . .' as one of White's best statements on the nature/use of history – which is indeed a relativistic one. Secondly, however, I disagree with Kansteiner's fear that relativism might facilitate a Nazi reading of the past. It seems to me that whether we like it or not the kind of relativism which White articulates is a fact of life. Rorty's position on the relationship between relativism and possible Nazi interpretations is probably the only plausible position for an anti-Nazi to take up. See above, pp. 125–7.

 7 ibid., p. 72.
 8 ibid., p. 73.
 9 ibid., pp. 72–3.
10 ibid., p. 73.
11 ibid., p. 64.
12 ibid., p. 64.
13 ibid., p. 65.
14 ibid., p. 66–8 *passim*.
15 ibid., pp. 68–9.
16 ibid., p. 69.
17 ibid., pp. 70–2.
18 ibid., p. 72.
19 ibid., p. 73.
20 ibid., p. 73.
21 ibid., p. 81.
22 ibid., p. 81.
23 ibid., pp. 81–2.
24 ibid., p. 82.
25 White, *Tropics of Discourse*, p. 50.
26 White, 'Foucault Decoded: Notes from Underground', in *Tropics of Discourse*, pp. 230–60; 'Foucault's Discourse: The Historiography of Anti-Humanism', in *The Content of The Form*, pp. 104–41.
27 For some interesting views on the possibilities of Foucault which go in different directions, see, for example, B. K. Marshall, *Teaching the Postmodern*, London, Routledge, 1992, *passim* and Patrick Joyce, 'The End of Social History' in *Social History*, 20, 1, 1995.

28 Kansteiner argues that whilst in his post-1987 writings White begins to blur the distinction between 'the facts' and 'the plot structures' in an attempt to meet critiques of his relativism, nevertheless, the type of history which White likes is still close to the discontinuous histories he previously preferred. As Kansteiner puts it, White still argues that conventional historical narratives of continuity, etc., constitute an anachronistic form of knowledge, quoting White to this effect: 'It seems to me that the kinds of anti-narrative non-stories produced by literary modernism [and postmodernism] offer the only prospect for adequate representation of the kind of unnatural events that mark our era and distinguish it absolutely from all the "history" that has come before it', Kansteiner, *op. cit.*, p. 286. Kansteiner's comment on this is that White therefore always tends to be 'most appreciative of historians or theoreticians who acknowledge the chaos of the primary historical field and take this meaninglessness as a challenge to construct history in a politically and socially responsible fashion without completely erasing the traces of this construction in their texts' (p. 284).

I would make one comment here on White and narrative/non-narrative. I think that, despite White's critique of the sort of narrative he doesn't like, the sort of 'non-narrative narratives' he does are there to fulfil the same (or similar) purposes as narratives do for Rorty. Rorty, to recall, wants us to replace arguments by useful fictions; by useful narratives linking (say) the present to an imagined future. Similarly, White wants us to use the past and to tell of its sublimity and discontinuity to help us realise his sort of utopia. In that sense, both invent the pasts they think their futures need. It therefore seems to me that White isn't arguing against narratives *per se* (it may, after all, be 'almost natural' for humans to narrativise) but only that we realise our narratives are always constructed and not found and that we beware of other people's suasive narratives if we are to change our lives in the direction we like.

29 H. White, *Metahistory*, Baltimore, Johns Hopkins University Press, 1973, p. xi–xii.
30 ibid., p. 5.
31 ibid., p. 6.
32 ibid., pp. 6–7.
33 White, *Tropics of Discourse*, pp. 92–3.
34 For two very different arguments about 'translation' see, G. Steiner, *After Babel*, Oxford, Oxford University Press, 1975; I. Chambers, *Migrancy, Culture, Identity*, London, Routledge, 1994; esp. chapters 1, 2 and 5.
35 White, *Tropics of Discourse*, p. 94.
36 ibid., pp. 94–8.
37 ibid., p. 99.
38 White, *Metahistory*, p. 7.
39 White, *Tropics of Discourse*, p. 63.
40 ibid., p. 64.
41 White, *Metahistory*, p. 14.
42 White, *Tropics of Discourse*, p. 64.
43 White, *Metahistory*, p. 14.

44 White, *Tropics of Discourse*, p. 66.
45 ibid., p. 66.
46 ibid., p. 67.
47 White, *Metahistory*, pp. 20–1.
48 White, *The Content of the Form*, pp. 44–7.
49 ibid, pp. 42–3.
50 White, *Metahistory*, p. 9.
51 ibid., p. 9.
52 White, *The Content of the Form*, p. 48.
53 White, *Metahistory*, p. 21.
54 White, *Tropics of Discourse*, p. 68.
55 ibid., p. 69.
56 ibid., p. 70.
57 ibid., p. 72.
58 ibid., p. 94.
59 ibid., pp. 94–5.
60 ibid., p. 95.
61 ibid., p. 95.
62 White, *Metahistory*, p. 34.
63 ibid., pp. 30–1.
64 ibid., p. 429–30.
65 What I am advocating here – that we might at least start thinking about applying White's approaches as laid down in his main works and his later 'revisionist' essays – is to recommend something that has not really been tried. I pointed out in the Introduction (p.5) that White is generally little known or read in this country, and that whilst he has been subject to much debate in America, few historians in that country have wanted or been able to, as Kansteiner has shown, 'imitate him'. I am not advocating, of course, a slavish 'White school of historiography', but I do think that despite the many detailed criticisms levelled at aspects of White's work – criticisms which would have to be considered and integrated where necessary into any approach – his general position (Metahistory-style as I have tried to outline it) could be fruitfully developed so that our reflexiveness about the nature of historical representation might be increased. As to where White has moved on since the late 1980s, his concerns seem to be centred on a re-thinking of his 'relativism' and the usefulness of the 'middle-voice' as a mode of 'representation'. See especially White's essay 'Historical Emplotment and the Problem of Truth', in S. Friedlander (ed.) *Probing the Limits of Representation*, Cambridge, MA, Harvard University Press, 1992, pp. 37–53.
66 White, *Tropics of Discourse*, p. 99.

Further reading

In a typical bibliography, works already cited in the text are noted again and then supplemented by other works which may be relevant to the areas covered by the text but not directly cited. The result is a comprehensive list of works in alphabetical order. Whilst such a list is valuable, it is also rather unhelpful; for example, it doesn't inform the reader as to the degree and type of relevance the new works have to the arguments run in the text; it doesn't order the works in, say, their difficulty or the development of specific themes, and so on and so forth.

This Bibliographical Note does not therefore take the usual form. It does not include any of the works already cited in the notes. What I have done is to give a few examples of further reading under the following three categories:

(1) *Books on Postmodernism.* Here I list about a dozen introductory books on postmodernism, all of which have extensive bibliographies of their own and which between them offer a good coverage of the current debates, etc.

(2) *Books on History and Postmodernism.* Here I list a few works which I have found especially useful when thinking about the relationship between history and postmodernism and which again offer a good coverage of the sorts of argument which constitute 'the debates'.

(3) *Articles on History and Postmodernism.* Here I give a few titles of articles which seem to me to have a direct bearing on history and postmodernism in ways which will hopefully be familiar after having read the arguments of this current text, along with the names of several journals which also frequently carry articles relevant to this whole area.

A final point. After this book was written I read three works which, had they been published earlier, or had I had the opportunity to read them beforehand, I would have discussed at some length. These works, which ought to be considered, are *Telling the Truth About History* by Joyce Appleby, Lynn Hunt and Margaret Jacob (W. W. Norton, New York, 1994); *The Illusion of the End* by Jean Baudrillard (Polity, Oxford, 1994) and A. Callinicos, *Theories and Narratives: Reflections on the Philosophy of History*, Polity, Oxford, 1995. In 1995 Norman Geras' two-hundred page critical, engagement with Rorty is to be published by Verso: *Solidarity in the Conversion of Humankind*. A summary of Geras' position *vis-à-vis* Rorty is in his 'Language, Truth and

Justice', *New Left Review*, 209, 1995, pp. 110–35.

BOOKS ON POSTMODERNISM

Bauman, Z., *Intimations of Postmodernity*, Routledge, London, 1992.
Berman, M., *All that Is Solid Melts Into Air*, Verso, London, 1982.
Callinicos, A., *Against Postmodernism*, Macmillan, London, 1990.
Connor, S., *Theory and Cultural Value*, Blackwell, Oxford, 1992.
Docherty, T., *After Theory: Postmodernism/Postmarxism*, Routledge, London, 1990.
Docherty, T. (ed), *Postmodernism: A Reader*, Harvester Wheatsheaf, Hemel Hempstead, 1993.
Habermas, J., *The Philosophical Discourse of Modernity*, M. I. T. Press, Cambridge, MA, 1987.
Harvey, D., *The Condition of Postmodernity*, Blackwell, Oxford, 1989.
Nicholson, L., *Feminism/Postmodernism*, Routledge, London, 1990.
Norris, C., *The Truth About Postmodernism*, Blackwell, Oxford, 1993.
Tester, K., *The Life and Times of Postmodernity*, Routledge, London, 1993.
William, P., and Chrisman, L., *Colonial Discourse and Post-Colonial Theory*, Harvester Wheatsheaf, Hemel Hempstead, 1993.

BOOKS ON POSTMODERNISM AND HISTORY

Amico, R. D', *Historicism and Knowledge*, Routledge, London, 1989.
Ankersmit, F. R., *Narrative Logic: A Semantic Analysis of the Historian's Language*, Martini Nijhoff, The Hague, 1983.
Elam, D., *Romancing the Postmodern*, Routledge, London, 1992.
—— *Feminism and Deconstruction*, Routledge, London, 1994.
Emarth, E. D., *Sequel to History: Postmodernism and the Crisis of Representational Time*, Princeton University Press, Princeton, 1992.
Foucault, M., *The Archaeology of Knowledge*, Pantheon, New York, 1972.
Lloyd, C., *The Structures of History*, Blackwell, Oxford, 1993.
Palmer, B. D., *Descent Into Discourse: The Reification of Language and the Writing of History*, Philadelphia University Press, Philadelphia, 1990.
Rosenau, P. M., *Post-modernism and the Social Sciences: Insights, Inroads and Intrusions*, Princeton University Press, Princeton, 1992.
Rattansi, A., and Westwood, S., (eds) *Racism, Modernity and Identity: On the Western Front*, Polity, Oxford, 1994.
Scott, J. W., *Gender and the Politics of History*, Columbia University Press, New York, 1988.
Wilson, A., (ed) *Re-Thinking Social History*, Manchester University Press, Manchester, 1993.
Van Der Dussen, W. J. and Rubinoff, L. (eds), *Objectivity, Method and Point of View*, E. J.Brill, Leiden, 1991. (An interesting range of essays orientated around W. Dray's theoretical work; see especially A. P. Fell's contribution on Ankersmit in '"Epistemological" and "Narrativist" Philosophies of History', pp. 72–86.)
Young, M., *White Mythologies: History Writing and the West*, Routledge, London, 1990.

ARTICLES ON HISTORY AND POSTMODERNISM

Over the years the journal *History and Theory* has often addressed the issues of poststructuralism, postmodernism, and narrative and the works of Hayden White (White being a long-time member of/advisor to the Editorial Board). Some relevant articles include:

Ankersmit, F. R., 'The Dilemma of Contemporary Anglo-Saxon Philosophy of History', 25, 1986.
—— 'Historiography and Postmodernism', 28, 1989.
Carr, D., 'Narrative and the Real World: An Argument for Continuity', 25, 1986.
Norman, A.P., 'Telling It Like It Was: Historical Narratives on Their Own Terms', 30, 1991.
Strout, C., 'Border Crossings: History, Fiction and Dead Certainties', 31, 1992.

In a similar fashion, the journal *Social History* has recently been discussing the impact of postmodernism on history. In addition to the articles already cited, others worth looking at include:

Joyce, P., 'The Imaginery Discontents of Social History', 18, 1, Jan. 1993.
Laurence, J. and Taylor, M., 'The Poverty of Protest: Gareth Stedman Jones and the Politics of Language – A Reply', 18, 1, Jan. 1993.
Mayfield, D. and Thorne, S., 'Social History and its Discontents: Gareth Stedman Jones and the Politics of Language', 17, 2, May 1992.
Patterson, T. C., 'Post-structuralism, Post-modernism: Implications for Historians', 14, 1, 1989.

Similarly, the *American Historical Review* has had its postmodern numbers/articles. See especially Vol. 94, 3, June 1989, for essays by D. Harlan, D. Hollinger, A. Megill, T. Hamerow, G. Himmelfarb, L. Levine, J.W. Scott and J. Toews.

OTHER ARTICLES

Easthope, A., 'Romancing the Stone: History-Writing and Rhetoric', in *Social History*, 18, 2, May 1993.
Norris, C., 'Postmodernising History: Right-wing Revisionism and the Use of Theory', in *Southern Review*, 21, 1988.
Partner, N., 'Making Up Lost Time: Writing on the Writing of History', in *Speculum*, 61, 1986.
Wilson, A. and Ashplant, T. G., 'Whig History and Present-Centred History', and, 'Present-Centred History and the Problem of Historical Knowledge', in *The Historical Journal*, 31, 1, 1988, and 31, 2, 1988.

Journals to consult for articles on the areas discussed in this work include:
Gender and History, Economy and Society, New Left Review, History Workshop Journal, Political Theory, The Oxford Literary Review, New Formations, Textual Practice.

Index of names

Printed in the United Kingdom
by Lightning Source UK Ltd.
122286UK00001B/39/A

9 780415 097253